A St. John's Book 1989

Flight of the ENOLA GAY

Paul W. Tibbets

Buckeye Aviation Book Company
P.O. Box 974
Reynoldsburg, Ohio 43068

Theodore J. Van Kirk
Navigator

Paul W. Tibbets
Pilot

Thomas W. Ferebee
Bombadier

A St. John/Tibbets Book 1989

FLIGHT OF THE ENOLA GAY

Copyright © by Paul W. Tibbets

All rights reserved. No part of this book may be reproduced or transmitted in any form or by any means, electronic or mechanical, including photocopying, recording, or by any information storage and retrieval system, without permission in writing from the publisher, except in the case of brief quotations, embodied in critical articles and reviews.

ISBN 0-942397-11-8

Book cover design by Brent St. John and Joe Coulter.

Printed in the United States of America.

Published by
Buckeye Aviation Book Company
P.O. Box 974
Reynoldsburg, Ohio 43068

To the memory of my mother, Enola Gay Tibbets, whose quiet faith and support gave me courage in many trying moments of combat, this book is dedicated.

Paul Warfield Tibbets

I wish to acknowledge the special contribution of both Clair Stebbins and Harry Franken who pursuaded me to share my war experience to benefit future generations.

It was their enthusiasm, continuous encouragement and meticulous research that created a permanent and detailed account of the important events in which I participated.

Contents

Introduction 1
1 *Strange Destiny* 5
2 *From Corn Belt to Sun Belt* 11
3 *Target: Hialeah* 19
4 *A Dose of Discipline* 24
5 *The Big Decision* 32
6 *Winning My Wings* 40
7 *Fort Benning* 49
8 *Skeet-shooting with George Patton* 55
9 *Flying Low* 62
10 *Flying Fortress Training* 66
11 *Code Name Bolero* 74
12 *Yankee Doodle Goes to Town* 80
13 *Close Calls and Milk Runs* 89

14 *Mark Clark's Secret Mission* 101

15 *Ike Goes to War on a Two-by-Four* 107

16 *Bombardment in Africa* 113

17 *Marauders in Algiers* 121

18 *The Norstad Incident* 127

19 *Reunion* 137

20 *Flying Blind* 140

21 *Testing the Super Fortress* 146

22 *My Secret Air Force* 151

23 *The Air Base at the End of Nowhere* 161

24 *Escaping the Shock Wave* 168

25 *The Green Hornet Line* 175

26 *Manhattan in the Pacific* 181

27 *Taunts and Jibes* 190

28 *Last-Minute Preparations* 198

29 *Using Every Inch of the Runway* 209

30 *"My God, What Have We Done?"* 218

31 *The World Gets the News* 229

32 *End of the War* 240

33 *Fiasco at Bikini* 245

34 *Testing the B-47* 254

35 *"Above and Beyond"* 262

36 *Trouble-shooting Years* 268

37 *Mission to India* 277

38 *The Sad Case of Major Eatherly* 282

39 *Executive Jet* 291

40 *Reflections* 303

  Index 311

"Mr. Tibbets"
—An Introduction

Behind a polished desk in his well-appointed office at Columbus, Ohio, Paul Warfield Tibbets is the very personification of a successful executive.

He is a pleasant-mannered man, handsome in a rugged sort of way, with black wavy hair and penetrating blue eyes that look appraisingly at you through dark-rimmed glasses.

Many of those who come to see him on business are not aware that he is literally a legend in his own time, a heroic figure to millions around the world and, unhappily, a symbol of nuclear evil to millions of others.

There is nothing in his office—no mementos on his desk or photographs on the walls—to indicate that he was once pictured on the front pages of newspapers and in magazines all over the world; that he led the first American daylight raid on Hitler's occupied Europe and the first mass attack across the Channel; that he was entrusted to fly Mark Clark on his celebrated secret rendezvous with the French in North Africa; that he flew General Eisenhower to Gibraltar for the start of the African invasion . . .

Or that he dropped the atomic bomb on Hiroshima!

As a colonel in the air force, he not only flew the first A-bomb mission, but he commanded history's only nuclear strike force and planned the strategy that brought an unexpectedly swift end to World War II. Depending on whose estimates you accept, the atomic bombings of Hiroshima and Nagasaki saved a half-million or possibly a million lives, both American and Japanese.

Old myths are slow to die. This is particularly true of the one which persists to the effect that the Hiroshima pilot and crew are living out their days in a dark world of doubt, assailed by guilt and remorse.

This tale, based on the unfortunate mental problems of one of the more than 40 pilots under Tibbets's command, was circulated, embellished, and deliberately distorted by a worldwide left-wing propaganda machine.

Like any soldier who has followed orders, Tibbets has no sense of personal guilt for his role in bringing atomic war to a world that had already indulged, throughout its history, in many other types of inhumane slaughter.

For his accomplishment, he was praised by military leaders and by President Truman. General Leslie R. Groves, the man responsible for the bomb-building project, wrote that "your performance was perfect."

The pursuit of perfection has been a lifelong obsession of Paul Tibbets.

With the war over, there were other assignments—some important, some routine. His expertise was useful to the air force and the Boeing Airplane Company in the development of the first successful jet bomber, the B-47. He was called upon to straighten out a couple of faltering air divisions. He was assigned to the NATO staff in France and to India as deputy commander of the American Military Mission.

But those tasks were beneath the capacity of a man who had been recognized as the world's most competent bomber pilot, as demonstrated in the skies over Europe, North Africa, and the Pacific. In combat and command positions, he had performed brilliantly.

Those who knew of his wartime record expected that Tibbets would eventually attain three-star or even four-star rank. But with the end of the war, traditional military politics took over. There was no longer a need for the Tibbets brand of perfection. At the very top, competent men remained in charge but, at the next level, many officers skilled in the art of pulling strings insinuated themselves into the diminishing number of key jobs.

Introduction 3

Tibbets had been too busy with important wartime assignments to polish apples. He had even made a number of enemies by standing up to superior officers when he considered it necessary. He had no patience with mediocrity, particularly when it threatened the success of a wartime mission or the lives of his men.

Retiring from the air force with the rank of brigadier general, he was soon invited to join Executive Jet Aviation Inc., based at Columbus, Ohio. Today he is the president of that company, which operates the largest jet air-taxi service in the world.

Whatever bitterness he harbored over his postwar experience in the air force is now largely offset by the success he enjoys in a business that enables him to pursue his lifelong love affair with the airplane. Only a few steps from his office door is the entrance to a large hanger where maintenance men are usually to be found working on two or three Lear jets. He manages the operation of this far-flung civilian air service with the same efficiency that made him famous as a World War II military commander.

Not many address him today as "general," even though the use of this title in retirement would be appropriate. By his own choice, he is "Mr. Tibbets" to his secretary and associates at Executive Jet. He has avoided capitalizing on his fame as the world's first atomic bomber pilot, although he has accepted speaking invitations from service clubs and schools in the Columbus area.

Without seeking publicity, he has granted occasional newspaper interviews but has avoided controversies or confrontations with "ban-the-bomb" activists whom he distrusts, not because he is unsympathetic to their abhorrence of war, but rather because of the flagrant anti-American bias which some such groups display.

As the son of Enola Gay Tibbets, he is proud that his mother's curiously melodious name is better known than his own. This red-haired daughter of an Iowa farm family had a profound influence on his life, and he never lost sight of the fact that she stood by him with confidence when he gave up plans for a career as a medical doctor to become a military aviator.

On the day before the Hiroshima flight, when it came time to choose a name for his B-29 bomber, his thoughts were of her. *Enola Gay* is also the title of a best-selling book about that historic mission.

Other books, and countless magazine and newspaper articles,

have been written about the development and dropping of the only two nuclear bombs ever used in warfare. Interviews with Tibbets by a *Chicago Tribune* writer resulted in a series of stories which appeared in that newspaper in 1968.

Until now, Tibbets has resisted suggestions by friends that he write his own account of the most cataclysmic chapter in the history of warfare. From the spear to the crossbow to the introduction of gunpowder and powerful explosives, his was the most fearsome of the many weapons that man has devised in a never-ending effort to improve the means of humanity's destruction.

This book is more than a story of the atomic bomb, however. Because of the misleading information that has gained worldwide circulation, the author has chosen to tell the entire story of his life so that readers may learn of the typically American background of this dedicated soldier who would rather fly civilian jets through a peaceful sky than drop bombs on enemy targets.

It is the story of a quietly efficient man who, with great skill and unquestioning faith in the judgment of those who led his country and its allies, brought a hasty end to the most terrible of all wars.

1 Strange Destiny

From the pilot's seat of my airplane, I saw the city shimmering 6 miles below in the bright sunlight of an August morning. Suddenly there was a blinding flash beside which the sun grew dim. In a millionth of a second, the shimmering city became an ugly smudge.

For eleven months I had worked day and night to plan the delivery of that bright and devastating flash. Now that I could say "mission accomplished," I was stunned.

What strange destiny had brought me over this alien island, half a world away from my birthplace in Quincy, Illinois, to keep this appointment with history?

My eleven companions and I were improbable choices to become the messengers of a war god more terrible than any who had walked this earth in all the centuries past. We were no Genghis Khans, no Tamerlanes, no Julius Caesars or Napoleons. Yet any of these ruthless warriors, whose deeds are written in blood across the pages of human history, would have trembled at what we had done.

Nothing in their experience as practicing agents of death and destruction would have prepared them for the awful sight I had just witnessed on the morning of August 6, 1945, and for which I was actually responsible.

I shall never forget the sight of that bright purple cloud boiling upward for ten miles above a dying city, which was suddenly blanketed by an ugly mass of black smoke that resembled, more than anything else I can think of, a pot of bubbling hot tar.

Awe and astonishment were my feelings as I viewed this scene. Although briefed in advance on the potential effect of this incredible new weapon, I was unprepared for what I saw. The shock was such that I don't remember what was said by me or my fellow crewmen at that moment, except that everyone reacted in stunned disbelief.

A movie reenactment of the historic flight had me saying, "My God, what have we done?"

I'm sure those dramatic words were not spoken, but they probably reflect the thoughts of all 12 men aboard the *Enola Gay*, a B-29 bomber that I had named for my mother.

We were certainly aware that thousands of people were dying at that moment on the ground below. It is not easy for a soldier to be detached from the misery he has created. Every fighting man with normal sensitivity, even if he has simply pulled a rifle trigger and slain a fellow soldier of another nationality, is painfully aware that he has brought tragedy to some household.

Let it be understood that I feel a sense of shame for the whole human race, which through all history has accepted the shedding of human blood as a means of settling disputes between nations. And I feel a special sense of indignation at those who condemn the use of a nuclear explosive while having no lament for the fire-bombing attacks in the same war on the city of Tokyo, where thousands of civilians were literally burned to death in a single night, and on Dresden, a great German city that was all but leveled in a dreadful mass attack.

Only a fool speaks of humane warfare. There is no such thing, as General Sherman and other competent witnesses have testified. It has the smell of hypocrisy when self-proclaimed humanitarians draw a distinction between an acceptable and an intolerable brand of human cruelty. Let those who honestly desire peace among nations also condemn all forms of international terrorism that are meant, by their perpetrators, to set the stage for war.

As often happens after a cataclysmic event, rumors have spread that some form of divine retribution has overtaken a majority of those who participated in the Hiroshima attack. It has been implied that some of us have died mysteriously and that others have fallen victim to disease or insanity.

For at least 20 years, the anniversary of Hiroshima would bring telephone calls from news media all over the country, ostensibly to request interviews but actually, and not so subtly, to inquire about my health and mental conditions. Always, the reporter seemed surprised and a bit disappointed to learn that I was leading a perfectly normal life and had no intention of repudiating my role in the historic event.

The Japanese seem to be more understanding. I was visited a number of years ago by newsmen from Japan and once submitted to a taped television interview which was broadcast in that country. In each case, the interviewers asked no hostile questions and gave no sign that they regarded me as a monster whose superweapon had destroyed two of their cities and killed 150,000 of their countrymen. Perhaps they understood, better than many Americans, that the nuclear strikes had shortened the war to the extent that Japan had been spared a far greater toll in the months ahead. They may have sensed the possibility that the bomb had saved their own lives.

Today's controversy over the use of the atomic bomb is interesting in view of the fact that in 1945, Americans were almost unanimously thankful that such a miracle weapon had been developed. The A-bomb ended the war and brought the boys home, and that was what counted. Thousands of those servicemen who returned to their families would have been dead had it not been for this terrible new instrument of war.

During the four years of the bomb's development, there was no suggestion that it should not be put to actual use. The scientists worked around the clock to perfect this weapon with full knowledge that, if they were successful, their handiwork would wreak appalling destruction on people and property.

President Roosevelt and Prime Minister Churchill were in complete agreement on the bomb, and both of these men are regarded as enlightened humanitarians. The ultimate order to drop the bomb came from President Truman. He did not hesitate despite last-minute suggestions from a group of scientists to warn Japan in advance and then make a well-publicized demonstration blast at sea, somewhere off that country's coastline. Neither the President nor his military advisers were willing to risk the fiasco that such a plan might have produced. First, there was the chance of failure. Second, the Japanese might well have decided to prevent the demonstration by shooting down the bomb-carrying plane.

Pacifists and leaders of left-wing thought in this country and overseas pointed the finger of shame at the United States during the Cold War years for having unleashed a cosmic dragon upon the world. They sought to haunt all Americans with a feeling of guilt over the dead in Hiroshima and Nagasaki. Just as we were exhorted during the war to "remember Pearl Harbor," we were now being counseled to "forget Hiroshima."

Aware that this outcry might have a psychological effect on the lives of those who participated in the mission and its planning, President Truman summoned me to the White House one day and said: "Don't you ever lose any sleep over the fact that you planned and carried out that mission. It was my decision. You had no choice."

His advice was appreciated but unnecessary. This was exactly my view from the start. But it was good to know that we had a president with the guts to take the heat. I have often thought of the well-known sign on his desk: "The buck stops here."

Some have said that American guilt was compounded by the fact that the bomb was used against the Oriental race. It was implied that we would not have employed it against Caucasians.

This is nonsense. The bomb was conceived in part by refugees from Nazi tyranny. Germany was already known to be working on such a weapon and Japanese scientists were engaged in similar advanced research. When I was assigned to organize a bomb group and devise a method of delivery, the war in Europe was in full fury.

My instructions were to create an elite bombing force, comprised of the best pilots and bombardiers in service, with the understanding that, when trained, they would be divided into two groups: one to be sent to Europe and the other to the Pacific.

There was no Japanese target priority. All our early planning assumed that we would make almost simultaneous bomb drops on Germany and Japan. However, we had not reached the point of discussing the most likely targets in Germany at the time the war in Europe was over, for completion of the bomb was still three months away.

It is my belief that Berlin would have shared the fate of Hiroshima if the war in Europe had still been in progress in August 1945.

From the pilot's seat of the *Enola Gay*, I saw Hiroshima in the moments before it disappeared. The city has now been rebuilt; for that I am glad. I visited the ruins of Nagasaki soon after the attack by another plane of the squadron I commanded, and saw for myself the terrifying results of the atom.

In the three decades since these events, the so-called "Little Boy" and "Fat Man" bombs we dropped have become obsolete, as has the method of delivery. In the United States, hundreds of missiles with nuclear warheads many times more powerful are poised and zeroed in on Soviet targets. In Russia, an estimated equal number are aimed at our cities and military installations. Nuclear-armed submarines from both sides range across the world's oceans. Like it or not, we live a precarious existence under the shadow of the atom.

In that context, it is probably no wonder that the United States appears embarrassed by its invention of nuclear warfare. However, the world's smaller and weaker nations might well ponder the probable consequences if the secret had fallen first and exclusively into the hands of an aggressor nation.

During World War II, when the atomic bomb was developed, it's a safe guess that 99.9 percent of the American people would have said "yes" if the question of its use had been put to a vote. No one suggested that our war effort should be less than 100 percent. The enemy wrecked Rotterdam and Coventry and fire-bombed London. We made rubble out of Dresden, Essen, and Berlin. The Germans and Russians fought a battle that destroyed Stalingrad. Our bombers in the Pacific laid waste a dozen or more Japanese cities, killing untold thousands of civilians in nighttime terror raids. Our purpose was to bring the empire to its knees. We didn't very much care how we did it.

Yet today, our employment of this war-ending weapon remains a matter of controversy, kept alive by a relatively small number of people. My B-29 bomber, *Enola Gay*, was allowed to suffer from weather and vandalism for years in a remote section of Andrews Air Force base outside Washington, D.C. Today it is in a Maryland warehouse partially restored through the work of a volunteer hobbyist, Vince LoPrinzi, an Allegheny Airlines pilot. The Smithsonian Institution, which holds title to the plane, had no space in its new Air and Space Museum for an aircraft of this size. It is now scheduled for permanent display in the National Atomic Museum at Kirtland Air Force base, Albuquerque, New Mexico, where exhibition facilities are being expanded.

By contrast, the *Enola*'s sister plane, *Bock's Car,* occupies a conspicuous place of honor in the Air Force Museum at Wright-Patterson Air Force base near Dayton, Ohio. There is no apology for the display of this plane, which I assigned to carry the plutonium bomb to Nagasaki. This exhibit is a leading attraction in a museum that is jammed with military aircraft dating back to before World War I.

There were disappointments and frustrations in my military career that need not be dwelt on here because they will become apparent to the reader of this autobiographical narrative. The fact remains that my 30 years in the service were rewarding in many ways.

It was no infatuation with military life that led me to give up the prospects of a medical career to join the Army Air Corps in the pleasant, peaceful days before World War II. On reflection, I am sure that I gave no more than a passing thought to the prospect of ever being involved in deadly combat. It was, rather, my love affair with the airplane that drew me into service. And that love affair has continued throughout my life.

2 From Corn Belt to Sun Belt

I grew up in the prairie states of Illinois and Iowa. Quincy, Illinois, a medium-size city with broad tree-shaded streets running down to the Mississippi, was my birthplace. This was Mark Twain country, but the steamboats that made the broad river a thing of romance and adventure for the boy from nearby Hannibal, Missouri, had grown scarce by the time I came along. There were no rafts, no Tom Sawyers. Automobiles were beginning to change the face of America and the life-style of its people. And then there were the exciting new airplanes, which dad assured me were very dangerous.

When I was nine, my youthful horizons were broadened when father discovered Florida. Delighted by the wondrous fact that one could live there all winter without having to shovel snow or fire a furnace, he moved the family to Miami. I didn't realize until then how much he despised northern winters.

But the move to Florida did not sever my ties with the corn country. I went back to Iowa every summer for a long vacation on my uncle's farm, where I learned almost everything there was to know about farming from the milking of cows to the castration of pigs. From my uncle, I also learned to shoot a rifle and shotgun and hunt rabbits and other small game.

I was the first child of Enola Gay Haggard and Paul Warfield Tibbets, who were married in 1913. A sister, Barbara, came along five years after me.

Mother and dad met when he was traveling across Iowa as a salesman for the family wholesale grocery business, which had its headquarters in Chicago and branches in Des Moines, Davenport, and Sioux City. Mother's home was the small town of Glidden in the west-central part of Iowa. She came from a family of farmers, while dad's side of the family was involved in the mercantile business and banking.

My birth date was February 23, 1915. I was too young to remember World War I except that dad was away for a couple of years when I was a very small child. I remember his coming home in uniform after serving overseas as a captain with the 33rd Infantry Division.

We moved around a great deal during my boyhood. When I was three, the family moved from Quincy to Davenport, and a couple of years later we bought a house in Des Moines. It was a big, white, two-story house with green shutters. In one corner of the large living room was a glamorous new piece of furniture: a Zenith Superhetrodyne radio with four dials for tuning. It became a family hobby, repeated in households across the country, to see how many distant stations we could pick up, carefully making a notation of each with its call letters and "wave length." Frequently, we would stay up late at night to listen to the Kansas City Night Hawks.

Our Des Moines house was at the top of a small hill on Waterbury Road, in what you would call a good neighborhood. One of our neighbors, Allen Munn, was prominent in Iowa politics and, during the time that we lived there, was elected to the office of state treasurer. I remember the campaign and the visits of many leading politicans to his house.

My father's mother was a Warfield, a family of considerable prominence in Quincy. Great-grandfather John D. Warfield, whom I vaguely remember, owned a couple of banks and a streetcar company. Two of his sons, my great-uncles, went to Chicago and established a wholesale coffee and spice business. My father went to work for the firm as a youth, and it was through this job that he met mother.

On the somewhat reluctant testimony of my grandmother, confirmed by my dad, it seems the less said about Grandfather Tibbets the better. He was a dentist and an avid collector of Oriental rugs. Grandmother, whom I called "Gummie" as a child, was a soft-spoken woman who never said an unkind word about anyone, to my knowledge, except her divorced husband. Goaded by the mention of his name, she once said, "If there is a hell, I hope he roasts there."

Their divorce and its aftermath had a traumatic effect on dad's early life. Grandfather moved to San Jose, California, and literally forced dad, who was only 14 at the time, to accompany him.

In revolt, he ran away a couple of times and had to be returned by the police. Grandfather finally gave up and dad returned to Illinois, living with his Grandfather Warfield for some years. Meanwhile, his mother married a showcase manufacturer, C. Arthur Fifer, and together they traveled all over the world. They were ardent golfers and won a number of trophies at the sport.

During this time I had become a great favorite of Grandmother Fifer, who seems to have set out deliberately to spoil me. I had only to mention a desire and she made it come true. Her gifts included bicycles and, when I became old enough to drive, an automobile.

Perhaps because of his own parental problems, dad went out of his way to be my friend and companion. But this attitude didn't prevent him from being a strict disciplinarian. If he told me to do something, his order had to be obeyed. If I stepped out of line, he punished me with a leather strap. But spankings weren't frequent. They were effective because they came only when deserved.

As a result, we didn't have any serious problems and certainly no misunderstandings of consequence. I knew he meant what he said, and the occasional welts from the leather strap were there to remind me. He told me in later years that I was no problem—certainly not like my sister Barbara, who was inclined to challenge his authority.

I never challenged dad because I respected him and regarded his word as law. Perhaps this accounts for my later acceptance of military discipline. Father's understanding of discipline stemmed from his education at a military academy in Missouri, an experience that predestined me for military academy life as a teenager.

By this time we were buddies. Dad was handsome, with a head of black curly hair. He never looked his age and, when I got to be 16, he enjoyed passing me off as his younger brother. His youthful appearance was embarrassing to my mother when she was sometimes mistaken for his mother.

Mother was a redheaded Iowa farm girl, very quiet and withdrawn. Although she enjoyed the company of friends and neighbors, she didn't join in a conversation with enthusiasm unless she was with people she knew intimately. She was a better listener than a talker.

I had always understood that her melodious first name was of Indian origin. But I learned in later years that she derived her name, Enola Gay, from a character in a novel her father was reading shortly before she was born.

Her family came from Holland in the 1880s, while the Tibbets are of Welsh and Irish extraction, settling first in Massachusetts and then Maine.

Mother was a half-inch taller than dad, a difference that was exaggerated when she wore high-heeled shoes. Neither had a college education because, even though their families could have afforded it, schooling beyond high school wasn't considered essential among many midwestern families in the early part of this century.

Father's decision to move the family from Iowa to Florida came on an impulse. In the winter of 1923–24, his mother invited him to Florida, where she and her husband always spent the winter. He boarded the train at Des Moines in a blizzard and arrived in Miami two days later in bright sunshine. When he saw the palm trees and felt the warmth of the Florida sun, he decided on the spot that this was for him. As he remembered it later, he thought, "Boy, I like this. I hate the snow back home so why live there when I don't have to?"

Dad, a good businessman, immediately explored the opportunities in the Sunshine State, which was just then in the midst of its first big boom. He cut loose from the family grocery business back home and promptly found a partner, Bob Smith, with whom to launch a Miami-based firm known as Tibbets and Smith, Wholesale Confectioners. Theirs soon became the largest business of its kind in the state.

I was the first member of the family to join dad in Florida, arriving by train on July 4, 1924. Mother remained behind, with sister Barbara, long enough to close out the Des Moines residence and pack the furniture.

Those first few weeks in Miami, with dad and me baching it in a small apartment, were memorable. For the first time in my life I was on my own from morning to night. Miami was a city of only 40,000 at that time—not much larger than Quincy—and had only a dozen paved streets.

I would go downtown to the office with dad in the morning, he would give me 25 cents spending money for the day, and I would blow 10 cents of it for a matinee movie. Another 10 cents went for a milk shake, and what nine-year-old boy could ask for more, with a nickel left over for incidentals? My favorite screen fare was any cowboy picture, usually starring such actor heroes as Tom Mix, Buck Jones, and William S. Hart.

Almost immediately, father caught the deep sea fishing fever. He found a day on the water relaxing and the battle with game fish exciting. Every Sunday, he and a friend would charter a fishing boat and head for the Gulf Stream, which flows only a few miles off the southern Florida coast.

When I arrived in Miami, the Sunday fishing ritual had begun and I was given to understand that I would be a regular member of the boating party. The idea of a day at sea was appealing to my youthful imagination, and I climbed aboard eagerly that first Sunday. For a midwestern boy who had never seen an ocean, there was the promise of new adventure.

Disillusionment came soon after we pulled away from the dock and the boat began to pitch and toss, gently at first, and then with a more determined rhythm that played tricks on my landlubber stomach. Before we were more than a mile from shore, I was sick. Dad wasn't sympathetic. He and his friend went on fishing and enjoying themselves while I held my head in misery, upchucking at intervals and wishing for the moment late in the day when we would head back for shore.

Father made light of my unhappy experience and assured me that the tendency to seasickness would soon wear off. So it was back to sea and a day of misery the next Sunday, and the next—in fact, until mother finally arrived from Iowa. It wasn't until years later that I outgrew my queasiness aboard a boat or ship, and I have never forgotten the misery of those Sunday fishing trips. It is both strange and fortunate for my later career as a flier that I never suffered from the airsickness that afflicts some airplane passengers. I have always felt completely at home and comfortable in the air.

These were Florida's boom years, but at my age I could not take in the excitement of the land-buying fever that was converting Miami from a sleepy seaside settlement into a bustling metropolis. The whole east coast of Florida was a 450-mile strip of sand, washed by an ocean that beckoned wealthy fugitives from the rigors of northern winters.

What Florida had to sell was sunshine, and the northern vacationers—many of them hard-headed businessmen back home— were quick to see the possibilities of large-scale land development. Most of the wintertime visitors came to Florida by train in those days, while others made the four-day voyage from New York on such coastal steamships as the Clyde Line's *Comanche* and *Arapahoe*. Some braved overland travel in their Packards, Pierce-Arrows, and Stutz Bearcats, following such early semi-improved north-south roads as the Dixie Highway.

I remember the hundreds of real estate offices, many of them on Flagler Street and others in hotel lobbies. Fast-talking salesmen from New York came south to make a killing on land that sometimes doubled in value in three months. The oranges and grapefruit for which the state had been famous were almost forgotten in the new scramble for land and riches.

To the east, across an expanse of shimmering water called Biscayne Bay, was a sand dune that was being developed under the name of Miami Beach. A causeway was built to connect this narrow strip of real estate with Miami. Only vaguely aware of the excitement in the Florida air at that time, I was content to live and play and go to school in this frantic wonderland of palm trees and sunshine that was borded on the east by the Atlantic Ocean and on the west by mangrove swamps inhabited by alligators, water moccasins, long-legged birds, and mosquitoes.

Father's business flourished as the area grew, and he somehow managed to emerge financially solvent although not wealthy when the land bubble burst in 1927, three years after we had moved there. Meanwhile, since this was the era before air conditioning, my mother and sister and I escaped the heat of Florida summers by returning to Iowa for prolonged vacations.

Then came two devastating hurricanes, and the confectionery business took a bath both times. Dad, a realist who had made some cautious real estate investments without falling victim to the get-rich-quick frenzy of the period, decided it was time to sell. After rebuilding on the wreckage, he had the confectionery operation back on its feet by 1930, when he sold it to a large Tampa cigar and tobacco firm that had been trying to buy him out for a couple of years.

Dad's decision to sell the Florida business was not entirely the result of the hurricanes or the sudden end of the land boom. He was receiving urgent SOS messages from relatives in Illinois, pleading for his help in disposing of the family-owned grocery houses.

Actually, he had seen the handwriting on the wall before he left for Florida six years earlier. He watched the early development of chain stores and their mass-buying capabilities, which spelled financial doom for operations such as the one the family had managed with great success during the early part of the century. His uncles and cousins, who were then running the business, would not listen to his warnings that they would have to modernize and change their methods completely if they were to avoid disaster. They regarded him as a young upstart who didn't know what he was talking about.

Now the relatives who had shunned his advice were turning to him for help. They were ready to sell the business, but not at a sacrifice. Since his forecasts of a decline in profits had proved correct, the family reluctantly agreed that he was best suited to engineer a favorable deal.

Dad returned to Chicago, went over the books and found things in worse shape than he had imagined. Before he could sell the business at a decent figure, he had to put it back on its feet.

This was not a happy assignment. Turning things around involved some drastic changes in management. He had to dismiss a number of old friends who weren't able to adjust to new methods of marketing. During this period, he spent many sleepless nights.

Patience finally paid off, and he managed to sell three of the family grocery houses at a profit. The relatives, pleased with the money they were paid for their stock, began to regard dad as a business wizard who had saved them from financial disaster. They were equally pleased a short time later when he sold the Chicago business, which dealt in coffee, spices, and chocolate, to the National Tea Co.

The rescue enterprise consumed four years. As soon as it was over, father gathered up the family and headed back to Florida. These were Depression days, but he returned to Miami with newfound confidence in his business skills. Never a gambler, he dabbled around a bit, buying and selling properties and being satisfied with modest profits.

Meanwhile I was growing up. In 1928, when I was about to enter the eighth grade, dad decided it was time to send me to military school. For the next five years I was a cadet at the Western Military Academy in Alton, Illinois, only a few miles up the Mississippi River from St. Louis.

3 Target: Hialeah

Among the thousands who attended the races at Hialeah track one week in January 1927, there must be many still living who remember being bombarded each afternoon with candy bars dropped from a low-flying airplane. They would be surprised to learn, at this late date, that the "bombardier" was a schoolboy who, 18 years later, would pilot a real bomber to Hiroshima with a cargo of death instead of chocolates.

As I look back on both events, I'm obliged to report that the mission to Hialeah was more exciting than the one to Hiroshima. There is nothing to match the thrill of a 12-year-old boy's first airplane ride.

This was the golden age of aviation. The old biplanes with their fabric-covered wings, wooden propellers, and open cockpits were more exciting to watch and more thrilling to fly than today's limousinelike aircraft, in which pilots and passengers occupy enclosed cabins and never feel the wind on their faces or hear the weird music of the piano wire that held the wings together.

Like all barnstorming pilots of the twenties, Doug Davis wore a leather jacket, whipcord breeches, leather helmet, and goggles. I don't remember that his costume included a white silk scarf but, if not, it was his only shortcoming as a celebrated member of the barnstorming clan.

Davis was under contract that year to the Curtiss Candy

Company for the purpose of flying low over public gatherings, such as country fairs and horse races, and dropping Baby Ruth bars like manna from heaven on the people below. Before the year was over, he had introduced the new candy in this manner to the inhabitants of 40 states.

The assignment brought him and his Waco 9 airplane to Miami, where he called upon my father, who was still operating his confectionery business. As Florida's principal distributor of Curtiss candy, dad became the contact for the pilot.

I was in dad's office when Davis arrived and introduced himself. To say that I was excited would be an understatement. Here was an honest-to-God aviator, and what more could a kid ask than to see one of these heroic figures in the flesh? I managed to interrupt with a few questions about the life and adventures of a pilot.

"Did you ever loop the loop?"

"Sure, son, lots of times.

"Does a tailspin make you dizzy?"

"Well, maybe a little bit sometimes."

Davis and dad sat down and talked about the candy-dropping stunt. Since it was the racing season at nearby Hialeah, the track would be crowded. And since it was midwinter, the sandy shore of Miami Beach would be filled with swimmers, many newly arrived from the north to enjoy the Florida sunshine. Accordingly, it was decided to unload the candy bars on the race track crowds and then make a pass at the swimming area. First it would be necessary to attach small paper parachutes to each of the paper-wrapped confections. This would be easy.

Next, Davis mentioned that he would need someone to go along to throw the candy bars overboard.

"I can do that," I said with unconcealed eagerness.

Dad was basically skeptical about airplanes. After all, the newspapers were filled with reports of barnstorming pilots losing their lives in plane crashes.

"The boy's never been up in an airplane," he said, citing my inexperience rather than his fears as an excuse.

Davis was reassuring. "He looks like a bright boy," the pilot said. "He won't have any trouble."

I chimed in with assurances of my competence, of which I really wasn't certain.

Under this double-barreled pressure, dad gave in. We went to the

36th Street airfield, where Davis had tied down his plane. It was the most beautiful thing I had ever seen. The wings were red and the fuselage white, the predominant colors of the candy bar wrapper. There was also some blue trim. I scrambled into the cockpit and asked a lot of questions. I'm sure he had heard them all many times before but he answered them patiently.

We were to make our first flight the next afternoon. That evening I helped fasten the parachutes to the candy bars.

I didn't sleep much that night. I was the luckiest boy in Miami. The next morning I was back at the field, examining the wonderful airplane in great detail. Davis was there to fill the tank with gasoline and tinker with the engine. In those days pilots were always making adjustments of one sort or another.

I was ready to take off and said so, but the pilot explained that there was no use flying over an empty grandstand. "We'll have to wait till the races start and the crowds get there," he said.

It was about two o'clock in the afternoon—time for the second race of the day—when we thundered into the air from the sod runway and I was viewing my home city of Miami from a new perspective.

No Arabian prince ever rode a magic carpet with a greater delight or sense of superiority to the rest of the human race. I could see the unfortunate earth-bound mortals crawling around like ants on the ground below.

The flight was an important event in my life—more important than I realized at the time—because it was then that I subconsciously opted for a career in the sky. Nothing else would satisfy me, once I was given an exhilarating sample of the life of an airman.

With the lose-fitting helmet held onto my head by the chin strap, I watched eagerly as Davis swung the nose of the plane in the direction of the famous racing oval only five miles away. It didn't take me long to become oriented, for I knew Miami and its surrounding area quite well by this time.

Beside me in the front cockpit was a case of candy bars, each with its own tiny white parachute. My responsibility was clear. When Davis throttled down the engine and banked so that the grandstand was visible on the left side of the plane, I was to begin throwing out the candy bars by the fistful.

The race track appeared ahead of the whirling propeller. We

seemed to be moving very slowly. But as I leaned forward to get a better view, the wind slapped me in the face and I realized that we were moving at considerable speed. We were less than 500 feet above the ground.

The stands were filled with people and the horses could be seen warming up on the track as Davis put the plane into a shallow bank, as he had explained that he would, to give me the best opportunity to get rid of our chocolate cargo.

I reached into the carboard container and came up with a fistful of candy. Just before we passed over the grandstand, I began frantically to unload the bars, one handful after another. No bombardier with a Norden bomb sight at his command ever took more careful aim than I. Miraculously, it seems now, most of them came reasonably close to their target. I watched with pride and excitement as the parachutes floated toward the earth, many of them headed for the grandstand or the infield directly in front of it.

Before they reached the ground, however, we were well past the stands and Davis was circling back for another "bomb run." Now I could see the people below scrambling for the goodies, and I knew it was a successful mission.

There was no time for self-congratulation. We were making a second pass at the grandstand and I had more candy to drop. After the third circle, when I unloaded still another batch, Davis straightened our course and soon we were over downtown Miami, then crossing the bay that separates the city from the sand spit where in the last decade the new resort area of Miami Beach had sprung up.

There were hundreds of sun worshippers and surf splashers stretched out on the sand or paddling around in the water. Davis roared low over the beach, perhaps giving some of the bathers a thrill and others a fright. As we raced north at no more than 200 feet altitude, I pelted the beach with candy bars, then stretched as high in the cockpit as my seat belt would permit to watch the mad scramble below.

We repeated the operation every day that week. I don't know whether it helped dad's confectionery business, but thousands of people in the Miami area got to know the name of the new Baby Ruth bar.

Doug Davis went on to become an airline pilot and a famous air race winner. He had learned to fly in World War I, after which, like many of his fellow sky warriors back from France, he joined the ranks of the barnstormers who flew into and out of pasture fields all over the country, delighting small children and frightening their parents. It was during this period that he was engaged by the Curtiss Candy Company for the chocolate bar promotion.

Soon after, he joined Eastern Air Lines and became its most celebrated pilot in those pioneering days of air transport. He was chosen to pilot many of Eastern's inaugural flights over its rapidly expanding route system through the eastern and southern states. The aircraft he flew at that time was the lumbering Curtiss Condor biplane, the largest passenger aircraft then in service. By 1932 he had logged more than a million air miles and, although his steady job was with the airline, air racing became his hobby.

A crash took his life at the National Air Races in Cleveland in 1934. He was leading the Thompson Trophy race after seven laps when his Wedell-Williams racer spun into the ground. Roscoe Turner went on to win the 12-lap race at a speed of 248 miles an hour.

Davis was enshrined in the Aviation Hall of Fame at Hammondsport, New York, in 1972. His candy-dropping operation is the subject of an illustrated exhibit at the Smithsonian Institution's Air and Space Museum in Washington. It was one of the many colorful footnotes to the history of aviation during the frantic decade of the twenties, but it had a special meaning for me because it influenced my future. I was thus introduced to flying, a delightfully incurable disease from which I have never recovered.

4 A Dose of Discipline

It was a sunny morning in early September, 1928, when father and I arrived at the entrance to the Western Military Academy in North Alton, Illinois. I was about to become a cadet, and this would be my home for nine months out of each of the next five years. I had never seen the place before and had only a faint idea of what barracks life would be like.

At the gate, an upperclass cadet directed us to the large main building, a three-story red brick that housed the administrative offices, classrooms, infirmary, study hall, and the living quarters of the superintendent and his family. This was on the right side of the quadrangle, while on the left were the barracks, consisting of five three-story brick buildings, each with 30 rooms.

The quadrangle was a neatly trimmed lawn shaded by large oak trees. Visiting parents were certain to be impressed with the pleasant surroundings in which their sons would obtain an education plus a good dose of discipline.

Father and I had come by train from Florida to St. Louis, then had taken an interurban to Alton, only 20 miles to the north on the Illinois side of the Mississippi River. From the end of the interurban line, we went by taxicab to the academy, which occupied considerable acreage on a hill at the edge of Upper Alton, one of the city's several satellite communities.

The academy people lost no time in introducing the newcomers to the routine that we would be following daily in the months to come. After being measured for a dress uniform and receiving a service uniform that fit reasonably well, I attended my first class the same afternoon. The next morning, I participated rather awkwardly in my first drill.

Except for the insignia, our uniforms were an exact copy of those worn at West Point: gray with black stripes down the trouser legs. There were military-type caps for normal wear and shako-style headpieces, complete with plumes, for dress parades.

In addition to the main building and the five barracks, the academy's facilities consisted of a basketball gymnasium, with a swimming pool in the basement, and a recreation area large enough for two football fields and three baseball diamonds, all surrounded by a half-mile cinder track. There was also a drill ground, of course.

Occupying a prominent place on the quadrangle was an ancient cannon that was fired twice daily, at reveille and retreat, and on special occasions as a salute to visiting dignitaries. I viewed it with interest, not realizing that one of my future tasks would be to clean the barrel with soap and water after each firing, then give it a light coat of oil.

After depositing me at the school, dad took a train to Chicago, where he would be joined a couple of weeks later by my mother and sister. They were to live for the next three years in a rented apartment on Chicago's South Side while father applied himself to the difficult task of rescuing, then selling, the family's faltering mercantile business.

I soon became resentful of the regimented world into which I had been thrust. Finding myself in a restrictive if not prisonlike atmosphere, I fired off a protest to my parents. The letter, written in a moment of indignation or depression after only two weeks at school, consisted of a summary of grievances against the academy, its system, and its personnel. No doubt other parents received similar letters, inspired in part by homesickness and in part by resentment over the discipline that was so rigidly imposed.

My protest fell on deaf ears because, even though mother may have been sympathetic, father had long ago decided that I should attend a military academy. He valued his own youthful experience at Blees Academy in Mexico, Missouri, and considered it a sure way to "mold character." Of one thing I am certain: I wasn't sent to military school for training to become a soldier. War seemed the remotest of possibilities in those peaceful days of the late 1920s.

My first roommates were Hubert Sadowski, a quiet but determined young fellow of Polish extraction, and Federico Jiminez Fernandez, a frail, dark-complexioned Mexican with a fiery temper. We became close friends before the semester was over. This was my first association with people of different ethnic backgrounds, and the experience at the age of 13 gave me an understanding and sensitivity that have been useful throughout my life.

Although possessed of no more than average skills in athletics, I was an enthusiastic baseball and football player at the academy and also participated in wrestling. In football, my lack of size prevented me from making the varsity squad until my senior year when, having suddenly gained more weight, I worked my way up to first substitute status.

As an outfielder on the company baseball team in our intramural program, I collided one day with my roommate, Kendall Richardson, as we both ran for a fly ball. Both my front teeth were bent back into the roof of my mouth, but a dentist managed to put them back in place and fasten them with a brace so that I had them for another 20 years. Finally, they started giving me trouble and had to be replaced by a bridge.

During my first year, hazing was humiliating and occasionally painful. Upperclassmen frequently required us to "assume the angle" by bending over our metal army cots while they flogged our backsides with brooms. More often, they would order us to stand rigidly at attention while being subjected to verbal abuse and ridicule.

Hazing was theoretically employed as punishment for wrongdoing, careless attire, or a room that was not tidy. An upperclassman with white gloves would examine shelves or table tops for signs of dust. If nothing was out of order, the frustrated inspector would order his hapless victim to raise his foot, whereupon he would brush his white gloves across the shoe sole. When the inevitable smudge would appear on the fingertip of the glove, he would exclaim, "Ah, the floor's dirty!" And punishment would follow.

More humiliating than the hazing by our peers was the punishment inflicted by the tough-minded commandant of cadets, Major Frank Henderson, a World War I cavalry officer whose receding profile earned him the nickname "the chinless wonder," spoken only out of his hearing by cautious cadets. Although feared and disliked by many for his stern methods of dispensing discipline, Henderson had a reputation for fairness. He played no favorites.

When he reviewed a line of cadets standing at attention on the long walkway in front of the barracks, he examined every uniform with a critical eye, also taking note of the stance and demeanor of each individual. If a blouse was frayed or a shine was visible on a trouser seat, the cadet was sent back to barracks for a change. If he showed up at a future review in the same outfit, the major would whip out a knife and slit the offending article of clothing. I suffered this indignity a couple of times.

In much the same manner as a convict accepts prison life, I became reconciled to the restrictions imposed by the military school. After my letter of outrage failed to wring a sympathetic response from my parents, I determined to make the best of what to me was an undeserved personal misfortune. Like my fellow cadets, I took eager advantage of what few privileges were permitted. Aside from furloughs at Thanksgiving, Christmas, and Easter, these consisted of a two-hour leave off-campus each Wednesday, and four hours on Saturday.

We would stroll the streets, flirt with the better-looking town girls, or stop in the drugstore for an ice cream soda. On Saturdays we would invariably watch a shoot-'em-up Western at the town's only movie theater, where the admission price was 10 cents. Sometimes we would squeeze in a picture show during the brief Wednesday leave, with the result that we would often have to rush from the theater before the show was over and race back to the campus. When the rules said two hours, they didn't mean two hours and one minute.

My most unforgettable showdown with Major Henderson came in my junior year as the result of my freehanded interpretation of school regulations forbidding a cadet to have an automobile. Thanks to the indulgence of Grandmother Fifer I had a 1931 Chevrolet, blue with black fenders and a beige canvas top.

The rules said quite clearly that a cadet enrolled at Western was not permitted to operate a motor vehicle. I drove the car to Alton in the fall and stored it in a downtown garage, my purpose being to have it available when time came for Thanksgiving furlough. As I remember it today, I considered this to be a legal circumvention of the rules, but I must have had some misgivings because I never reported the possession of a car to academy authorities.

When time came for the Thanksgiving furlough in 1931, I planned to drive to Quincy for a visit with grandmother and her husband. Before leaving the campus, each cadet was required to fill out a form stating his destination and indicating the form of transportation.

Major Henderson was a great one for detail, even to the point of checking every line on all the forms that were submitted. When he noticed that I was making the trip to Quincy "by car," he summoned me to his office.

"Is your grandmother coming to pick you up?" he asked.

"No sir," I replied, offering no explanation.

"Then who are you going with?" he insisted.

I explained that I had a car in a downtown garage.

The major fixed me with a penetrating stare and thrust out what little chin he possessed.

"Don't you know that it's against regulations to have a car?" he demanded.

I looked back at him in the most innocent manner I could muster and gave him my interpretation:

"I know, sir, but the rules say I can't have a car at school. I don't have it at school. It's downtown."

We stared at each other a moment and he dismissed me with a wave of the hand. He was watching the next day as I paraded out the gate and climbed into a taxicab that took me downtown to the garage.

When I arrived at grandmother's house in Quincy, a telegram from Major Henderson was waiting. It said: "Your grandson is absent from the academy. We don't know where he is but advise his immediate return."

Grandmother was upset but grandfather, upon seeing that I had arrived safely, started laughing.

Showing me the telegram, he asked, "What are you going to do about this?"

My alternatives had run out. "I'd better get back to school," I said. "I'll leave the car here in Quincy."

I returned to Alton by train. When I reported to Major Henderson, he didn't say a word.

A Dose of Discipline

It was customary, after Monday noon mess, to announce the names of cadets who had become subject to discipline during the past week.

I was not surprised when my name was read. So it was back to Henderson's office. There were several others ahead of me.

When my turn came to face him, I saluted and stood at attention.

"Didn't I tell you you couldn't drive that car?" he demanded.

"Yes sir."

"Then why did you do it?"

My answer was as straightforward as I could make it. "Because you told me to get rid of it and I told you I was going to."

I thought I detected a glint of humor in his eyes as he said: "It's going to cost you. I'm going to give you 50 hours on the detention squad. No double-time."

That meant I had to work 50 hours at assigned tasks. The custom of granting double-time for difficult chores was not to apply in my case.

To emphasize the seriousness of my offense, he added, "You're also going to lose three days off your Christmas furlough."

"Yes sir," I replied before saluting and leaving the office. I may have imagined that there was a trace of disappointment on his face, perhaps because I hadn't pleaded for leniency.

For the next few days, when I went to study hall after classes were over, I sat silent as Major Henderson asked the customary question: "Anyone want double time?" This was the opportunity for those on discipline to volunteer for the more arduous and less pleasant chores for the purpose of shortening punishment. Double-time jobs included such things as cleaning up the chemistry laboratory or washing blackboards. I didn't lift my eyes when he made his daily offer because he had specified that I was not eligible for it.

On the following Saturday afternoon, I was the only cadet in the study hall, the others having taken the customary four-hour leave for which I was not eligible. I was surprised when he asked, as if there were a roomful of students: "Anyone for double-time?" When I looked up from the textbook I was readng, no doubt with a puzzled expression, he summoned me to his desk.

"Go and get your old clothes," he commanded, "and report to my office." I left in a hurry, wondering what was in store for me.

"Come with me," he said when I reported to him a few minutes later. I followed him to the garage where he kept his car, a big shiny LaSalle. It was his pride, always polished to a high luster.

"Get under there and wipe off all the grease," he ordered, with emphasis on the word *all*. It turned out to be a big job because he believed in keeping the underside of the car and the engine as spotless as the exterior.

After that I was given all the double-time work I wanted and soon had atoned for my sin of having that car in a downtown garage.

However, when Christmas vacation time approached, I didn't submit my name as required of those who were taking the usual holiday furlough. I remembered the three days that he had erased from my furlough time.

Finally came the day when the furlough period began. At midafternoon, all the cadets had left except myself and several boys from Mexico City who were not attempting the long trip home.

A staff member came to my room to say that Major Henderson wanted to see me.

"What are your plans?" the commandant asked when I arrived at his office.

"I have none," I replied.

The major hesitated a moment, as though wrestling with an important decision. Then he asked, "How long will it take you to pack?"

When I told him I would need 15 minutes, he said, "Well, hurry up. There's an interurban to St. Louis in 20 minutes and I'll get you to the station in time to catch it."

I hurried. We made it and I didn't lose a single day from my furlough, which I spent with the family in Chicago.

Major Henderson had milked his punishment decree for all it was worth. But the quality of mercy that he dispensed with feigned reluctance took the edge off the bitterness I had felt over the automobile incident.

The fairness with which this veteran soldier administered justice made a lasting impression on me. The memory of how he handled difficult situations at the academy would provide a model for my own behavior when I came into a position of command in World

War II. At this time, however, I had no thought of ever becoming a soldier.

The enrollment at Western in my final year was 328 cadets—which, I believe, was an all-time record. The superintendent was Ralph L. Jackson, who had the rank of full colonel in the Illinois National Guard, although he was an educator rather than a military type. Major Henderson was the real backbone of the school. He was both feared and respected by the cadets. The other staff members were, for the most part, World War I veterans who also held commissions in the Illinois National Guard.

I saw Major Henderson only once after graduating from the academy. That was in 1943, upon my return from Europe for reassignment during World War II. Having a brief layover at Scott field, not far away, I decided to revisit the academy at Alton.

Wearing the silver leaves of a lieutenant colonel on my shoulder straps, I entered his office. With its collection of old weapons on the walls, it was practically unchanged from the day I had been summoned there as a rule-breaker 12 years before.

This time, when he turned and saw who I was, he leaped from his swivel chair, snapped to attention and gave me the most memorable salute I ever received. After a warm handshake, we sat down and talked about old times for more than an hour.

A few years later, Henderson left the school to organize a youth rehabilitation project in cooperation with the St. Louis police department. They would round up problem children, literally street urchins, and Henderson would undertake to rehabilitate, educate, and find jobs for them. Unfortunately, his death occurred while he was at the peak of this useful career.

It saddened me to learn that Western Military Academy, faced with declining enrollment, closed its doors in the early 1970s. Many other institutions of this type have met the same fate in recent years.

I have always felt that my five years at the academy, distasteful though they were at times, were useful in preparing me to cope with the problems I was to face in the years ahead.

5 The Big Decision

The University of Florida at Gainesville, where I enrolled in the fall of 1933, was a comparatively small school, with a student body of 2,800 men. Coeducation had not yet been introduced.

Nevertheless, after five years of iron-fisted discipline in military school, college provided a freedom that I found difficult to handle. Imagine the incredible luxury of being able to come and go as I wished! No hassle over having a car on campus. No one cared what I did as long as I showed up in class at the appointed time. There were no mess calls to answer, no morning reveille, no drills or parades, no punishment for unshined shoes or wrinkled trousers.

My new environment should have been paradise for a youth who had been fettered so long by military academy restrictions, but adapting to my new freedom was actually a problem. I held my professors in awe, because that was the way I had been taught to regard teachers and drill masters. If my English professor had told me to jump out the window, I would probably have obeyed in the belief that he was serious.

After a couple of months, I adjusted to my new status as a liberated student. In fact, I overadjusted. In this freewheeling atmosphere, it became difficult to understand that the real purpose of going to college was to acquire an education. Until then, discipline had been imposed by top-sergeant types who regulated my time: so much for classes, so much for study hall, so much for physical exercise, and so much for sleep.

Now I had the everyday use of the Chevrolet roadster that grandmother had given me two years before and that I had been prevented from having at Alton. It was a snappy car for its day, and the girls with whom I became acquainted—there were plenty in the Gainesville area, even though not in the student body—were partial to college men with motor cars.

When I wasn't out raising hell or playing poker with fellow students, I was having dates, going to dances or the movies, or parking along one of the lonely roads around Gainesville. "Necking" was the word for what boys and girls did in parked cars in those days.

I joined the Sigma Nu fraternity and entered into all the undergraduate social activities that college life offered in the early thirties. In these first years of the Great Depression, as history refers to the period, I was almost unaware of the economic calamity that had befallen the country. In fact, I was unaware of many things with which I should have been concerned, including my studies. Although I had learned to accept discipline at the academy, I had not been taught how to impose it on myself. As a consequence, I almost flunked out of school.

Grades were sent to parents in those days, and when I went back home to Miami for Christmas vacation, I found dad in a state of frenzy over my first semester performance.

"Look," he said when he sat down with me in the living room for a serious talk, "you've reached that point in life where nobody's going to tell you what to do any more. You've got to make your own set of rules. But if you're going to amount to anything, you have to settle down and study."

He made it clear that, since he was paying the tuition, it was my job to see that he got his money's worth. He also mentioned pointedly that I would never be admitted to medical school, as the family had planned, if I didn't qualify in my premed studies.

It was true that I had treated college as a lark and now it came to me forcefully, as dad pointed his finger and pounded the table, that I was not living up to his expectations; in fact, I was letting him down. I was even more sensitive to my mother's obvious disappointment. Although she did not chastise me for my shortcomings, as father had, it was clear that she had been hurt by my failure to take my schooling seriously.

I had no choice except to get a grip on myself and turn things around. Father may have been firm, and sometimes even harsh, but he was always fair. I knew I deserved the chewing-out and resolved then and there to buckle down and study. My grades improved the second semester, but the year's averages were so low that I found myself on academic probation.

We went north and spent most of the summer in Quincy. By this time, dad was so pleased by what he sensed was my determination to improve that he rewarded me with a new car. It was a silver metallic Airflow DeSoto, a sporty model that would become the envy of my college classmates when I returned to Gainesville in the fall.

My newfound determination to make a good record in school began paying dividends. My grades improved remarkably. They were mostly B's with an occasional C, and the letters from home indicated that dad and mother were happy. Physics and chemistry were my favorite subjects.

While keeping up with my studies, I did not find it necessary to neglect the extracurricular facet of college life. My interest in airplanes was rekindled on trips to the Gainesville airport, where a charter and flying service was operated by a deputy sheriff. Whenever I had a few dollars to spare, I spent them on flying lessons.

Actually, I had learned the rudiments of flying from Rusty Heard at Miami's Opa Locka airport the summer before enrolling at the university. I had hung around the field, changing tires and fueling planes, to earn enough money for lessons. Rusty, who was later to become a well-known captain with Eastern Air Lines, soloed me in a Taylor Cub after five or six hours of dual instruction. Now, at Gainesville, I was getting more instruction and adding to my flying experience.

Since my boyhood, it had been taken for granted that I was to become a doctor. Until my father broke the tradition, there had been a medical doctor or dentist on the Tibbets side of the family for many generations. Perhaps it was because he felt a bit guilty for lapsing into the occupation of business that dad was determined I would be educated for the practice of medicine.

I offered no objection because the prospect of becoming a doctor was appealing to me. On my grandfather's farm in Iowa during the summers of my boyhood, I had been fascinated by such things as the birth of animals and the castration of pigs. The sight of blood gave me no squeamish moments.

Because it was generally known that I would someday become a doctor or surgeon, I was permitted to view the profession from the inside, so to speak. The family had a number of doctor friends, several of whom had invited me to watch them at work, even in hospital operating rooms. The intensity of my interest never failed to impress the doctors, who more or less accepted me as a fledgling member of their profession.

Since the University of Florida did not have a medical school at that time, the sophomore year was to be my last on that campus. To complete my premed studies, father had decided that I would enroll at the University of Cincinnati and, after a year, enter its well-known medical college. His decision to send me to Ohio rather than a medical school nearer home came about through his friendship with Charley Crum, a former Ohioan who was retired and living in Miami.

Each summer, when our family went north to Illinois or Iowa, we were accompanied as far as Ohio by Charley Crum and his wife. We would stop at Cincinnati and visit Charley's nephew, Dr. Alfred Harry Crum, a urologist whose brother, Louis, was a student in the University of Cincinnati's medical college.

It was decided that I would live with the Crums, who had a big three-story house in the Clifton area, not far from the university. Louis and I shared the top floor with our own kitchen, living room, and separate bedrooms. Dr. Crum operated two clinics that specialized in the treatment of venereal diseases. He was also on the staff of a major Cincinnati hospital.

I spent the weekends working as an orderly in the hospital, picking up a little money on the side by mopping floors and cleaning up. On Saturday nights I would be in the emergency room, helping to move people around when they were brought in from accidents. I got the feel for hospital operations and saw some of the least-pleasant aspects of a doctor's task.

Sometimes Dr. Crum would take Louis and me to his clinics, where we would help treat people with venereal diseases. I was soon able to use the hypodermic needle with the dexterity of a real doctor, administering shots for gonorrhea and syphilis. I would wear a white suit and smock, and no one knew me from one of the doctors on duty.

I remember that in those days we treated syphilis with an arsenic solution injected directly into the bloodstream. The treatment consisted of six weeks of arsenic, six weeks of bismuth, followed by six weeks of treatment with still another solution. The female patients would have their vaginas swabbed out with potassium permanganate.

Social disease was a hush-hush thing in the 1930s. Patients came reluctantly because they were ashamed. The treatment was long and there was no guarantee of a cure. To make matters worse, the disease was usually in its advanced stages when a doctor saw the patient. The 36-week course of treatments was unpleasant for the patients, and we saw many a sad case.

After a successful first year at the University of Cincinnati, I came to realize that I was losing my enthusiasm for a career in medicine. I can honestly say that my new attitude was not caused by my contacts at Dr. Crum's clinics with the seamier side of the profession. There were three other reasons.

First, I discovered that it was a killing profession. Physician friends of Dr. Crum, many of them less than 50 years old, were dying off from heart attacks and other problems induced by hypertension and overwork. I could see that the demands of the profession were excessive.

Second, Dr. Crum was constantly complaining that the country was drifting toward socialized medicine. "A doctor's not going to be his own boss in a few years," he said many times. This was 40 years ago, and it has turned out that he was premature in his prediction.

The third and probably the most important reason was my growing infatuation with the airplane. Having already learned to fly in Florida, I spent much of my spare time in Cincinnati at Lunken airport, taking lessons and renting airplanes an hour at a time for the sheer fun of flying.

Now I was faced with a dilemma. There were the family's wishes to consider. Against these, I began to weigh my own doubts about the depth of my commitment to a career in medicine. I was well aware that becoming a doctor required complete dedication. One cannot accept a responsibility that often involves the matter of life or death unless he is capable of shutting outside thoughts from his mind.

As I gave deeper thought to the vexing question, I became aware that an aviation career, my alternative, also required dedication. Perhaps not of the same sort, but there was a skill involved in flying that called for the same commitment to excellence if one were to survive.

Dr. Crum seemed to sense that my interest in flying was beginning to supersede my enthusiasm for a medical career. Around the table at nightlong poker games in which I frequently participated, the doctors often talked of difficult operations and newly discovered medications. My contribution to these conversations often related to a new flying experience.

One day when we were alone, Dr. Crum surprised me by saying, "I'm not so sure you want to be a doctor."

I wondered how he had sensed something that was not entirely resolved in my own mind.

"You may be right," I said. "I'm not exactly sure of it myself."

I admitted that I had been giving serious thought to dropping out of school.

"Then why don't you do it?" he asked.

"Frankly," I replied, "I'm afraid of what my old man would say."

Dr. Crum was blunt. "To hell with the old man. He's lived his own life and he didn't ask you what he should do." The doctor, who had given me a great deal of good advice, for which I was grateful, sensed that aviation had become my principal interest. "If you want to fly, go ahead," he advised.

His words were welcome, but I still had misgivings. Even though it was apparent to thoughtful people that the aviation industry had a bright future, the romantic notion of becoming an airplane pilot did not include any immediate promise of finding a job.

As I groped for a decision in the fall and early winter of 1936, a recent event was taking air travel from the adventure category to one of safety and reliability.

The introduction of the Douglas DC-3, the first truly dependable airliner, was destined to revolutionize air transportation.

There were problems, however, when it came to finding a job in commercial aviation. First, there was the training and experience that would be needed to qualify. I was sure that dad would never foot the bill for what he would certainly consider an irrational and harebrained venture.

This left only the Army Air Corps which, I had learned, was looking for volunteers capable of surviving the rigorous training to become a pilot. Here was my opportunity to fly, and to do it at government expense.

Just before Christmas, I wrote to the Adjutant General and received an application to become a flying cadet.

On the train ride to Florida for the holidays, I tried to think of a way to break the news to dad. I felt sure he would blow his top and possibly threaten to read me out of the family. Mother would be disappointed but placid.

Coward that I was, I decided to postpone the showdown until after Christmas.

Mother quickly sensed that I had something on my mind. My lack of enthusiasm in answering questions about college must have been the tip-off. She asked a few perceptive questions and I finally told her of my decision. I was surprised that she didn't seem even slightly upset. It was apparent to her that my decision came after considerable soul-searching.

Looking at me for a moment without saying anything, she placed her hand on my shoulder and said, "If you want to fly, go right ahead and do it, because I know you will be all right."

Her words reflected the faith and trust that were part of her nature. They were said bravely, because I knew she had no great confidence in the safety of flying. I also knew that she would worry. But her faith that I would be all right helped me through many a hazardous situation in a flying career that was to take me into many unfriendly skies.

Neither she nor I gave thought to the possibility that I would ever be flying in combat. War seemed very remote in the mid-thirties. Even though I had attended military school, my decision to become a soldier was simply a device to get into an airplane.

Having successfully passed the hurdle of telling mother, I now faced the more fearsome task of breaking the news to the old man. I called him "old man" with no disrespect because it was a term then widely used by the younger generation which, a few years before, had invented the expletive, "So's your old man!"

His reaction was not what I expected. Possibly he had sensed my change in attitude, as mother had. I don't remember his exact words, but they weren't harsh. He simply let me know that he regarded me as some kind of a nut. Perhaps the fact that I had already made application to the Air Corps convinced him that there was nothing he could do to deter me.

The difference between the reactions of mother and father had to do with their estimations of my survivability. Mother expressed confidence that I would be all right. Dad was sure I would be dead in a short time because he didn't believe the airplane was here to stay.

The die had been cast and I was on my way to a career in the sky. It was fortunate that I was confident, even cocky, in those days. Otherwise I would have worried over the possibility of washing out of the military pilot training program. The thought of failure never occurred to me.

6 Winning My Wings

Back in Cincinnati after Christmas vacation, I watched every mail for a reply to my flying cadet application. The official-looking brown government envelope finally arrived in early February. It contained a notice to report to Wright field at Dayton, Ohio, for my physical examination.

I was the picture of health and passed the exam without difficulty. Asked when I would be ready to start in flying school, I answered with one word: "Now."

Actually, things don't happen that fast in the army. First I was required to report to Fort Thomas, Kentucky, for formal induction. Military aviation was not a separate service in those days, and so I would become a member of the Army Air Corps.

The results of my physical examination and my application for pilot training arrived at Fort Thomas ahead of me. After taking the oath, I had another brief wait before being ordered to report to Randolph field at San Antonio, Texas.

Although enthusiastic, I had no illusions about the career I had chosen. It was 1937 and the nation was still in the Depression. Jobs were scarce, particularly among young people. Many were smart enough to see that there was a future in aviation, but few could afford the expense of civilian flight training, so they turned to the military, as I had.

As a result, the Air Corps had more applicants than it could handle within its limited peacetime budget. The screening process was rigorous and the washout rate among candidates was high. It was the old question of supply and demand, and the supply was considerably greater than the demand for aviation cadets. Many of those who were washed out of the program were probably quite capable of becoming good pilots.

I was determined to succeed. America's military training program was the best in the world. Not only would we get first-rate experience in progressively better equipment, we would also get uniforms, food, medical care, a place to live, and regular pay while learning.

Looking back, I realize that I had many things going for me in getting into the Air Cadet program. I had more college training than most of the applicants, and I had limited experience with civilian flying. I had also been to military school.

Randolph had a "dodo" system that almost amounted to hazing. Applying pressure to the newcomers to see what our reactions would be was, I suppose, an effective way of singling out the weaklings or those who might be emotionally insecure or mentally unstable. You were a "dodo" for three months. While many of the cadets sweated out this period, it was like water off a duck's back for me. I had been a plebe for a whole year in military school and three months now seemed but a short time to put up with the army's form of torment. I knew what to expect, and I knew I could take it. The close order drill, the daily inspection, the constant pressure, and the threat of getting demerits or being washed out were all old stuff to me. And I have to admit that I was willing to take a lot of punishment if it would help me become a pilot.

As far as flying was concerned, I suppose I was about an average cadet. Through no fault of my own, I had three instructors before completing the primary phase of flight training.

I don't even remember the name of my first instructor. After a few preliminary lessons, he was transferred to meteorology school.

My next instructor was Lieutenant George Slater, a dapper fellow with a little mustache. He wore a Sam Brown belt, jodhpurs and riding boots, and always carried a swagger stick. He was the personification of the typical aviator of those days. The well-known joking admonition to remove your spurs before climbing into the cockpit of one of those old wood-and-rag airplanes could have been meant for him. He was cocky, but he had reason to be. He was a crack pilot and an excellent instructor.

Civilian experience didn't mean anything in military flight training. A cadet who might have flown the mail for years as a civilian pilot still had to have eight hours of dual instruction at Randolph before he could solo a military airplane. Those were army regulations. No exceptions, no excuses. The rule was a good thing in my case, even though I considered myself a moderately capable pilot as the result of my hours of instruction in Florida and at Cincinnati's Lunken field.

I had a little trouble with my first military airplane—a PT-3, ancient even by the standards of that day. The airplane, built by Consolidated back in the 1920s, was nothing but a fuselage and a pair of wings held together by what looked like baling wire. For shock absorbers the landing gear used a bungee cord, which was nothing more than a cable made up of several strands of rubber, the kind used in making rubber bands. The only instrument in the cockpit was an altimeter. On a panel out on the wing there were three other instruments: a tachometer to tell you how fast the Wright engine was turning the propeller, a cylinder head temperature gauge, and an oil pressure gauge.

In front of the open cockpit was a very narrow windshield that served almost like the needle ball on better-equipped airplanes. As long as your controls were coordinated, the tiny windshield would keep the blast of the propeller off your face. Slip or skid a little and the wind would slap you in the face, tearing at your helmet and goggles. This tendency would not have been a problem if the airplanes flew the way they should, but class after class of students bouncing in to landings had messed up the rigging of some of the trainers so that it was normal for them to fly through the air sideways. There was a joke that you could tell whether a student held too much or too little right rudder on takeoffs by which side of his goggles was more splattered with bug juice.

Despite the sometimes strange behavior of this airplane, things went well for me until it came time to solo. This should have been easy, since I had encountered no trouble when Rusty Heard turned me loose for the first time in a Taylor Cub at Opa Locka. But this airplane was no Taylor Cub. It seemed fragile, although the engine was more powerful. Somehow I developed a hangup whenever I tried to land.

For those who have had no experience with the old "tail-draggers," as they were called, let me explain what a landing was like in those days. The idea was to make a "three-point landing" in which the two wheels and the rear skid touch the ground at the same instant.

Such a landing required judgment and coordination. To achieve one, you chop the throttle and aim for the spot on the field where you intend to land, maintaining a good safe gliding speed during descent.

Near the ground, you pull back on the control stick. This slows the airplane. Ideally, you reach what is called the "stall speed," at which the airplane refuses to fly, when you are only a foot or less above the ground, whereupon the plane settles gently on the surface.

Two things can go wrong. If you fail to reach stall speed, you fly the plane into the ground. If you stall prematurely and run out of airspeed while 10 feet or more above the surface, you drop suddenly to a hard and sometimes disastrous landing.

I developed the haunting fear that either of these miscalculations would wreck the frail airplane and wash me out of the air cadet program. George Slater sensed this and decided one day to cure me of my timidity. As I came around for a landing and started to ease back on the control stick for what would certainly be a mushy landing, the stick suddenly jumped out of my hand and the instructor's voice came through the gosport to my earphones.

"I'll show you that you can't hurt this goddamned thing," he shouted. With that he jammed the throttle all the way open and pushed the stick forward. The two wheels smacked into the ground with such force that I expected the whole airplane to collapse in a mass of broken struts and torn fabric, with the hot engine ending up in my lap.

Instead, the plane took a mighty bounce. We leaped up higher than the tops of the hangars. And my heart flew right up into my throat.

At the top of the bounce, Slater didn't let the plane stall out. He simply gave it power and we started around the pattern again. I learned my lesson. The PT-3 was more rugged than I had thought. And my next two landings were so successful that, when we rolled to a stop after the second, the instructor climbed out of the cockpit.

"Now we'll see if you've really got it," he said, waving me on for my first solo attempt in a military training plane.

I was surprised but no longer afraid of failure. The solo flight went off smoothly, and I had cleared the biggest hurdle of the primary training program. I considered myself lucky to have had an instructor who knew how to straighten me out. A few days later, George Slater was transferred to West Point as an instructor in mathematics.

My next instructor was Neil Osborne, one of the quietest and gentlest men I ever knew . He was also a fine pilot. He had faith in himself and transferred that faith to me. His calm approach to the finer points of flying was just what I needed after the tussle I had been through. As a result, I completed the rest of the primary course with no problems.

Graduating from primary training in those days meant moving to the other side of Randolph field for the basic flying classes. We were given a new airplane, the BT-9, a low-wing monoplane with a little more power and speed than the primary trainer. It also had more problems.

One of the men who had enlisted with me at Fort Thomas and was with me on the train to San Antonio was Frank Fisch, a big, good-natured guy from Mansfield, Ohio, who had been a football player in the Ohio State University backfield.

At Randolph we became roommates. Frank was healthy and strong and, on the football field, he operated like a well-constructed machine. Off the field it was a different story. He seemed to lack coordination. He was a fine fellow, however, and I spent hours teaching him such basics as left-face and right-face and about-face. Luckily, he was taller than I so I didn't have to march behind him in formation. He was always getting out of step and skipping to get back in stride. He simply didn't have the rhythm to keep in cadence.

We had to drill with rifles. This was old stuff to me because of my years in the military academy. I was continually afraid that Frank would make a wrong turn and swat someone in the head with his rifle. Teaching him the manual of arms was about like teaching a monkey the touch system of typing.

He was completely unaware of the tricks to getting a room ready for inspection. I knew the inspecting officer wouldn't be satisfied until he found something wrong, and I was an old hand at the game of making his job a tough one. You'd better believe that I dusted the tops of the doors, and the inside as well as the outside of the bedsprings. I could milk the faucets in the washroom so there wouldn't be a drop of water for the inspector to complain about.

We got so good that one inspector, after looking everywhere else, used the age-old trick I had known at Western: rubbing the tip of his white glove over the soles of his shoes and, when the inevitable black smudge appeared, calmly noting in his report book that our floor was dirty.

Frank Fisch and I were opposites in many ways, so we used each other's strengths and weaknesses. We were ideal roommates and became good friends. We remained together when we shifted from primary to basic training.

The BT-9 was not only a hotter airplane than the PT-3; it was less forgiving. It had extremely bad stall characteristics. Some airplanes start to buffet and feel mushy 5 or 10 knots before reaching stall speed. Not so with the BT-9.

Fly it too slow and, with no warning at all, the nose of the airplane would dip and the stick would whiplash out of your hand, forward and left, sending the plane into a tight spin from which it was a struggle to recover.

Many modern civilian airplanes won't go into a spin. Some that you can force to spin just turn lazily with the nose a little below the horizon. To recover, you simply take your hands and feet off the controls and the airplane will pull out automatically.

The BT-9 wasn't that kind of an airplane. We had orders not to stall it unless we were at least 5,000 feet above the ground. We couldn't do a full-turn spin but were allowed to practice a half-turn. It took a good pilot 2,000 feet to recover from that.

Needless to say, the airplane didn't have a good safety record. The very first accident our group had after starting our basic training took the lives of my roommate and his instructor. This grievous blow was my first taste of the personal tragedies that a career military man learns to live with.

As Frank's roommate, I was designated an honor guard to accompany his body back to Mansfield for burial. It was a sad time in my young life, and I did a lot of thinking on that long train ride to Ohio and back. I talked to Frank's parents and stayed in Mansfield for the funeral services. All told, I was away from Randolph for five days.

When I returned, I found the instructors worried about the effect this experience might have on my flying and my mental attitude. I could tell that they were concerned by the questions they asked and by the solicitous way they treated me.

Finally one of the instructors, Roger Ramey, with whom I would cross paths many times in my future military career, came right out and asked what this accident was going to mean to me. I had already asked myself the question and had worked out the answer in my own mind.

"Well, I lost a good friend and that's not easy," I told him. "On the other hand, I have to look at it as one of the bad breaks of the game. On that basis, I'm not going to let it get me down. He's not the first good man killed in an airplane and he won't be the last. I'm going to do the best job I can."

I believe the tragic death of my friend Frank Fisch helped form in my mind a fatalistic philosophy that stays with me to this day. That attitude helped me in my own flying career and in the forming of command decisions that had to be made even though they sometimes meant that good men, some of them close friends, might lose their lives.

As it turned out, I performed better in basic training than I had in primary. They started teaching us basic instrument flying and I caught on very easily. I liked to fly by instruments and passed all the required check rides ahead of schedule.

There was a great deal of solo flight time in this phase of our training. Much as I liked to fly simply for the thrill of it, I never used these opportunities merely to bore holes in the sky. On every solo, I kept busy trying to improve my proficiency.

I stuck to the rules because I was convinced that they were the way to become a good pilot. I resisted all temptations to become a daredevil. I may have been one of the few cadets in my class who never flew under a certain Seguin River bridge that offered a challenge not easily resisted.

My hard work and determination paid dividends. When our class finished basic, I had the highest flying rating. The record was important at this point because the cadets with the best ratings were most likely to be given their choice of advanced training when we moved to Kelly field on the other side of town. There were just two choices: pursuit or observation. There was no bombardment in those days.

My inclination was to fly the fast fighters, or pursuit planes as they were called then. I was small and I thought of myself as a hot pilot. But Bill Seibert, a West Pointer before he went into flight training and became one of the company tactical officers at Randolph, advised me to ask for observation training.

He explained things this way:

"If you fly fighters, when you get through training you're going into the GHQ [General Headquarters] Air Corps. If you go there, I'll guarantee you that for at least a year you'll never fly an airplane alone. All of your flying will be in formation with someone else deciding where you go and how you get there. You'll be escorted on every mission. But if you choose observation, you're going to do most of your flying on your own and you'll be making your own decisions."

His reasoning appealed to my independent nature.

When I started as a cadet, there were 138 in my class. Of this number, only 58 graduated. Many had washed out. Others—too many others—met the same fate as Frank Fisch. A few decided flying wasn't for them and transferred to other army jobs.

It was expected that the top pilots of the 58 survivors would want to become fighter pilots. When I told my instructor of my decision to take observation training, he threw up his hands as if I had lost my mind. After I explained my reasoning, he acknowledged that I might have a point. But I am sure he was puzzled.

I must admit that I had some misgivings at the time. I wasn't nearly as comfortable with my choice as I had expected, for now I was separated, in training, from most of the top-rated cadets whose flying skills I respected.

I know now that Bill Seibert gave me good advice, and the decision was one of the most important of my life. If I had gone into fighters, I would most likely have been a single-engine pilot until I retired. With due respect for those who prefer this kind of flying, I must say that it was not for me. Observation training was important from my standpoint because it opened the door to multi-engine flying, an experience that would bring me to an unanticipated rendezvous with history in years to come.

Upon graduation from the advanced training program at Kelly field, I became a brand-new second lieutenant in the Army Air Corps. I had a pair of silver wings over my left breast pocket and 260 hours of flying in my log book.

I had looked forward to the moment when the lieutenant's gold bar was pinned on my uniform, but an almost equal thrill came with the arrival of my father from Florida to witness the graduation ceremony.

Dad had been the grudging skeptic when I announced my plans to give up medical school and enter the Army Air Corps, but my letters home, relating my successful advancement through the three stages of training in Texas, had apparently modified his attitude. If he couldn't have a doctor for a son, he would settle for a pilot.

He came early and I showed him around the field and introduced him to Ted Timberlake, one of my instructors, who later became a three-star general. Ted spent a lot of time with dad and laid it on rather thick about my promising career as a military flier. After all, I was graduating at the head of my class, and this was a matter of pride for dad.

After a long conversation with Timberlake, he broke down and confessed that I had probably made the right decision. "After being here and meeting some of these men you're involved with," he said, "I feel a hell of a lot better about this thing than I did. I can see why you like it and I think it's going to be great for you."

He was probably the proudest member of the audience at the graduation ceremony on that February day in 1938. I had won an important battle on the home front. Mother didn't come for the ceremony, but I knew all along that she was on my side.

7 Fort Benning

With the brand new gold bars of a second lieutenant on my shoulders, I reported in February of 1938 to Fort Benning at Columbus, Georgia, ready for anything they might have for a fledgling pilot at the home of the United States Infantry School.

Reporting to the 16th Observation Squadron at Lawson Field, I was assigned to Flight B. My operations officer was Lieutenant William H. Tunner, who was later to make a name for himself flying the Hump in the China-Burma-India theater and, after the war, as the man who ran the successful Berlin airlift.

I reported to Tunner along with Marvin Zipp, who had also been a classmate of mine at Kelly field. We learned that we were to replace two men who had recently been killed in an airplane crash.

Bill Tunner took us to the operations room. On the wall was one of those old Department of Commerce maps showing the locations of all approved landing fields. Tunner took a string and placed one end of it at Fort Benning. With a pencil attached to the other end, he drew a circle with a 100-mile radius.

"As soon as you've landed at every one of the fields in that circle, you'll be ready for your first cross-country trip," he told us.

There was a surprising number of airports in that circle. At least the map identified a lot of places as airports, but it was soon obvious that the map was out of date. Some of the landing strips were so grown up in weeds that they couldn't be seen from the air.

Marvin Zipp and I managed to hit about three of those fields a day, and it wasn't unusual to land in weeds as high as your head. Each day when we returned to Benning we would "x" out, on the map, the fields where we had landed. Miraculously, we managed to get in and out of every field in that circle without flipping the plane over on its back.

We were flying an airplane called the O-46, a high gull-wing built by Consolidated and powered by a 750-horsepower Pratt and Whitney engine. Its fuselage was long and narrow, and the landing gear was very high. For the first few hours, I had to get used to sitting so far above the ground. In the air it was a good, stable airplane, a real pleasure to fly.

For my first cross-country solo flight, I wanted to go back to Miami to show off a bit and let my parents know that I was trusted to fly off alone with an Air Corps plane. Bill Tunner gave me some good advice about the trip.

"When you get home, you are going to have the temptation to buzz the house. You may even feel like doing a slow roll or something reckless just to show off.

"Now take it from me. Don't do it!

"You may be a pretty hot-shot pilot but this is how hot-shot pilots get killed. A lot of guys have put on a show for their parents or a girl friend and spun into the ground right before their eyes. It's not a pretty sight and it's not the way to end your first trip home."

I learned later that five of my classmates who went to pursuit planes were killed on their first cross-country flights home.

I took Tunner's warning to heart, and on that first trip I was strictly a law abiding citizen. I did everything by the book and didn't even fly over my house. I landed at the nearest airport, Chapman field, having already telephoned my parents. They were waiting at the field when I got there.

Chapman was an army reserve field with one hangar and a 1,600-foot dirt runway, which I didn't use. I gained more landing room by coming down diagonally on the sod. It was not only the field nearest my home, but the only one in the area with army gasoline. (The field isn't there any more. Located along Cutter's ridge, it is now the site of a housing development.)

After I started flying larger planes, I couldn't get into Chapman. I then landed at old Miami airport at 36th Street, now Miami

International. It wasn't much of an airport then—just one runway of crushed coral rock and a CAA communications shack.

A later trip home resulted in one of the more memorable experiences of my early flying career: the first and only time I ever landed an airplane on a highway.

Returning from Miami to Fort Benning, I had a tail wind at first. Because of it I believed I could make the flight without refueling, even though the normal range of my plane was only a little over 500 miles, and my trip would cover 600 miles.

An unexpected head wind developed, however, and somewhere beyond Waycross I discovered that my fuel supply was dangerously low. There were fields in the area suitable for an emergency landing, but I didn't look forward to the prospect of spending the night in a farmhouse and having to telephone the base and explain my predicament to some unsympathetic superior officer.

Just as I had resigned myself to such a misfortune and was circling to land in a cow pasture, I spotted a nearby highway on which there was no traffic in sight. Up the road a short distance I could see a filling station.

With the gas tank nearly empty and no time to spare, I brought the plane down on the road, taxied to the filling station and asked the surprised attendant for five dollars worth of gasoline. He obliged and even volunteered to flag down a couple of approaching automobiles long enough for me to take off. I was back at the base only ten minutes behind my scheduled arrival time.

I didn't mention my experience for several days. When I finally got up the nerve to confess, the commander of our little air facility laughed and said I was just plain lucky. If that sort of thing happened today, there would be hell to pay.

There were several types of aircraft at Benning, none of them frontline equipment even for that day, but still quite suitable for building flying experience. In addition to the O-46, they had some BT-2s and a B-10.

It wasn't long before an C-47 arrived. This was the first 200-mile-an-hour airplane on the base and the first with retractable landing gear. Built by Douglas, it was also the military's first all-metal midwing airplane. Powered by a Wright engine, it performed well but had a strange pot-bellied appearance. It was designed for a crew of three, with the pilot up front, a gunner in the rear, and an observer in the belly.

I made my first truly long cross-country flight in an O-47, having been assigned to fly two infantry officers out to Hamilton field in California for the San Francisco World's Fair. We made many stops along the way because the airplane carried only a 3½-hour supply of fuel. By the time we reached the coast, my propeller was out of balance, causing the airplane to vibrate like a washing machine. Apparently I had picked up a rock at one of the dirt fields where we had landed. There was a big nick in the prop, and we had to send it back to be repaired and rebalanced.

We had planned to stay at Hamilton field for three days but ended up with an eight-day vacation in San Francisco. Ever since military aviation came into being, pilots have been inventing engine trouble or mechanical difficulties that needed to be fixed only when they reached some city or country with interesting vacation possibilities. But this emergency was legitimate and everyone knew it.

Romance came into my life not long after my arrival at Fort Benning. I had dated frequently in college but had not given serious thought to the fair sex until now.

It all started one night when Billy Beasley, a bachelor friend in our outfit, invited me to join him on a double date. There was to be a picnic on base and Billy's girl would bring along a friend. Her name was Lucy Wingate.

Lucy lived in Columbus and was clerking in a department store there. We hit it off from the start, and that first date led to another and then another. Within a couple of months, we decided to get married. For some reason that escapes me now, I didn't want my fellow officers to know of my plans in advance. Lucy and I obtained the marriage license at the courthouse in Columbus and arranged to have the notice kept out of the local newspaper. The wedding was strictly hush-hush. I didn't even notify my commanding officer, as I was supposed to, because I thought it was none of his business.

The ceremony took place on the evening of June 19 at a Catholic seminary in the village of Holy Trinity, Alabama, a short distance southwest of the Fort Benning reservation on the opposite side of the Chattahoochee River. Although nominally a Protestant, I was not a practicing churchgoer. Lucy was a Catholic.

I had obtained a 10-day leave and, from Holy Trinity, we drove on to Miami to visit my parents, stopping overnight at a hotel in a small town along the way. We made the trip in a shiny new gourd-green Pontiac sedan I had purchased in Texas four months earlier, after graduating from the Air Cadet training program.

I didn't tell my bride about the difficulties of life as an army wife because, quite frankly, I wasn't aware of them myself. There was no way of forecasting future events that would keep us apart for long periods of time—the war and a variety of unexpected assignments during the postwar years.

Dad and mother were just about floored when I arrived at home in Miami with Lucy, whom I introduced as Mrs. Tibbets. I had never confided to them that I was even considering marriage but, after the momentary shock wore off, they were quite gracious. By now they had become reconciled to the unexpected where their only son was concerned.

Returning from Florida, we set up housekeeping in one of the units provided on the base for married officers. My life pattern changed somewhat but the flying schedule continued to be exhausting. These were happy days. I was flying airplanes to my heart's content. The military life at this well-established army base was pleasant. Lucy and I made many friends, and there was a satisfying round of social activity.

An addition to the family arrived on November 19, 1940. Paul Tibbets III was born at the base hospital to swell an already impressive reproduction rate among the Fort Benning families. He was the 123rd out of 137 babies to be born at the base that year.

By late 1940, the role of the military was becoming more important than when I had reported to Fort Benning more than a year and a half before. The war in Europe was in full swing and the nation was divided on the question of whether we would be drawn in. The odds against involvement were shortening daily as America took sides openly against the Axis powers.

Meanwhile I had been introduced to multi-engine aircraft. By this time there was a number of B-10s at Benning. The B-10 was a twin-engine plane that was designed as a bomber. However, it was slow and not really suited to combat use. It was relegated to a utility role when the B-18 came along and replaced it as a bomber. Marvin Zipp and I, as young second lieutenants, were given a lot of the jobs that were done by the B-10 because the pilots with more seniority found them undesirable.

Because the B-10 would sit up there and chug along through the sky almost all day, it was often used for towing targets. Zipp and I would tow target sleeves for the ground troops at Benning and would sometimes fly down over the Gulf of Mexico and tow targets for the Coast Artillery anti-aircraft gunners.

One day I would fly the early morning mission and then land while Zipp took over for the midday target flight. Then I would fly again in the late afternoon. That meant we flew 10 hours one day and five the next, alternately, for the whole summer. You might think that we would weary of this flying routine, but we didn't. When there was no other excuse for flying, we would figure out different places to go for dinner. Through this daily flying schedule, we logged a great deal of multi-engine time, all of which looked good on our records.

About this time, the Air Corps took a look at these records in search of pilots with more than 1,000 hours of twin-engine time. I was high in the group, with about 1,500 hours in the B-10. Because of this, I was selected for the Third Attack Group at Savannah, Georgia. The group was just being supplied with the new A-20 Douglas attack plane. I was excited over the prospect of flying this hot new high-performance aircraft.

8 Skeet-shooting With George Patton

George Smith Patton, one of World War II's most colorful and legendary figures, was my hunting companion and skeet-shooting rival. We became personal friends, but I never presumed on this relationship because of the great difference in our military ranks. I came to be one of his great admirers because I had an opportunity to observe his military genius first-hand.

I was a mere second lieutenant and Patton was a lieutenant colonel when he arrived at Fort Benning in 1938. Even though we spent much time together on the skeet range and in his personal airplane, I always addressed him as "colonel." Only the most senior officers called him by his first name. Despite his well-known use of profanity and other colorful language, I never thought of him as an officer who would become famous around the world as "Old Blood and Guts." He was basically a very down-to-earth sort of man.

Colonel Patton's arrival at Fort Benning was an event never to be forgotten by those of us who were stationed there. He and Mrs. Patton brought with them a retinue of servants and a stable of saddle horses and polo ponies. Since boyhood, he had lived in the grandest of luxury and he saw no reason to modify his life-style while serving his country in a military capacity.

Patton's independence was born of the fact that he paid his own way. I was told that he drew only a dollar a year of his officer's salary and signed the rest over to the Army Relief. With all his millions, he would scream in fury whenever I won a few quarters from him on the skeet range. It wasn't that he cared about the money. He simply detested the idea of losing at anything.

With such a background, it is little wonder that Patton and his wife, Beatrice, who came from a wealthy New England family, could not easily adjust to the modest quarters normally assigned to them at various military posts. At Fort Benning, Patton paid a local lumber dealer, Jim Woodward, to build him a home according to a design drawn by Mrs. Patton. It was long and sprawling, with picture windows looking out upon a panorama of Georgia pines. Its paneled interior featured a huge fireplace of native stone. Less than three years later, upon being transferred to California, they donated the house to the army.

It was by rare coincidence that I, a very junior birdman, became acquainted with this brilliant pistol-carrying warrior who would later be recognized as the world's greatest strategist in armored warfare.

Because I was known to be a shotgun enthusiast, I was given the job of assisting Lt. Col. Bob Turley in the operation of the skeet range at the Fort Benning officers' club. I would arrive at 9:30 every Sunday morning and help Turley put things in order for the day's shooting. We would set the traps and load the houses with clay birds.

It was on one of those Sunday mornings that Colonel Patton showed up in a handsomely tailored shooting coat, carrying an expensive shotgun. He introduced himself and suggested that we have a match. Bill Golden, a wealthy manufacturer from nearby Columbus and a skeet shooter of considerable skill, came at about the same time.

Including Turley and me, we were a foursome who, starting that day, met at the range every Sunday morning for a couple of hours of spirited shooting competition. When Colonel Patton said, at the end of the first day's match, "I'll see you next Sunday," it was virtually a command for the rest of us. We usually had the range to ourselves because we were among the few shooters who did not attend religious services regularly.

Although the stakes were a mere 25 cents for each string of shots, you would have thought the world skeet championship was at stake. Patton took his shooting seriously, as he did every other activity in which he engaged, from polo games to tank battles. In this connection, it is worth mentioning that he finished fifth in the pentathlon event at the 1912 Olympic games in Stockholm.

Golden was the best shooter of our group and I was probably next, although Patton was skilled with the shotgun and carried off a fair share of the quarters. He thrived on this weekly competition and was loudly jubilant when he won. Victory was indispensable to his character.

Patton and I hunted together on the military reservation which was 25 miles square, covering an area of pine forests in what was once Georgia plantation country. It was well stocked with game that included wild turkeys, pheasants, and deer. There was also an abundance of quail and doves.

The master strategist stalked the game in much the same manner as his armored units would soon pursue the enemy. "You've got to be smarter than the pheasant if you're going to have one for dinner," he once told me.

While at Fort Benning, Patton was promoted first to colonel and then to brigadier general, but his rank made no difference in his relationship with junior officers. Although strictly correct and sometimes abrupt with his associates while on duty, he was "one of the boys" on the shooting range and in the field. There, he would drop his military stance and display the intensely down-to-earth side of his character. He had a keen sense of humor and was blessed with the ability to share a laugh at his own expense.

One incident that I remember quite well came in 1940, when Patton's outfit was demonstrating the speed, firepower, and maneuverability of some newly acquired tanks. Bleachers and loudspeakers were set up in the demonstration area, and a large number of officers from various units, in addition to tank corps students, turned out to watch the show.

The tanks clattered by in formation, then turned and smashed down a number of fair-sized trees. The instructors kept the spectators informed of what was happening. Patton himself took over the microphone at one point. He was a heroic figure in his whipcord breeches and shiny leather boots.

Inspired perhaps by the size of his audience, he was suddenly seized with the impulse to do something spectacular. On a nearby hillside was an abandoned farm-house in ramshackle condition. A tank had just come to a stop in front of the bleachers and its driver, a sergeant, was pointing out features that made this equipment superior to the old tanks.

Patton broke into the sergeant's lecture and said, "Now I'll show you what this tank can do. See that house over there? I'm going to knock it down."

The sergeant started to protest. "But sir," he said, "I wouldn't do—"

The general waved him aside and said, "Never mind, sergeant, I'm going to show these people something."

Before the sergeant could remonstrate further, Patton climbed through the hatch, let himself down into the driver's seat, and went roaring across the field and up the hill in a cloud of dust.

The old frame house shuddered as Patton's tank smashed into it at full speed. Splinters flew in every direction as one side of the structure collapsed. But the big tank failed to come out the other side as it was supposed to. The spectators watched in puzzled expectancy, and a couple of tank corpsmen, including the sergeant, rushed to the house.

A few moments later they emerged, accompanied by Patton. "Why didn't someone tell me there was a basement under that house?" asked the general, who was in good spirits despite his misadventure. Suddenly he realized that the sergeant had been trying to tell him just that. Striding to a microphone that had been set up for the demonstration, he showed no sign of embarrassment.

"There's a lesson in this," he told his audience of military personnel. "Always listen to your sergeant."

Patton had not been given the "Blood and Guts" nickname when I knew him, and none of the officers at Benning dared address him as "Georgie," a familiarity reserved for a handful of long-time personal friends and a few military associates of equal or superior rank, including General Eisenhower.

In addition to our skeet shooting and hunting, I sometimes flew Patton's private airplane. This turn of events began when he decided one day that the airplane would be a useful tool in developing tactics for the armored brigade that he had been sent to Fort Benning to organize. He wanted to observe tank maneuvers from the air and requested the Pentagon to authorize flight training and the assignment of an airplane for his personal use so that he could be his own "eye in the sky" when his tanks were operating on the ground.

The request was forwarded to Washington, and the reply came back negative. The usefulness of armored warfare on the grand scale that he had in mind was still questioned by old-school military leaders, despite the newly achieved success of German Panzers in Poland and France. The idea of supplying an airplane for the use of a tank commander was deemed preposterous by the unimaginative brass at army headquarters.

Patton was angry. After relieving himself of a few descriptive epithets, he said, "Then I'll buy an airplane and fly it myself." No one at Benning knew at the time that he had owned and flown an airplane some 20 years before.

He promptly carried out his threat, purchasing a plane from Ralph Swaybe, who ran a flying service at a small airport along the Chattahoochee river near Columbus. It was a two-place Stinson Voyageur, well suited for his purpose. He brushed up on his flying skills by taking lessons from Swaybe.

Seeing that he meant business, the military brass that had refused to assign him an airplane now became concerned that he might kill himself. There was no objection to his use of a private airplane, if only someone else were to fly it. Another second lieutenant, B.B. "Buckshot" Taylor, and I were assigned to take turns piloting the Patton plane. To qualify for the operation of a private aircraft, I first had to obtain a civilian license, which was no problem.

From then on, the Stinson became a familiar sight in the air over Fort Benning as we flew low above fields and forests where the armored units were operating. Our altitude was often no more than 100 feet and sometimes we skimmed the treetops as Patton kept an alert eye on the tank maneuvers. Sometimes he would curse and shake his fists in anger and often he would cheer and wave his hands in excited approval, depending on how well his tanks were carrying out their assignments.

Usually when I flew Patton over a war games area, we would take off from and return to an established airfield, but there were times when he wished to land near the scene of operations. For this purpose, his men on the ground would locate a suitable flat area, sometimes a cow pasture, and designate it for us with strips of white canvas.

We flew to Louisiana for the famous war games of 1941, in which

Patton demonstrated the effectiveness of armored warfare with a display of mobility that caught the conventional forces off guard. I remember very well his elation after out-maneuvering "the enemy" in one critical mock engagement. "That will show the bastards they can't stop a well-planned tank attack," he said as we skimmed a cypress swamp one day and watched his swift-moving armored columns close in for the "capture" of Shreveport.

The "bastards" embraced a large number of conventional army commanders, including particularly General Lesley J. McNair, who were determined to show that heavily armored equipment was not a decisive element in warfare. As director of the maneuvers, McNair was in a position to influence the official decision on the outcome, for the umpires, far from being unbiased, were under his orders. It was a "no-win" situation.

Patton was the very picture of self-confidence and he took the pettiness of the old guard in stride. History was on his side and he knew it. The people who really counted—General George C. Marshall, the chief of staff, and the rapidly rising colonel, Dwight Eisenhower—were impressed by the tank commander's performance. These were the men for whom Patton was putting on his spectacular show of armored maneuverability.

Although a hard-riding cavalry officer between wars, Patton constantly studied and devised tactics for armored combat, recognizing it as the wave of the future. This conclusion, I understand, was based on his experience with the earliest type of tank equipment in the Meuse-Argonne campaign toward the end of World War I.

Wounded in a show of personal heroism that involved more reckless courage than good judgment, he was awarded the Distinguished Service Cross for bravery under fire. At the end of the war, Patton was 33 years old and had attained the rank of colonel. In the peacetime army he dropped back to captain, and it was 18 years before he regained his eagles. He was a lieutenant colonel when I met him, although he became a brigadier general at Fort Benning. Rapidly winning recognition as a brilliant strategist and daring field commander, he was to attain four-star rank before the end of World War II.

His death in December 1945 came as the result of an automobile accident in Germany when, on a Sunday morning, he was on the way to a wooded area for a pheasant hunt. Beside him in his staff car was a shotgun which, to me, symbolized this amazing war hero more accurately than did the ivory-handled pistols for which he was famous.

He was tall, erect, and the very impressive picture of a military commander. I am glad to have known him in his nonmilitary role, for indeed he was able to throw off the mask of authority and relax in his favorite hobbies of shooting, polo, and horsemanship. My relationship with him was seldom that of a subordinate to a commander, for even while we were flying over a maneuver area, we were in his personal plane and I was a chauffeur with no responsibility for the operation except to place Patton in the position of greatest visibility.

It was a grandstand seat from which I was a spectator to the shaping of a strategy that had much to do with the defeat of the Axis armies in North Africa and Europe.

In addition to being a meticulous strategist and planner, Patton was an articulate speaker who frequently lectured on the subject of tank warfare. I attended one such lecture in which he and two fellow officers gave an illustrated analysis of Nazi armored successes in Europe. He supplied background information obtained by a careful reading of books written before the war by German Panzer generals Heinz Guderian and Erwin Rommel.

In view of my own role in the next and even more revolutionary transformation of warfare—the introduction of nuclear weaponry— it seems worth observing that Patton was among the first to recognize that the tactics he had helped to perfect had suddenly become obsolete.

He reached this conclusion almost immediately after learning, in April of 1945, that the United States was developing an atomic bomb. At that time the project was still secret to commanders in the Pacific, but Patton was told of it for two reasons. First, he was assigned to satisfy the curiosity of American military leaders about the progress that the Germans had made toward the development of atomic weapons. He found they were far behind the United States. Second, with the war in Europe nearing an end, he was anticipating a major role in planning and participating in the next big battle: the invasion of Japan. He was instantly aware that, if the atomic project was a success, there would be no such battle.

9 Flying Low

Towing targets in that B-10 at Fort Benning gave me considerable multi-engine experience, but the A-20 was a different and far more advanced airplane.

Arriving at Savannah in June 1941, I was assigned to be the engineering officer of the 90th Squadron of the Third Attack Group. The next few months were the most important of my career from the standpoint of learning to become a precision pilot.

There were no living quarters for married officers on the base at Savannah. Although I didn't know how long I would be stationed there, I rented an apartment in town so that Lucy and the baby could be with me.

The A-20 engines gave us problems at first and, as engineering officer, I had to figure out how to cope with them. The experience was useful in the future, for knowledge of engines is important to a pilot who stakes his life on their performance.

Our trouble in this case was caused by engine back-pressure. When we throttled back for an approach and landing, the oil would sometimes be pumped out of the oil cooler-breather. We found the solution before long.

As a pilot, I was learning a totally new type of tactical flying. I had been taught from my first days at Randolph that there was safety in altitude. If trouble developed, you had time to make decisions. There was time to bail out or possibly glide to a safe landing place. Altitude was money in the bank when the going got tough.

Now we were getting into a type of flying where altitude could be costly. High-flying planes could be picked up by a newly invented device called radar, which gave anti-aircraft gunners a chance to track you, even if you were above the clouds, and shoot you out of the sky.

A-20 flying was right down on the deck and, believe me, it was a thrill a minute. Our orders were to fly at no more than 100 feet above the ground on all tactical missions. The terrain over which we trained was the Georgia-Florida coastline, and across the swamps that abound in those states. There were few people there to complain about the noise, although the alligators and swamp animals must have been annoyed when we roared by only a few feet above their habitats.

The pilots I flew with during this period were the best. To qualify for this type of training, each of us had to spend a certain amount of time with a flight commander and then take a check ride with a squadron commander. We not only flew low, we were flying in formation. And I mean tight formation.

When we returned from one of these low-level missions we were expected to have chlorophyll on our propeller tips. If we weren't chopping grass and weeds with the props, we were too high. The Air Corps knew from reports out of Europe that the Germans were building flak towers all over their country and the occupied lands. The towers were 100 feet or less above the ground, and we were being trained to operate below the deadly fire from such installations.

The idea was to use the natural terrain as a shield. If there were trees, fly alongside them. If there were hills, fly between them. And all this with your wing tucked close to the one next to you. It was hard work and it was for people who loved to fly. Fortunately, I loved flying and this was right down my alley. We practiced and practiced until we were really sharp.

There were occasional complaints in Congress about flight pay for Air Force men. The argument was made that the infantrymen and others down there in the mud were having as tough a life as we were. Maybe tougher. Whenever a congressman started raising hell about flight pay, the Air Corps would invite him to Georgia for a personal indoctrination. The real purpose was to take him for a ride in the A-20. After flying across the deck at 200 miles an hour, fighting the turbulence and prop wash, he usually turned very pale and got back on the ground thinking we earned every dollar we got.

It was becoming apparent to many people that we were going to get into the war, but there were also many who refused to accept this possibility. We took part in all the military maneuvers of the day, including the Carolina war games of 1941. These demonstrations showed the public how poorly prepared the military was. We used old trucks with the word "Tank" painted on the sides. Some of the infantrymen carried sticks and logs to simulate rifles and mortars.

We worked our way up the East Coast in our A-20s, trying to show how inadequate the air attack warning systems were. We were just beginning to organize some sort of civil defense system. Air raid wardens, most of whom had little training in aircraft identification, were stationed on top of the taller buildings in the big cities. Our mission was to show how easy it was to get past them before they had time to send out an alert.

Theoretically, we wiped out most of the East Coast population. We would fly out over the water, drop to low altitude, and head for the city, ripping in across the waves as fast as we could come—full blower.

I remember our "attack" on Boston. Each of us took a street and flew alongside the taller buildings. I came in to the left of Boston Common and flew the length of Boylston Street. Paul Revere would have needed more than two lanterns to warn the good people of Boston that day. We were there and gone before they knew what had happened.

We ran the same kind of operation against New York with the same results.

These practice attacks made us expert at low-level formation flying, and fortunately we never had a serious accident. Sometimes my wing tip would be thrust between the wing and tail assembly of the next plane. Now and then a wing tip would make contact with the fuselage of the other plane and leave a slight dent. A few times, the propeller of one plane would start to chew up the aileron of the aircraft ahead of it. Take my word for it: there was no boredom in this kind of flying.

While I was doing all this with the 90th, orders came through promoting me to captain. I had received the routine advancement to first lieutenant while still at Fort Benning.

On a Saturday in the first week of December 1941, at Fort Bragg, North Carolina, we went up to fly attack missions over some ground troops as part of an army maneuver. The next day we flew back to Savannah.

It was a reasonably sunny day, and I had tuned my radio to a station in Savannah and was following the needle home. Every weekend pilot will understand this method of navigation. I don't remember what the station was, but I was able to find some music instead of the sermons that were on many stations that Sunday. Suddenly the music in my earphones ceased and a voice broke in.

A mile over the red clay earth of Georgia, I learned that the Japanese had bombed Pearl Harbor.

10 Flying Fortress Training

War was suddenly a reality. Many of us had expected it for months. But even those who were sure war would come did not know quite what to do now that it was here.

When I landed after hearing the news of Pearl Harbor, people were out of the buildings and all over the field. You would have thought that they expected a Japanese attack on Savannah that day.

I had received orders transferring me to the 29th Bomb Group in Tampa, and I was to report early in January. Because of the many hours I had logged in the A-20, I was selected for training in the new Boeing B-17, the four-engine "Flying Fortress." Meanwhile, the 29th moved to Savannah because of the fear that enemy submarines could surface in Tampa Bay and shell MacDill field.

Although I was looking forward to flying the B-17s, I would have to wait. Priorities changed and the four-engine bombers were suddenly taken away from the 29th and sent to the Pacific to replace those destroyed on the ground at Hickam field during the Pearl Harbor attack.

In their place, our outfit was supplied temporarily with the Douglas-built B-18, which had little value except as a trainer because its cruising speed was only 130 miles an hour and its ceiling 12,000 feet. One advantage, however, was its huge fuel capacity.

Because of the fear that our coastal cities would be attacked, it was decided to send all of the available B-18s to Savannah to be used for antisubmarine patrol. Every unit in the country that had any B-18s was instructed to fly them to Savannah, land them, and park them. The field soon filled up with these airplanes. We had so many it was decided that we would send a squadron to Fort Bragg and operate out of there. Our squadron commander, Frank Robinson, was in the hospital at the time and still hadn't moved up from Tampa. As a captain and the senior officer on duty, I inherited the job of moving the squadron to North Carolina.

I was given 33 airplanes and told to take my choice of men. Although I didn't know anything about their qualifications, I remember winding up with a lot of second lieutenants. The selection process consisted of putting people in airplanes and telling them to "fly to Fort Bragg."

Finally there remained on the ground one airplane and one man, a corporal named Orville Split. He had never been in a B-18, and I had only about three hours in the airplane. I told Orville he was going to be copilot on this trip. We cranked up the airplane and flew to Fort Bragg. No problem.

Orville readily took to flying, and he stayed with me as my B-17 radio operator all through Europe. He was a writer and remained in the air force as a civilian employee after the war, finally retiring as head of the magazine section of Air Force Public Relations.

The B-18 was a gentle airplane and everyone made it to Fort Bragg despite the widespread lack of experience. Then came the task of getting the squadron operational. We were assigned to patrol the East Coast from Cape May, New Jersey, to the Yucatan channel between Cuba and Mexico.

German U-boats were prowling the Atlantic only a short distance off the coast. People around Cape Hatteras saw as many as four separate fires off on the horizon on a single night—burning tankers that had been torpedoed by German submarines.

We were finally organized to the point where we put bombs in the B-18s and got them out over the ocean for nine-hour flights. This was no difficult task for the B-18 with its large fuel capacity. In fact, I once remained aloft on a single mission for 17 hours.

This long flight was part of a special assignment for the protection of a troopship that had lost a rudder off Jacksonville, Florida, on its way to the Pacific by way of the Panama Canal. It was a sitting duck for any submarine that might spot it.

Our services were limited to the daylight hours because we didn't have electronic detection devices. From dawn to dark, we hovered over the ship, flying a cloverleaf pattern for 3 miles in each direction from the disabled vessel. We carried four 500-pound bombs, but our inexperience with them was such that I'm not sure we could have hit a submarine if we had seen one.

We remained over the ship while it was being towed into Jacksonville harbor for rudder repair and even continued to fly a pattern over the harbor while it was moored there. As the ship headed south, our escort service continued. After all the time we had spent guarding the ship while it was disabled, we didn't want to lose it now. I got the job of flying cover on the last day it was in our area.

I picked up the ship just after daylight a short distance off Miami and hoped it would reach the Yucatan channel by nightfall. I set the fuel mixture controls as lean as possible and throttled the engines back to the point where the plane would barely stay in the air. All day long I was flying about 70 miles an hour, and I stayed with the ship until we couldn't see it any more in the darkness.

We got back to Miami a little after 9:00 P.M., and it just happened that this was one of only three nights in the whole year when the airport was fogged in. It was a beautiful night in the air and the city of Miami was visible from 50 miles away, but over the airport was a thick patch of fog. My fuel gauges were reading "empty," and I didn't know when the engines would sputter and die.

I made one pass at the airport and missed the runway. We started to go around and just then the copilot spotted a hole in the fog directly over the middle of the field. I pulled around and did a chandelle to the right, lowered the gear, dumped the flaps all the way down, chopped the throttles, and pointed the plane's nose at that hole in the fog. You could do that with the B-18, and with all that garbage hanging down in the slipstream you didn't gain airspeed when you dived at the ground. We touched the runway at no more than 50 miles an hour. It was one of the smoothest landings I ever made.

We managed to taxi to the fuel pits before the engines stopped. I don't know how much fuel was left, but if we had missed that hole in the fog, I'm sure we would have bellied in somewhere among the alligators.

When the Army Air Corps asked for bids on a "multi-engine bomber" in 1934, most manufacturers assumed they wanted an advanced version of the twin-engine airplane and went to work accordingly. Clair Egtvedt, engineer of the Boeing Airplane Company, was looking further ahead than that. He envisioned a four-engine bomber that would have the speed of a fighter, armament to fight off attackers, and a bomb load measured in tons.

Boeing started to work on an airplane called Model 299. It was a big, fast, complicated airplane. The first one flew so fast from Seattle to Wright-Patterson Air Force base at Dayton that it was on the ground ahead of the welcoming committee that was supposed to greet it. (That airplane had a tragic ending. It crashed and burned on a test flight from Wright-Pat because the pilot forgot to unlock the controls before takeoff.)

Model 299 was the largest land plane of the time. Some critics said it was too big and too complicated for regular Air Corps crews to fly safely. But the army was impressed and ordered 13 more of the planes, which were given the designation B-17. It was a wise decision. Those airplanes were the first of thousands to come off the production line.

The airplane had great growth potential. Although its size was not increased appreciably through the eight models that were built, its range, speed, payload, and performance were continually improved.

On the ground it was a cumbersome-looking airplane—the biggest and one of the last of the tail-draggers. In the air, with its gear tucked up, it was a thing of beauty. Four Wright Cyclone engines pulled it along at a commendable speed, and it bristled with machine guns in every direction. Little wonder it was named the "Flying Fortress."

With the start of the war, production of B-17s began at plants all over America—engines, radios wiring assemblies, guns, wing assemblies, lights—millions of parts that were assembled into bomb-carrying airplanes.

I was ordered to MacDill Air Base near Tampa as the first officer in the new 97th Bomb Group (Heavy). The B-17s were beginning to arrive, as were the fliers who were to pilot them. When the table of organization of the new group began to take shape, I was made commander of the 40th Squadron. My job was to take the new airplanes and the new pilots and make a fighting outfit of them.

Most of the pilots assigned to me were new second lieutenants who had just completed advanced training in "multi-engine" school. This was the course for those who would be going into bombardment or transport squadrons.

The fliers had learned to pilot the UC-78, a very basic wood-and-fabric twin-engine airplane. Although we didn't have a very high regard for that plane, you can still see a few of them sitting around airports to this day. They were commonly referred to as the "bamboo bomber". We also called them "Mexican Messerschmitts" or "termite's delight". Although they taught a pilot how to fly an airplane with two engines, they didn't do much more. They were a far cry from the B-17, so it was decided we should give the pilots transitional training in some intermediate airplane. That's where the B-18 came in handy.

It was decided to give each pilot three six-hour transition periods in the B-18. Then we started giving him six-hour cycles in the B-17. There was no specified training time for the B-17, some pilots picking it up quicker than others. We couldn't afford to wash out many pilots at this stage, so we kept working with them until they were competent to handle the airplane. The idea was to get everyone qualified in the bomber so we could move to Sarasota, where our outfit was supposed to pick up its equipment, get combat-ready, and prepare to move overseas. Here we were putting the crews together: the navigators, bombardiers, radiomen, engineers, and gunners.

It was an exhausting job. I found myself flying as much as 18 hours a day training and checking crews. When I got on the ground, there were the administrative duties of a squadron commander to look after. I tried to get six hours sleep out of every 24, but it didn't work out that way. Lucy and the baby were living in Tampa at this time, and there were periods when I couldn't get home to see them. Sometimes I would go for days without even taking off my clothes.

I worked in one of the hangars at MacDill and had some space in a tower that was full of B-17 tires, parachutes, and other miscellaneous equipment. I learned that, if you sit down in a B-17 tire, put your head on one side and hang your feet over the other side, it makes a fairly decent bed—if you're tired enough.

It seemed there were always more things to do than there was time to do them. We had six weeks to get ready for the move to Sarasota and we made it, but just barely.

At Sarasota, it was the same thing all over again. We were given six weeks to get ready for overseas. There wasn't sufficient time to get the crews assembled into smoothly working units, but we made a stab at it.

Our orders came in the middle of the night, as orders often do. We were to leave in the morning for Fresno, California. No details. Most of us wondered what Pacific island would be our eventual destination.

We were flying the "D" model of the B-17. These planes didn't have the ball turret gun in the belly or the side-mounted guns in the nose. There was a single .30 caliber machine gun forward in the bombardier's compartment, in addition to the top turret .50 calibers, the waist guns, and the tail gun. We were ordered to stop in San Antonio to have the rest of the weapons mounted.

We had been so busy teaching our pilots simply to fly the B-17 that we had not done any formation flying with the big plane. So I started sending the crews out individually for San Antonio. As a result, we had airplanes landing all over the state of Texas. It was embarrassing. We were in sad shape if our navigators couldn't even find San Antonio. It was one thing to get lost over Texas, where landing strips were plentiful, but quite another to stray off course over the Pacific, where a navigation error would most likely mean disaster.

Upon reaching our Texas destination, I got in touch with Ellington Air Base, where they taught bombing and navigation. An instructor was sent to give our crews a crash course. For them, there was no night life and no trips down to Mexico while our planes were being modified.

No one liked the medicine I prescribed. It meant long hours of work when they would have preferred the pleasures of San Antonio

72   THE TIBBETS STORY

bars and bordellos. There were lectures every day and, at night, I took my navigators to the roof of the Gunter hotel to train their sextants on the stars in the cloudless Texas sky.

My gunners were required to strip their weapons time after time until they could do the job blindfolded. I had learned the importance of gun care as a boy in military school. My men didn't care for the monotony of such constant practice, and some were bold enough to say so, but many took the trouble to thank me months later when their experience paid off in the skies over Europe. A few of them may be alive today because of what they learned during the "Battle of San Antonio," as they called it.

We finally got to Fresno and waited for orders which, we assumed, would take us to some island in the Pacific. Then came the word that no one had expected. We were told to fly to Bangor, Maine!

Our change of direction reflected indecision in high places. It was understandable, of course. Since Japan had attacked us at Pearl Harbor, some of our leaders wanted us to throw all our strength into the Pacific war. But a wiser view prevailed. We would fight with equal vigor on two fronts. In early 1942, the B-17s would be considerably more useful in Europe than in the Pacific, where we did not then have bases from which to bomb the Japanese homeland effectively.

Back across the country we went, one airplane at a time, with an overnight stop at Scott field, Illinois. Everyone made it to Bangor without mishap. The San Antonio training had paid its first dividend.

We still didn't know what Uncle Sam had in mind for us, but I was determined we'd be ready. We were a heavy bombardment squadron but we didn't have any bombs. Even if we had bombs, there were no ranges nearby where we could practice.

I knew we would have to cross the ocean to get to war and, since there were no landmarks in the ocean, my next step was more navigation training. We started night navigation practice from Bangor. Our planes were in the air almost every night.

One clear June night—it was about 2:00 A.M.—I was on the ramp at Bangor waiting for two planes to return from a practice mission when a DC-3 landed and taxied up to where I was standing.

"We've got some freight for the 97th Bomb Group," the pilot told me as he climbed out of the plane.

"I'll take it," I said. "I'm the 97th Bomb Group. Part of it, anyway."

They opened the door of the Gooney Bird and shoved out four big packing cases. Each was about 7 feet long and 3 feet on each side. They hit the ground like they weighed a ton. I signed a receipt and the plane left to go back to wherever it came from.

I rounded up a couple of enlisted men and we pried open one of the boxes. It was full of Thompson submachine guns. I counted the guns in one box and figured we had enough to supply the pilots, bombardiers, and navigators of two squadrons.

By this time we had four squadrons in the 97th. Mine and the one commanded by John Knox were at Bangor. The other two were now at Westover in Massachusetts. I divvied up the guns with John and kept one for myself. That was one piece of military equipment I kept throughout my military career and even into civilian life.

Whoever sent those machine guns must have known something I didn't. Within a few days we were ordered to move our squadrons to England.

11 Code Name Bolero

When you look at a flat map of the world, based on what is called the Mercator Projection, it appears that the shortest way from the United States to Europe is directly east across the Atlantic ocean.

The perspective is different when you look at a globe, which shows that the shortest way to Europe is an arc that runs a considerable distance to the north and then curves back south again. Fortunately, there are some land masses poking down out of the Arctic that are very close to this so-called "Great Circle" route. Also, quite fortunately, those lands were in the hands of our allies during the war.

It wasn't an ideal part of the world for flying an airplane, but there was no choice. And in the summer it never gets very dark at night along this northern route. Although there had been nighttime navigational instruction, there was no satisfactory way to prepare relatively inexperienced airmen for the problems they would confront on their flight across the North Atlantic where the weather was unpredictable and landing sites scarce.

The B-17s that flew from New England to old England were piloted by boys in their late teens and early twenties, and were guided by navigators of the same age. Most had never before flown out of sight of land. In fact, a majority had never seen an ocean until recently.

We lightened the planes as much as possible in order to get in and out of fields with short runways. However, we had to take on adequate fuel as a safety margin in case of unfavorable weather.

The route across the ocean was set up so that even the fighter planes, with their limited range, could make it. Because the fighters didn't have a means of navigation over water, each B-17 was assigned to escort from two to four P-38s. The ground crews, the gunners, and all of the support equipment were sent to England by ship, taking their chances with the German wolf-pack submarines that roamed the North Atlantic. Movement of the 97th Group, consisting of 49 B-17s, started on June 15. Sandwiched into our flights were 80 twin-engine P-38 fighter planes and 52 C-47s, the reliable old Gooney Birds. The bombers carried only skeleton crews but the Goonies made the flights with full crews, each also carrying a load of freight.

The aircraft left Bangor in small groups, flying when weather permitted. Conditions were treacherous on the route, particularly since we didn't have all the reporting stations we needed in the Arctic, where much of the North Atlantic weather is born. Some Air Corps people had estimated that we might lose as many as 10 percent of our planes en route.

It had been planned to send along some single-engine P-39 fighters, but this idea was vetoed at the last minute. The pilots went by ship and left their planes behind. Upon reaching England, they were supplied temporarily with Spitfires.

The first leg of the flight out of Maine was easiest. We flew over forests for most of the 700-mile hop to Goose Bay near the east coast of Labrador.

The next leg of the trip was most hazardous because of uncertain weather and the difficult locations of the airfields on the southwest coast of Greenland. Some planes waited at Goose Bay as long as three days for a break in the weather before takeoff, then were forced back by fog or icing conditions that had not been forecast.

Under agreement with Denmark, the United States had established two bases in Greenland. One, near the southern tip of the big ice-covered island, was given the code name of Bluie West One, abbreviated on the maps to BW-1. It was 776 miles from Goose Bay. The other, farther up the west coast, was Bluie West Eight. Its distance from Goose Bay was 1,002 miles, a longer over-water haul for the fighters with their limited range.

BW-8, just north of the Arctic Circle at Sondre Stromfjord, was originally meant for use only when the weather was bad, or the traffic congestion too great, at BW-1. But because the more southerly base was often fogged in, BW-8 became a very busy airfield, even though using it meant that departing east-bound planes had to fly over Greenland's high and desolate ice cap on their next leg to Iceland.

Luckily, the weather was good for my flight and I reached BW-1 without incident, along with the two P-38s that accompanied me. I shall never forget my first view of Greenland. In June, the slopes leading down to the sea are green with Arctic mosses and vegetation; hence, no doubt, the name for the world's largest island. Beyond the coastal mountains I could see the beginning of the eternal ice cap, which stretches flat as a table for a distance of 1,300 miles northward and reaches a thickness of more than 2 miles in places.

There was little time to dwell on the grandeur of the view, however, because the approach to Bluie West One required complete concentration. I had been briefed on the method of threading my way up the fjord and was told that it would be "hairy," a word that was just then coming into use to describe a difficult flying operation. Even so, I was unprepared for this experience, as were many other pilots encountering Greenland's landing strips for the first time.

The approach began at the entrance to a long fjord, an inlet of water that twisted between steep cliffs for more than 20 miles, and at the end of which was our runway. We began our letdown, according to advance instruction, as we approached the fjord, which was reasonably wide at its entrance.

It soon narrowed, however, and before I knew it there were steep slopes on each side and a narrow channel of water beneath. Then came the first of several tricky turns. A number of canyons branched off from the main fjord, and I had to watch our map closely to avoid following one of them. To do so would lead to a dead end with no way of escape. Close behind me were the two P-38s, their pilots trusting my leadership over a dangerous path that no one in my plane had ever seen before.

The rule was never to enter this fjord without finding out by radio what the weather was like at the airstrip at the end of the line. Once you were flying between those cliffs, you were committed. There wasn't room to turn around and the mountain at the end of the fjord was a towering obstacle over which a B-17 could not climb. The more maneuverable P-38s might have managed to get out if their pilots were lucky.

Many pilots said a prayer as they flew up that fjord with the cliffs just off their wing tips, the water below, and a low overcast above. They knew the airstrip was open when they started in and hoped it would still be that way when they got there.

On the glidepath to the runway, a rocky island rose 60 feet out of the water. The landing strip itself sloped uphill toward another cliff. Since the island was on the line of flight, it was necessary to skim over it and land quickly. Because you had to get out of the field the same way, the downhill run on takeoff was a bonus.

Before the war was over, many an American airplane came to grief in this fjord. Nevertheless, BW-1 was important to the difficult task of transferring American air might to Europe. Thousands of bombers, fighters, and aircraft of every description made fueling stops at this isolated base on Greenland's forbidding shore. The many pilots who landed there successfully never stopped talking about their experience.

There was little on the ground at BW-1; just a mess hall, a weather shack and some crowded huts for sleeping. Across the fjord, in easy view, was the Eskimo village of Narsarssuak. It was strictly off limits. The Eskimos had never been in contact with the germs we might be carrying, and army medics were afraid we might bring an epidemic that would wipe out the village.

Leaving BW-1, we flew around the southern tip of Greenland and headed across the water for Iceland. Greenland is a land of ice whereas Iceland, brushed by the Gulf Stream, is comparatively green although much of its volcanic soil is a reddish purple.

We landed at Reykjavik, took on a new load of fuel, and headed for Prestwick, Scotland, 846 miles away. This final stretch of the Atlantic crossing was, as the British would say, a cup of tea.

The first B-17 of our outfit, still unnamed and carrying the tail number 19085, landed at Prestwick on July 1. I arrived a couple of days later. On July 27, Colonel Newton Longfellow brought in the last B-17 of this first large-scale ferrying operation, which had been code-named *Bolero*.

The B-17 that touched down July 1 was the first American-manned tactical aircraft to reach the United Kingdom in World War II, with the exception of a single B-24 Liberator that had flown over in May. Its arrival marked the beginning of a long stream of planes that would swarm across those cold northern skies until Germany was finally defeated almost three years later.

Our airplane was met at Prestwick by a British navigator who would guide us to our new home in England at a base called Polebrook, a short distance northeast of London. The runway on which we landed had recently been a potato field.

The crossing had been achieved with a remarkable safety record. Nine planes were forced to turn back because of weather on a day when 18 had taken off from Goose Bay. Six returned safely but three were forced to land in Greenland. All the crews were rescued.

On July 15, six P-38s and two B-17s came down on the icecap near the east coast of Greenland. Again, all the crews survived. The problems were communications and weather, twin difficulties that would plague the long over-water operation throughout the war.

Throughout the ferrying procedure, the airmanship was superb. Considering their inexperience and inadequate training for such an adventure, these youthful American crews and their aircraft proved that they had what it takes to win a war.

At Polebrook, the enemy was only a channel-crossing away. Ready or not, we were in the war.

Unfortunately, there were those in the leadership of the 97th who didn't seem to realize this. No sooner had we settled at Polebrook than they began yielding to the temptations that they discovered in the immediate neighborhood.

The people of England were glad to see the first American combat fliers arrive, and some who lived in the neighborhood of our base promptly showed their appreciation in a way that also turned out to be demoralizing to our operation. The Rothschilds had a big estate nearby that soon became a social center for our officers. The cocktail hours expanded into afternoon drinking bouts that often lasted late into the night.

I was determined that my squadron would be ready for action when the time came. And the time was not far off. It had been drilled into me from the days at the military academy, and by my dad, that the place of an officer was with his troops. That's where I stayed. Major John Knox shared my philosophy, and the other top officers in the outfit were inclined to leave us alone when they saw we didn't intend to join them in riding to the hounds, enjoying high tea, and hitting the free Scotch all night.

The Polebrook situation soon came to the attention of our top military leaders in Britain, with the result that the 97th commander was replaced. His successor was Colonel Frank Armstrong, a no-nonsense officer who quickly straightened things out.

Part of the problem was described by Beirne Lay and Sy Bartlett in their novel, *Twelve O'Clock High*, which became a popular movie. The fictional general in that story, Frank Savage, is based on the real-life Frank Armstrong.

Those who read the book or saw the picture may remember that, when Savage arrived to take command, security on the base was lax, many of the key officers were absent, and no one knew where to find them. He found a squadron commander with the rank of major on duty. In reality, I was that major, having been promoted from captain during our stopover in San Antonio earlier in the year.

Armstrong promptly appointed me his executive officer. From that time on, morale and efficiency improved at Polebrook, although the Rothschilds and other party-givers in the neighborhood lost some interesting American guests.

12 Yankee Doodle Goes to Town

The bomb-bay doors of *Butcher Shop* opened and we were on our bomb run.

The navigator had done his job well. Now I turned over control of the B-17E to the bombardier crouching ahead in the Plexiglas nose. The railroad marshaling yards at Rouen, an important city near the Channel coast in northern France, were moving in toward the crosshairs of his Norden bomb sight.

"Bombs away!"

As the bombardier spoke those words into the intercom, our 1,100-pound load of high explosive bombs dropped away from the airplane. For the first time, heavy bombers of the Eighth Air Force were attacking Hitler's expanding domain, which he called "Festung Europa." For the first time, I was engaged in an act of war against the enemy. We had been making practice bomb drops off the English coast, but this was the real thing.

It was a few minutes past 5:00 P.M. on August 17, 1942.

This was not only a first for me and my crew and for the 11 B-17s that were following us on this mission to Rouen. It was also the initial daylight raid by an American squadron on German-occupied Europe. This mission, of which I was the leader, was a small beginning for us, but the beginning of the end for Hitler. Of the 18 B-17s that took off on that late afternoon mission, 12 flew directly to the primary target and six made a diversionary run westward along the French coast. We operated under heavy fighter protection from Spitfires of the Royal Air Force.

In the 995 days of air war against Germany that followed, the Eighth Air Force would drop 4,377,984 bombs of all types on Europe, plus 25,556,978 4-pound incendiaries—a total of 701,300 tons of ordnance, delivered by 332,645 bombers.

The Eighth would lose 41,786 bomber crewmen killed or missing, and an additional 1,890 would be seriously wounded. Then General Carl Spaatz would announce that the strategic bombing of Germany had ended. There were no more targets.

The record of the Eighth Air Force was built largely on the success of that first raid over enemy territory and those that followed in the late summer and autumn of 1942. Many people, particularly the skeptical British, doubted that the B-17s could conduct daylight raids successfully over a heavily defended enemy Europe.

As pilot of the first plane on the first raid, I was very much aware that we had to prove our accuracy from high altitudes. We also had to prove that we could operate without prohibitive losses.

The eight days prior to the flight were tense with anticipation. We were young men fresh from the United States with sufficient military training but with no experience in actual warfare. It was a simple matter to release practice bombs and to fire machine gun bullets at targets towed by friendly aircraft, but what was it like to be fired at? We had learned to fly in tight formation, but could we keep our positions when under attack by enemy aircraft? We didn't know but we would soon find out.

We thought of all these things as we sweated out, quite literally, the orders to take off.

Our first order came on August 9. Ammunition was loaded aboard our 18 aircraft. To say that we were keyed up is an understatement. We didn't sleep much that night. Shortly before scheduled takeoff time the next day, the weather closed in. Rain dripped from low clouds for a full week. It was a period of letdown during which nerves came to be frayed. Finally there were signs of clearing skies and a flight alert was called on the night of August 16. Takeoff was set for the next afternoon, and this time the weather was fair.

General Spaatz was on hand with staff officers from the Eighth and from the RAF to watch the takeoff. Needless to say, the British officers wore an air of skepticism. They had warned against our foolhardy insistence on daylight flights into the unfriendly skies where Goering's Luftwaffe lay in wait. In addition to the brass, the takeoff was witnessed by 30 members of the American and British press. It would have been a hell of a time to blow a mission.

Butcher Shop, which led the first flight into the air, was not my regular airplane and I was not flying with my regular crew. Rounding out a hastily assembled "pickup" crew was Colonel Frank Armstrong, my immediate superior, who occupied the right-hand seat as my copilot. My future missions would be flown in the *Red Gremlin* with my regular crew, including navigator Dutch Van Kirk and bombardier Tom Ferebee, who would finish the war with me.

The plane that is best remembered from the first attack was *Yankee Doodle*, which led the second formation of six B-17s. On board this plane was Brigadier General Ira Eaker, head of the Eighth Bomber Command. The official war histories will record that General Eaker led the first American daylight raid on occupied Europe. This is a matter of military protocol, for although I led the attacking formation—and all others in which I participated while stationed in England—the highest-ranking officer on the flight is officially credited with being the leader.

It was just past midafternoon when we lifted off into sunny skies. All the planes were in the air at 1539 hours (3:39 P.M.). We started our climb for altitude immediately and had reached 23,000 feet, in attack formation, by the time we left the coast of England and headed south across the Channel. It was comforting to see the British Spitfire V's crossing and crisscrossing protectively above our formation as we set out on our first venture into enemy skies.

Three of our planes carried 1,100-pound bombs for the locomotive workshop at the Sotteville marshaling yards at Rouen, the largest railroad switching facility in northern France. RAF reconnaissance photos showed concentrations of more than 2,000 freight cars there. It was a focal point for traffic between the Channel ports and the west. The heavy bombs were for the locomotive repair shops. The other nine planes carried 600-pound bombs to be dropped on the Buddicum rolling stock repair shops.

Important though it was, this was a comparatively short mission in terms of miles flown. Rouen is only a few miles up the Seine from the port city of Le Havre.

We caught the Germans by surprise. They hadn't expected a daytime attack, so we had clear sailing to the target. Visibility was unlimited and all 12 planes dropped their bomb loads—36,900 pounds in all. Our aim was reasonably good, but you couldn't describe it as pinpoint bombing. We still had a lot to learn.

At least half the bombs fell in the general target area. One of the aiming points took a direct hit, and there were a number of bomb craters within a radius of 1,500 feet. Bombs intended for the other aiming point fell about 200 feet to the south. While the results did not come up to our expectations, our accuracy was considerably better than that achieved by the RAF in its night attacks, or by German bombers in their raids on England.

By the time we unloaded our bombs, the enemy came to life. Anti-aircraft fire, erratic and spasmodic at first, zeroed in on our formations as we began the return flight. Two B-17s suffered slight damage from flak. Three Me-109s moved in for the attack but were quickly driven off by the Spitfires that accompanied us. The only German planes I saw were out of range, and I got the impression they were simply looking us over.

A feeling of elation took hold of us as we winged back across the Channel. All the tension was gone. We were no longer novices at this terrible game of war. We had braved the enemy in his own skies and were alive to tell about it.

Back at Polebrook and Grafton Underwood, the VIP's were sweating out our mission. So were our ground crews. Their ordeal would be repeated many times in the months and years ahead as men on the ground strained to hear the first drone of the engines and then, when the returning planes came into view, counted to see if any of their comrades were missing.

All 18 planes got back safely that day. Our only casualties were caused by a careless bird. Approaching our home base, one of the planes struck a pigeon. The bombardier and the navigator suffered slight cuts from the shattered Plexiglas. I don't know whether the pigeon was one of ours or one of theirs. Nor did I hear whether the two crewmen ever received their Purple Hearts.

The last B-17 from the mission touched down at 1900 hours (7:00 P.M.). The British brass—those generals and war experts who had warned us against venturing across the Channel in daytime—were as elated as were our own commanders. General Eaker received a jubilant note from RAF Air Chief Marshal Sir Arthur Harris: "Yankee Doodle certainly went to town."

In all fairness, it must be noted that the British skepticism was based in part on their experience with a number of early model B-17s that had been supplied them before we were able to get our own units in operation. They experienced losses in combat mainly because they used the plane as it wasn't meant to be used.

The British had flown the B-17 singly instead of in formation, thus losing the advantage of concentrated firepower from several planes against enemy attackers. Moreover, they were unable to get enough bombs on target to cause substantial damage. It should also be mentioned that their B-17s were not equipped with the highly accurate Norden bomb sight, a piece of sophisticated equipment that deserves much of the credit for the destruction of Germany's industry and transportation centers in the 32 months between our flight to Rouen and the end of the war in April 1945.

The importance of that first raid in establishing a pattern for air warfare over Europe cannot be overstated. British newspapers had been openly critical of American plans to use the B-17 in the daytime, and even our first day's success was not enough to change their opinions. They gave most of the credit to our RAF fighter cover and predicted that our effectiveness would be limited to the range of the escort aircraft. Indeed we did welcome this assistance, although it was later proved that the B-17 was quite able to defend itself when necessary.

Two American generals, Carl Spaatz and Ira Eaker, put their careers on the line by insisting on daylight bombing. Eaker had been a fighter pilot before Hap Arnold sent him to England to study the British bomber command and assess the potential for hitting the enemy around the clock. In spite of advice to the contrary from the British, he concluded that daylight bombing was a gamble worth taking.

It was his idea that the Germans could be pounded to defeat with B-17s hitting them in the daytime and the British Halifaxes and Lancasters coming over at night. This put tremendous pressure on the enemy defenses, which had to be on constant alert, with no time to relax or regroup.

The seven weeks of training between our arrival in England and our first raid paid off handsomely. I shudder to think of the results had it not been for the intensive practice afforded during this period.

In the States, we had learned to fly the B-17 and that was about it. The bombardiers and gunners arrived in England with insufficient training. The RAF people recognized this too and were helpful in getting us ready for combat.

Their fighters were sent up day after day so that we could practice rendezvous procedures with escort aircraft. The RAF even got some planes into the air to tow targets so that our gunners could develop skill in firing their weapons and operating the turrets.

For all this help, however, we soon learned that it would have made more sense to provide this training over the broad expanse of Texas and other western states instead of trying to cram our learning experience into the limited airspace over England. Crews arriving in Europe later in the war would be better trained before leaving the ZI (Zone of the Interior, the World War II designation of the United States).

There was just no place over the densely populated English countryside where it was safe to fire our guns. The lead and brass were bound to fall on an inhabited area. The people had lived through the Battle of Britain and they didn't need anything dropping on them out of friendly airplanes. As a result, we had to confine our gunnery to "The Wash," a broad inlet of the North Sea that came between Lincolnshire on the north and Norfolk on the south.

Returning from our first high-altitude practice run, several gunners in our squadron reported that their weapons had malfunctioned. I took one look and discovered the cause. The heavy grease with which they were coated had thickened in the subzero temperatures at 20,000 feet, virtually freezing the action.

To solve the problem, I went back to something I had learned as a boy in military school when we fired black powder in a little cannon every morning and night. I called all the gunners together for an elementary lesson in the care of their weapons.

"Listen carefully," I said. "This may save your lives some day over France."

To begin with, I told them to take their weapons apart and wash everything in hot water and GI soap in order to remove all traces of the factory grease.

The next step was to take a small quantity of gun oil in the palms of their hands, then lightly rub every part of the gun. This left the metal covered with a light film of oil, protecting it against rust without gumming up the action, even at 20 below zero.

After every practice mission, I ordered the men to repeat this tedious operation. Since the guns were now functioning well, some thought it was nonsense to do the same job over and over again. My strict enforcement of this gun-care order didn't make me popular with the men who had to do the tiresome job. Although muttering under their breath, and perhaps referring to me among themselves as a finicky old s.o.b., they soon came to know their guns so well that they could take them apart and put them together blindfolded.

There came a day when they would thank me, grudgingly perhaps, for being so demanding. A few weeks later they were to see B-17s from other squadrons shot out of the sky because their guns jammed at a crucial moment when under attack by enemy fighters. My own outfit suffered some losses, but fewer than most, and never to my knowledge because of defective weapons.

There is nothing more embarrassing, or potentially fatal, than to have a gun jam at the moment a Messerschmitt is boring in for the kill. After the first time we were within shooting distance of a German fighter, I never had to remind my gunners to keep their equipment in working order. Cleaning their weapons between flights came to be looked upon as life insurance.

It wasn't our gunners alone who needed training. When we arrived in England, our pilots and copilots had never flown at altitudes above 10,000 feet; yet we were to do our bombing at 20,000 feet.

There's quite a difference, as our crewmen were to learn. At 20,000 feet, you need oxygen. Most of our people didn't understand the oxygen equipment and didn't know how to use it. Many were even afraid of it. I have to admit that the masks were about as uncomfortable as anything I've ever worn. After several hours at high altitude on a long mission, your nose and face and chin can get raw and a little sore. Worse than that, from my standpoint, the mask also kept me from puffing on my pipe, a hardship that seemed rather grim at the time.

Many of the B-17 pilots had received little training in formation flying, and even I had never experienced tight formation flying at the altitudes we would maintain on our missions over Europe. Controls are more sensitive and the plane has a tendency to wallow around a bit in the thin air of the stratosphere.

It was an education for all of us to keep our wing tips close to those of the planes adjacent to us. It wasn't easy under those conditions, because it required a steady hand on the controls, but it was necessary. With a tight formation, the entire unit was the "fortress." It was something the German fighters couldn't penetrate because it concentrated the firepower of our weapons. But let some holes appear in the formation, or let one of the planes straggle, and there were going to be sad telegrams home from the War Department.

Frank Armstrong had taken the group apart and put it back together again in a matter of little more than two weeks after taking command of the 97th. By mid-August, he was able to report that 24 crews were available for combat missions. Then came our attack on Rouen and the ice was broken. A busy time was ahead for all of us.

Some interesting sidelights on these early air attacks were brought out in a discussion, in Heidelberg in 1976, involving General Eaker, Dr. G. B. Metcalf, chairman of the board of the United States Strategic Institute, and Albert Speer, Hitler's minister of armaments production.

Speer said the bombings started a second front long before land forces crossed the Channel because they kept some 900,000 Germans tied down along the "West Wall" to protect against our raids.

These included anti-aircraft gunners, fire fighters, and workmen needed to repair damaged factories. The Germans never knew what targets we would hit next, so they had to provide defenses for their homeland and all of occupied Europe.

"Without this great drain on our manpower, logistics and

weapons, we might well have knocked Russia out of the war before your invasion of France," Speer said.

He wondered, however, why we started with small numbers of planes rather than wait until we had as many as 1,000 bombers available for daylight attacks.

General Eaker explained that it was necessary to get our planes into action in Europe and show immediate results in order to counteract the pressure from some quarters in America to send the planes to the Pacific.

"If we had not begun operations against the Nazis, this Pacific deployment would have taken place," Eaker said, also pointing out the importance of the experience gained in the first feeble cross-Channel attacks.

"We learned during those early operations how to operate bomber forces under the conditions that then prevailed," he said. "If we had waited for the arrival of a thousand bombers before making attacks on German-occupied Europe, it probably would have been a tragic disaster."

13 Close Calls and Milk Runs

I led nearly every mission while the 97th remained in England during the late summer and early autumn of 1942, even though Frank Armstrong often went along. We had a nerve-wracking schedule.

Detailed planning for a mission would start shortly after midnight, as soon as we had learned the targets for the day. First we would have to decide the size of the formations and which planes would fly where. Then we would select the route for our fighter escort and the point at which we would join up with these British protectors. There were literally hundreds of details.

The crews were usually up before dawn for a detailed briefing on the day's mission. Then they would move off for breakfast at the mess hall. After eating, they would go to their planes and check the bomb loads and ammunition before climbing aboard.

Takeoff time depended on the distance we were to fly that day. The first mission, already described, took place in the late afternoon because the target was comparatively near the French coast. A majority of our takeoffs, however, came soon after sunrise.

After our first raid, which caught the Germans off guard since their defenses were geared to the nighttime attacks by British bombers, we found the skies full of flak and enemy fighters. Antiaircraft batteries took a bead on us almost as soon as we crossed the Channel. Consequently, it became our practice to climb to full cruising altitude before setting out from the English side of the Channel. The ascent was painfully time-consuming because a fully loaded B-17 doesn't climb very fast.

As the size of our raiding force gradually increased, squadrons from more bases across the English Midlands joined the morning takeoff ritual until the skies over the island literally echoed with the full-throated roar of many engines. It must have been heartening for the people of this beleaguered island to know that our aerial armadas were carrying the first waves of retribution to an enemy that had so recently visited destruction on London, Coventry, and many other English cities.

General Eaker, who had flown with us on the mission to Rouen, was more than a mere sightseer. Before long we were receiving directives on how we could do the job better. Because that first raid was accomplished without the loss of a plane, he feared overconfidence. He demanded tighter formations.

Having analyzed the night raids by the Royal Air Force, and having participated in our initial flight, he had formed a positive idea of what it would take to make an attack successful. He was also looking forward to the day when we would be striking deep into Germany on flights that would have to be made without fighter escort. He saw strategic bombing as the major factor in defeating the enemy.

Two days after the Rouen raid, we were in the air again. This time our target was the German Drucat airfield at Abbeville on the French coast at the mouth of the Somme. We launched 24 airplanes and 22 reached the target, two having to turn back with mechanical trouble. It was another short mission designed to prepare us for the more hazardous and tiring assignments ahead.

All of our raids at this time were set up in cooperation with the British, who assisted in selecting the targets. The planning behind the first Abbeville raid was to take the pressure off the British in their planned commando attack on Dieppe. We blasted hell out of the German aircraft dispersal area at Abbeville, according to the RAF fighters that flew over to photograph the damage the following day.

The next day we were in the air again. This time, 12 planes took off to bomb the Longueau railroad marshaling yards at Amiens.

This was a key point in the flow of war matériel to the German army in France. Eleven planes reached the target.

At this point, the top brass decided to give priority in target selection to aircraft factories and repair depots. The long-range purpose was to limit the enemy's ability to defend against our attacks. Next in line was railroad transportation, particularly the marshaling yards. Third priority went to submarine installations on the coast of Holland and France.

On August 21, we went after the Wilton shipyard on the outskirts of Rotterdam. It was the most modern installation of its kind in Holland and was used by the Germans to service naval vessels, including submarines.

We had our first snafu on this raid. The Spitfires arrived at the rendezvous point on time but the 12 B-17s were late, due to a communications failure. By the time the bombers got there, the fighters had burned up so much fuel, circling and waiting, that they could escort us only halfway across the Channel.

When word of the situation reached the commanders back at home base, they decided to scrub the mission. By this time we had reached the coast of Holland and our fighter escorts were well on their way home. We were in a difficult situation when a couple of dozen Me-109s and FW-190s caught us by surprise, seeing that we were without fighter protection.

A running fight started as we raced back across the Channel and the enemy planes, with superior speed, darted into our formation from all sides. Miraculously we reached home without the loss of a plane, but the pilot and copilot of one B-17 were seriously wounded and several of our aircraft were badly shot up. The copilot died later.

Although it was a nightmare experience, this mission gave us new respect for our B-17s, their durability, and their firepower. So effective was our concentrated fire that the attackers were repeatedly compelled to veer away and seek another angle from which to attack. Finally they turned back as their own fuel supplies ran low. Our gunners shot down two of them.

We learned some important lessons from this mission. One was the need for split-second timing and coordination between bombers and fighters. The Germans also learned that B-17s are no sitting ducks, even when unescorted.

92   THE TIBBETS STORY

We were suffering structural damage to our airplanes on almost every mission, but the B-17s were limping home and landing safely with their crews. Airplanes returned from missions so badly shot up that it was a miracle that they held together. "Coming in on a wing and a prayer" was more than the mere title of a popular wartime song.

More crews were becoming combat-trained and, only three days after the mess-up on the way to Rotterdam, we were off on another 12-plane mission. This time all our bombers got through to the shipyard of the Ateliers et Chantiers Maritime de la Seine at Le Trait. The damage was heavy, although not to be compared with the sort of destruction that was to come later when we were to put much larger formations over the targets.

Three days later we made it back to Rotterdam. Seven of the nine planes got through, but damage to the target was disappointing. The German shipyard and U-boat facilities were well constructed, and it was difficult to cause substantial damage with the bomb loads we were carrying.

It was on our next mission—the target was a railroad marshaling yard in the north of France—that my formation lost its first airplane. The blow came as a personal shock to me because the pilot, John Lipsky, was one of my favorites. Up to this time, the war had seemed little more than a game in the sense that we flew out in the morning and came back a few hours later after dropping our bombs and eluding enemy flak and fighter fire.

We knew the flak was for real and the shells from the German attacking planes were dangerous, but we had come to consider ourselves supermen whose skill in the sky would always bring us back safely. That was the state of our overconfidence up until the moment we saw Lipsky's airplane spin out of formation, burst into flames and make that last grim, smoking dive to earth.

Now at last the war was a bloody reality for all of us.

The very next mission came close to sending me and my crew on that same swift dive to eternity. This was the closest call, the most frightening brush with death that I was to experience in all my wartime missions over Germany, Africa, and the Pacific.

We were on our way back from a successful attack on a German installation at Le Trait, near the border of Belgium and France, when we were suddenly jumped from above by the enemy's prize interceptor outfit, a squadron of yellow-nosed Messerschmitt 109s about which we had been warned.

These had been described to us as Goering's own fighter outfit, sometimes called "the Abbeville boys" because they were based at an airfield near that French city. The yellow-nosed 109s were flown by the best trained and most daring pilots in the Luftwaffe.

The guns from all our planes were spitting fire like mad as the enemy planes dived at us from three directions, ripping holes in the wings and fuselages of our B-17s. We were staggered by the attack and, although several of our planes were heavily hit, it appeared that the worst was over and all would be able to limp home.

Suddenly, from twelve o'clock—directly ahead—a yellow nose streaked toward my plane on what appeared to be a collision course. What you do under these circumstances is almost automatic. There's a place where thinking stops and instinct takes over. I yanked at the controls to change our course and avoid the fiery line of tracers that I could see streaming in our direction.

Just then, a 20 millimeter cannon shell ripped through the right-hand window. There was an explosive sound and a section of the instrument panel disappeared. At that moment, I felt the sting of flying metal, several fragments imbedding themselves in my right side.

Suddenly I discovered that my copilot, Lt. Gene Lockhart, had suffered a more serious injury. A portion of his left hand had been torn off by the exploding shell and blood was spraying over what instruments were left in the shattered cabin.

I struggled with the controls and somehow managed to keep the plane on course even though the whole airframe shuddered from repeated hits. This, I thought, must be why they call the B-17 a Flying Fortress.

At a time like this, when life and death hang in close balance, a disciplined crew works automatically. It becomes a matter of survival. There are no textbooks to guide you in the split-second reactions that have to occur. Every combat situation is different. Ours at that moment was desperate. It was no time for panic, but panic came. And from an unexpected source; not from one of my crewmen, whose collective behavior made me proud.

On many of these missions, we had been obliged to carry "passengers," usually senior officers who wanted to go along "for the ride" as a means of getting a combat mission on their records.

On this day, our passenger was Col. Newton D. Longfellow, who had a tough-guy reputation among his subordinates. Half his outfit was scared to death of him. If there was anyone in the air force who could fight the war singlehandedly and come out on top, Newt was the man. Or so it was said.

Even though he was a passenger on this flight, Longfellow doesn't deserve to be considered in the joy-riding category I have described. He was fixing to become a bomber commander, but this was his first taste of combat. He was an old-timer in the context by which veteran officers were judged, for many who had attained senior rank in this war were little more than boys. Promotions come fast in an expanding wartime air force.

Colonel Longfellow, who was based nearby, came to Polebrook one day for a visit and I made his acquaintance. We became friends and, since we had a mutual interest in squash and handball, he came to Polebrook often to play on the British-built squash courts there.

When he told me one day that he would like to fly a mission with our outfit, I said "fine." That's how he happened to be standing between me and my copilot at the time the cannon shell from the Me-109 burst through the instrument panel.

In the frenzied moments that followed, all of the cocksureness and bravado that had struck fear into the hearts of Newt's subordinates suddenly left him. Reacting with blind frenzy, he reached over my shoulder and grabbed a handful of throttles and turbo controls, sapping the power of our engines at 25,000 feet.

Now there was chaos in the cabin. I was trying to fly the plane with one hand and keep Lockhart from bleeding to death with the other. While he held his shattered hand above his head, I grasped his wrist tightly with my right hand and tried to maintain level flight at the same time. This was when my squash-playing friend, Colonel Longfellow, got into the act. He was trying to be helpful, but the result was just the opposite.

This was the kind of problem I didn't need at that moment. With Lockhart's blood spurting over the cockpit and a stream of ice-cold air whipping through the gaping hole where the instrument panel had been, I shouted to Newt to lay off, but he wasn't capable of heeding my order.

Although he outranked me—I was a major at the time—I was the airplane commander and the success of our flight was my responsibility. I faced the need for a quick decision. If we were going to save our plane, and more than incidentally our own lives, I would have to put the visiting colonel out of action.

Releasing my grip on Lockhart's wrist, I braced myself and delivered a backward shot with my elbow to Longfellow's chin. It was a hard, powerful, and well-aimed blow, and the colonel was out cold. He landed on the floor at the feet of the sergeant who was manning the ball turret gun. Just then, the gunner's skull was creased by a machine gun bullet from one of the attacking planes, and he fell crumpled in a heap on top of Longfellow.

The gunner's weight and the cold air in the shattered cockpit soon returned the colonel to consciousness. His panic gone, he promptly grabbed a first aid kit and put a tourniquet on Lockhart's arm. I took the opportunity to readjust the controls and put the plane back in level flight at the head of our formation, which had been busted as the result of Longfellow's seizure of the throttles.

Our plane and others in the squadron had fought off the enemy attackers with considerable skill. My engines were all functioning despite holes in the cockpit, wings, and fuselage. The Channel came into view, and the mission had been a success despite our close call. Longfellow spent the next half-hour ministering to the injured. Having done what he could for Lockhart's hand, he bandaged the head of the turret gunner who was lying on the floor unconscious. After lifting Lockhart out of his seat and making him as comfortable as possible on the floor, with a parachute pack for a pillow, Longfellow took over the copilot's duties to help me fly the plane.

When you have wounded aboard, you fire a Very pistol on final approach to the runway. Newt did that, and as we rolled to a stop, ambulances moved in beside us to speed the injured men to the base hospital.

As we climbed out of the plane, Newt looked at me with a sheepish smile on his face. "I sure as hell goofed that one," he said. "Paul, you did the right thing. If I ever do it again, I hope the same thing will happen."

"I'm sorry," I replied, "but I had to fly that airplane and I couldn't be fighting you at the same time."

We remained the best of friends. I knew there would be no second-time panic for Newt Longfellow. He reacted as many brave men do when confronted with their first combat crisis. It's the sort of experience that steels a man for the sort of hell that war often becomes.

He went on to become an outstanding plane commander, participating in many of the bombing missions which, in the next three years, had the cumulative effect of destroying Germany's war-making capacity.

As for the injured men aboard my plane in that furious combat over northern France, all recovered in good time, although there were some uneasy moments in the case of Lockhart, who had lost a large quantity of blood.

A ceremony was arranged soon after the mission so that General Spaatz could present the Purple Heart to those who were wounded. I was in that group but, quite frankly, I was embarrassed by all the fuss. My injuries consisted of a couple of punctures on my left wrist and several inside my left leg just above the knee. All were little more than skin-deep.

This event was as much for public relations as to honor the wounded. We wore our Class A uniforms and the press was invited. I was standing next to Lockhart, and all the photographers were attracted to him because his left hand was heavily bandaged and splinted. As a result, I was prominently pictured in newspapers around the world. We got a full page in *Life* magazine.

Beirne Lay remembers my reluctance to take the time required to arrange the formal ceremony. "Damn it," I told him, "I've got a war to fight and I don't have time for parades and ceremonies." Lay was on the staff of General Spaatz as public relations officer at the time, and he firmly reminded me that he also had a job to do.

One of the missions I was planning came on October 9, a raid in which the principal target was Lille. The operation was important because it would be the first time we were able to put more than 100 bombers in the air for one raid. Again, I was to fly the lead plane.

Much of Germany's strength in France depended on the heavy industries of Lille. The main targets were the steel and engineering works of the Compagnie de Fives-Lille and the locomotive and freight car works of the Ateliers d'Hellemmes.

We put up 115 airplanes, including seven that made a diversionary sweep to Cayeux. One hundred and eight headed for Lille, but only 69 of us reached the target. Thirty-three were shot down or had to abort. Six ran into trouble and dropped their bombs on secondary targets.

This raid was a landmark in aerial warfare. I'm told that it marked the first time the German high command took public notice of the Flying Fortresses, even though we had been over occupied Europe more than a dozen times.

It was also the first time that many of the RAF fighter pilots took us seriously. They finally came around to realizing that the B-17 was a war machine that could damage the enemy substantially by pinpoint bombing from high altitudes. Up until then, many of the British fighter pilots thought the chief use of the B-17 was to get the German fighters into the air so the Spits would have something to shoot at. Before the B-17s came, the RAF was having trouble picking fights in the air over Europe. They welcomed us as fighter bait because the Messerschmitts and Focke-Wulfs couldn't ignore our raids on their airfields and industry.

The raid on Lille also tested our ability to put a big raid together. We learned the difficulty of getting more than 100 planes up to bombing altitude and maintaining formation to the target and back.

For the first time we were joined by B-24s of the newly operational 93rd Bomb Group. Twenty-four of the twin-tailed Liberators, as they were called, were in our 108-plane formation, and 14 were among the 33 planes that were shot down or had to turn back.

It was no wonder! The German fighters didn't even take a second look at the B-17s. They must have had some good intelligence on the Libs, because they bored in from underneath with machine guns firing, then broke off and came back for another attack. They had to know that the early-vintage B-24 had little protection against a belly attack.

My God, I thought, it's like sitting up here and watching a movie. There were airplanes all over the sky, bombers and fighters coming apart in the air, smoke streaming from engines, and parachutes blossoming all over the place.

Because of the inexperience of some of the groups that flew that day, and because of the heavy and constant fighter attack, our accuracy was not equal to that of previous missions. But with so many planes in the air, many bombs did fall on target and the damage to industry and rail installations at Lille was severe. We dropped 147 tons of 500-pound high-explosive bombs on the target and more than 8 tons of incendiaries.

We had been told that our daylight missions were justified if the loss rate could be held to no more than 10 percent. With such losses, we figured we would be hurting the enemy more than he was hurting us. We could replace crews and airplanes faster than they were being shot down.

The 97th was well below the 10 percent loss figure, however. We had proved many times that we could defend ourselves and now, after the Lille raid, we had demonstrated that mass daylight bombing was practical. From now on, the size of the raiding force would rapidly increase until Germany's defenses were overwhelmed. The pattern was set for the destruction of the enemy's ability to make war, even though victory was still two and one-half years away.

Because our bases in England were the closest thing to a war front that Allied newsmen could cover in those days, we were besieged by correspondents from all the major newspapers and press services of England and the United States.

As the leader of most of the raids in the early days of American bomber attacks, I was singled out a number of times for interviews. One such report, by DeWitt Mackenzie of the Associated Press, was carried by hundreds of American newspapers in October, 1942.

"You can talk about your new weapons with staggering efficiency, but this fresh world conflict produced no greater marvel than the adaptability of our young airmen—most of them mere boys in years—to the complicated science of waging war from the skies," he wrote.

After describing the "fierce nerve tension" to which the bomber crews were subjected, he went on:

"I was chatting with young Lieut. Col. Paul Tibbets of Miami, one of the European war heroes who was awarded the Purple Heart for his part in the August 24 raid over Le Trait, France.

"Tibbets told me that while he was waiting for his first raid he was sick with the thoughts of the civilians who might suffer from the bombs dropped by his machine."

He quoted me as saying that this feeling "probably dates back to my training days when we had it hammered into us constantly that in practice we must watch out for the folks beneath us."

The remainder of the newspaper story as it related to me follows:

"This reaction persisted during my first three raids. Finally, I got used to the idea but I am cautious. When I look at a 2,000-pound bomb in the bay of my ship, I know a lot of people may get hurt. My anxiety is for the women and kids."

The colonel paused for a moment and his eyes sought the far-off horizon. Then he added, hesitantly:

"You see, I have a three-year-old boy of my own at home. I hate to think of him playing near a bombed factory. That makes me careful."

We found this feeling about civilians cropping up strongly with Tibbets the other day in the American attack on the great industrial city of Lille despite the fact that this was his eighth trip through no-man's air. He was leading his squadron.

I asked Tibbets if he had any special impression during this raid.

"Yes," he replied, "this is the most heavily populated area we have attacked and our target was in the thick of it. I remember as we came above a great circle with a church beside it which was the guide for our target, it came over me that if we missed the target we would hurt a lot of people.

"I gave the bombardier a heap of mental support to get his target. We don't want to kill French people. We don't want to hit anything but our target."

The Miami newspapers, *The News* and *Herald* gave the Associated Press interview a big play, and the *News* used my picture in two columns with a heading that read: "Miami Hero Forgets Own Danger to Spare Civilians in Europe Raids." There was a subhead: "Col. Tibbets Cited as Example of U.S. Courage Under Fire."

This was the first reference to me as a "lieutenant colonel." I had been a major at the time of the Le Trait and Lille raids. The promotion had come in early October.

My concern about civilian deaths was not solely due to the fact that these people were French. My feelings in this regard extended to the enemy homeland including Japan where, three years later, the atomic bomb took such a heavy toll of civilians. By this time it had become an all-out war in which the civil population had become virtually a part of the front: in London, Rotterdam, Coventry, Essen, Berlin, Tokyo, and other cities where there was heavy loss of life.

With the coming of autumn, an important development in the war against the Nazis was shaping up, and I would soon be leaving England to participate in a complex operation: the invasion of North Africa. Many experienced fighting outfits of the Eighth Air Force were to be pulled out of England and assigned to the new 12th Air Force, which would carry the war to the south shore of the Mediterranean.

14 Mark Clark's Secret Mission

Operation "Torch" meant nothing to me in early October 1942, but it was a very important topic in the highest military and political circles of Washington and London. It was the code name for the scheduled Allied invasion of Northwest Africa. Americans would storm ashore from the Atlantic at Casablanca while a combined American and English force would come in from the Mediterranean at Oran and Algiers.

French North Africa was in the hands of the Vichy government of Marshal Pétain, established after the surrender of France to the invading Nazis in 1940. Now that area assumed strategic importance as General Bernard Montgomery halted the eastward advance of Marshal Erwin Rommel's Panzers in Egypt at El Alamein.

To head off a possible German move into the French-held area of Northwest Africa, our plans for an invasion required the element of surprise. Thus there could be no long period of softening military targets by aerial bombardment.

Military men who would become the leading heroes of World War II were involved in "Torch." General Eisenhower was to command the overall operation with Major General Mark Clark as his deputy. General George Patton would lead the invasion troops at Casablanca. Major General Jimmy Doolittle was in charge of the air forces taking part in the invasion.

No one knew how the French would react to invasion. Even

though a majority of Frenchmen prayed for our victory, the Vichy government existed only at the sufferance of the Germans and was thereby obliged to maintain a posture of neutrality. We considered it a puppet regime.

Since the fall of France, Winston Churchill had been exhorting the people of France, by radio, to have faith, promising to cleanse Europe of the Nazi pestilence. In one particularly eloquent address, delivered in both the English and French languages, he described Hitler as "this evil man, this monstrous abortion," and said, "Now, what is it we British ask of you in this present hard and bitter time? What we ask at this moment in our struggle to win victory which we will share with you, is that if you cannot help us, at least you will not hinder us."

Now came the opportunity to test the French. Would they help? If not, would they refrain from hindrance? Allied hopes were raised in mid-October when the French commander in Algiers, General Charles Emmanuel Mast, sent word secretly through the U.S. State Department's Robert D. Murphy that he would welcome the opportunity to talk with a top-ranking American general.

The Allies seized upon this meeting as a chance of eliminating the danger of French resistance to our invasion forces. At a high-level conference on October 17 at No. 10 Downing Street, it was decided to send Eisenhower's deputy, General Mark Clark, to Africa for a secret meeting with General Mast and a number of other French leaders who would support an Anglo-American effort to clear the Germans from the south shore of the Mediterranean, where they occupied Tunisia, Tripoli, and western Egypt.

In addition to Clark, the mission would consist of General Lyman Lemnitzer, head of the Allied Forces Plans Section; Col. A. L. Hamblen, a shipping and supply expert; Capt. Jerauld Wright, the navy's liaison officer for "Torch," and Col. Julius C. Holmes, head of the civil affairs branch for "Torch" planning. As a former State department officer, Colonel Holmes spoke French fluently.

The idea was good—to carry it out was risky. But risk is an element of war and I soon found myself involved in an operation so bizarre that I still wonder how it turned out to be successful. Time was running short, for our troop landings were scheduled to take place within three weeks.

Consequently, the secret mission to Africa was planned one day

Mark Clark's Secret Mission 103

and put into action the next. After meeting with Churchill, General Eisenhower called General Carl "Tooey" Spaatz, commander of the Eighth Air Force, briefed him hurriedly on the plan, and told him that two B-17s would be needed. He said they must be flown by the two best pilots available.

The same day, I received a call from Spaatz telling me I had been designated to fly General Clark to Gibraltar in my plane, the *Red Gremlin*. Wayne Connors was chosen to fly Lemnitzer in the *Boomerang*.

"Be ready to leave early tomorrow," Spaatz said.

Connors and I were briefed in detail that night. The plan, as described to us, was to fly General Clark and his party to Gibraltar, where a British submarine would be waiting to take them across the Mediterranean for a rendezvous with the French at an isolated farmhouse along the coast 60 miles west of Algiers near the town of Cherchell.

The party was to be divided between two planes so that the mission could be completed even if one of the aircraft were lost.

Extravagant deceptions were devised to conceal our plans. First, it was made to appear that Clark had gone to Scotland. That night, he arrived at our Polebrook base wearing lieutenant colonel's insignia instead of his two stars. He and members of his group were hidden in a tiny barracks, out of sight of any of our personnel who might have recognized one or more of them.

Because of the danger that we might be picked up by German radar installations in Brittany or the northwest tip of Spain, our guns were loaded and ready. To avoid attracting attention, we would not have fighter cover out of England. We were instructed not to land in Spain or Portugal, regardless of what emergencies might occur in flight. Our instructions in that case were to ditch at sea and hope for the best. Lemnitzer carried all the secret documents for the session in a heavily weighted tube that would be thrown overboard to sink to the bottom.

Our passengers had breakfast at 6:30 A.M., then were brought in staff cars to our planes, which were waiting and ready to go. The weather was excellent for our purpose; there were clouds in which we could conceal ourselves from visual sighting.

I remained thus concealed in the clouds for some distance south of England. It was at least three hours before we broke into the sunshine, well out to sea and beyond sight of land. There were no difficulties en route, and as we approached Gibraltar, a flight of Spitfires came out to escort us.

"The Rock" looked just as it does in the insurance ads, overlooking the narrow strait between Europe and Spanish Morocco. The recently built mile-long runway was on a neck of land connecting British-held Gibraltar to Spain. In fact, the road to the Spanish border crossed the middle of the runway. To halt motor traffic when aircraft was taking off or landing, there were movable barriers like those at a railroad crossing.

Ours were the first B-17s to land at Gibraltar. We were sure that German agents had the airstrip under surveillance from nearby Spain, and we wondered what they were thinking.

It was important, of course, that they not suspect the real nature of our mission. Wayne landed first and I was close behind. Our passengers left the planes without wearing coats or hats. Cars with drawn shades were waiting to take them to the governor's house.

What followed for us was a period of nervous waiting and, for members of the military mission, an adventure of the kind most often found in spy novels.

With the coming of darkness, the American party boarded a small British submarine that would take them eastward along the southern coast of the Mediterranean for their rendezvous with General Mast and his fellow French conspirators. Clark later reported that a submarine crewman was heard to say that "we're going on a screwy mission with some Americans."

Our orders were simply to await their return but to stand by for a hazardous rescue operation should something go wrong. There was the chance that Clark and his party might be betrayed or that the secret meeting place might be discovered.

If our people were somehow prevented from returning by sea, we were to fly over and drop some bombs several miles from the rendezvous point to divert attention. Then I would land near the farmhouse—there was a level field not far away that was believed suitable—pick up our passengers and take off as quickly as possible. If we had to go in at night, the landing area would be outlined by flare pots. That was the plan, at least, although there was some doubt about who would light the flares if things went awry.

I had many misgivings about the possibilities of an air rescue.

Would the field really handle a B-17 landing and takeoff? If the Vichy authorities had discovered the meeting and prevented our officers from reaching the submarine, would we have to fight off a police or military contingent?

We had our doubts, but it was war and we were ready to try anything. Eisenhower and Churchill thought the gamble worthwhile. Our designation by Spaatz as the best B-17 pilots in the air force was flattering. If misfortune befell this secret mission to Algeria, we would be tested. Naturally, we hoped there would be no need to find out if the hastily drawn-up contingency plan would really work.

The operation turned out to be a comedy of errors which, with more than a little bit of luck, ended happily. The meeting with the French, although cut short by unforeseen circumstances, set the stage for cooperation by a substantial number of French forces when the invasion occurred the following month. We had reason to take pride in the fact that the mission eventually saved a considerable number of lives and played an important part in lighting the "Torch."

The 450-mile voyage from Gibraltar to the North African rendezvous point was an uncomfortable one for our people in the cramped confines of the H.M.S. *Seraph*, described as one of Britain's smaller and slower undersea boats.

Although it cruised on the surface at night, it had to run submerged during the daylight hours. Arriving late for the scheduled rendezvous, the submarine remained offshore submerged for a full day before contact was made the next night by flashlight signal from shore. Our people made it to the beach in collapsible "folboats," one of which capsized, spilling its occupants into the surf.

The meeting went well but was cut short by a warning that police were on their way. The French officers scrambled from the house and headed back to Algiers by car, while General Clark and his group hid in a wine cellar, which they locked from inside. The police, who had apparently been tipped off by suspicious Arab servants who had been sent from the house before the Americans arrived, searched the place from cellar to attic but didn't get into the locked room in which our officers were hiding.

It was 4:00 A.M. when Clark and his party, having emerged from the wine cellar, managed to make contact with the waiting submarine and launched their canvas boats under difficult conditions in the raging surf. In the scramble, Clark lost his pants and a money belt containing several hundred dollars in Canadian gold coins, which he had carried in the hopes of bribing his way out of trouble in case of capture.

Once at sea, the submarine radioed Gibraltar that all was well and those of us who were waiting for word breathed a sigh of relief. The British sent a Catalina flying boat to meet the *Seraph* and bring the bedraggled party back to base by midafternoon. General Clark got a message off to Eisenhower, took a hot bath, and before midnight was aboard the *Red Gremlin* for a flight back to London.

A few days later, he and Eisenhower were summoned to Buckingham Palace and Clark described his experiences to King George, who was amused by the story of how he lost his pants.

15 Ike Goes to War on a Two-by-Four

Less than a week after returning with Mark Clark, I was ordered to assemble a fleet of six B-17s for another airlift to Gibraltar. This would be the start of "Torch." Our passengers would be the American and British commanders for the opening of the new front in North Africa. My own passenger in the *Red Gremlin* would be the supreme commander of the operation, General Eisenhower. Mark Clark would fly in the *Boomerang* with Wayne Connors.

On November 2, we flew from Polebrook to Hurn airport near the city of Bournemouth on England's south Channel coast. It was there that we would meet the military leaders who came from London by an 11-car special train, arriving early the next day.

As often happens in England in the fall, the weather was foul. On the morning we were scheduled to leave, the fog was of pea-soup thickness and even the birds were walking. There was a fine mist in the air. A successful takeoff seemed out of the question, and it was decided to wait until the next day when, it turned out, conditions were even worse.

Throughout the day, we received updated weather forecasts at 30-minute intervals, all of them pessimistic. General Eisenhower was becoming edgy. It was decided to leave the next morning come hell or high water. This was November 5, and the first landings in Africa were scheduled for early on November 8.

We were out to the flight line early. The mist had turned into a steady rain but the fog was still thick. Conditions were even worse than on the two previous days.

With our raincoats buttoned around our necks, Eisenhower and Jimmy Doolittle and I were standing beneath a wing of the *Red Gremlin,* looking at the sky and hoping for a break. We were joined by Wayne Connors and another B-17 pilot, John Knox.

The supreme commander looked at his watch for perhaps the hundredth time and then turned to Doolittle. "Jimmy, what should we do?" he asked.

"It's Paul's show," Doolittle replied.

Eisenhower looked at me.

"If it was just the crew and me, I'd go," I told him, "But I've got to think about you and your staff."

"Well, son," the general said. "I've got a war about to begin down there and that's where I have to be."

"Okay, sir. Let's go."

With that, we climbed aboard and started the engines. The other crews and passengers took the cue and began boarding their assigned aircraft.

A jeep with a "Follow Me" sign led us from the revetment to the runway. Believe me, we needed that jeep to find our way. We could barely see our own wing tips.

The plane was crowded with staff members and Eisenhower was wedged between me and the copilot on a two-by-four that we had installed so he could fly up front and see what was going on in the cockpit. The hard wood was softened only a little by a blanket.

The B-17 was built to carry bombs, not passengers. It was noisy and uncomfortable and I have often thought that only under the most austere wartime conditions would a commanding general ride to his battle post on a hard wooden plank.

As we prepared to take off, Eisenhower could see how nearly impossible the weather conditions were, but he never said a word or expressed a doubt about our decision.

The jeep got us to the end of the runway, where I lined up the plane on the runway heading with the help of the gyro compass. Even if you can't see the edges of the runway, you can use the rudders to maintain that gyro heading and make a zero-zero takeoff. Zero-zero means no forward visibility and no ceiling.

We were able to glimpse the runway lights faintly on either side as we picked up speed. These were the wartime lights visible from low level, or on approach, but not from overhead.

As we broke ground, the lights disappeared. We were in thick

Ike Goes to War on a Two-by-Four   109

gray soup with rain pelting the Plexiglas. I climbed to 200 feet and leveled off. That would be our flying altitude until we passed the Brest peninsula. By flying low, we would remain beneath the beam of the German radar on the coast. The fog that was our enemy a few minutes before was now a friend. We were hidden from German fighter planes that sometimes roved out to sea in this area.

We finally flew out of the fog and mist into bright sunshine. The sea was a deep blue, and far to our left could be seen the coast of Portugal. I climbed to 8,000 feet. Eisenhower's spirits seemed to be lifted and he started talking.

For the next two hours, we engaged in what was to me a highly interesting conversation. As an army man, he disclosed a keen understanding of air power and its uses. Knowing that I had been the leader of most of the bombing attacks on the continent, he discussed their effects and questioned me about the details.

He also talked of the importance of Operation Torch, in which he recognized that air power would have a major role, along with Patton's armored forces. The heavy tanks would lead the way along the coast and strike the German Panzer units in the west while the British under Montgomery were forcing Rommel's retreat from Egypt.

Our commander's comprehension of large-scale military strategy left me, a 27-year-old lieutenant colonel, with confidence that the coming operation was in good hands.

This day-long flight to Gibraltar, a distance of 1,200 miles, was one I would never forget. Neither would Eisenhower. He came to the Pacific in 1946 and stopped briefly on the island of Kwajalein, where I was stationed at the time of the Bikini atomic tests. When he got off the airplane, he wanted to know where Paul Tibbets was. Unfortunately, I was on a flying mission at the time, but I heard plenty about it when I got back. Other officers wanted to know how Eisenhower happened to know me. I told them of our flight together to Gibraltar.

When we landed at Gibraltar early in the evening, it was not the same place I had left less than two weeks before. The airfield had become the scene of bustling activities. We had to circle almost an hour before landing because of the congestion. Troop-carrying planes were everywhere.

So much activity should have been a tipoff to German watchers from nearby Spain that something big was about to happen. Fortunately, they misinterpreted it as a buildup to reinforce the British garrison on the island of Malta.

Eisenhower was greeted by the governor, Lt. Gen. Sir F. N. Mason MacFarland, who turned over Government House to him as his temporary headquarters. He didn't expect to be there long. His offices were in the damp, dimly lighted tunnels of the Gibraltar fortress. He referred to his office as a "dungeon" and complained of the constant "drip, drip, drip of the surface water." But there was no place else available and the supreme commander made the best of it, expecting to be in Africa soon.

I was ordered to stand by to provide additional staff transportation as needed. Plans for the invasion appeared to be going well.

Meanwhile, there was sad news about one of the planes in our B-17 airlift from England. John Knox had taken off 45 minutes after we left and his plane never reached Gibraltar. To this day no one knows what happened to the plane and the men aboard. One of his passengers was Maj. Gen. Asa Duncan, a fine airman and a real gentleman who had been chosen to play a major role in the air war in Africa.

The plane in which Generals Doolittle and Lemnitzer were passengers had a close call. Taxiing for takeoff, its hydraulic system failed and for a moment it appeared ready to crash into one of the other planes on the ground as pilot John C. Summers and co-pilot Thomas F. Lohr frantically pumped the useless brakes. To avoid a collision, they rolled off the taxiway and cut all four engines. Takeoff was delayed until next day, after the hydraulic system had been repaired.

Not long after leaving the coast of England, the plane was spotted by a flight of four Junkers JU-88s, which split into two elements and flew alongside the B-17 for a short distance. Because of the heavy load for this flight, the waist guns had been taken out of the bomber. Only the top turret, the ball turret, and the tail guns were in place and loaded; there was no way to fire at the enemy planes while they were alongside.

Finally, the Junkers pulled ahead and turned to attack. Summers threw the plane into an evasive maneuver as the enemy aircraft approached head-on. As the JU-88s circled to renew the attack, Summers tried valiantly to outrace them. The Germans opened fire

Ike Goes to War on a Two-by-Four   111

and a 20 millimeter shell exploded in the B-17 cockpit, wounding Lohr. Another shell knocked out the No. 3 engine.

Lohr left the cockpit to have his wound bandaged and Doolittle took over as copilot. Lohr recalled later than Lemnitzer provided a flask that helped overcome his pain, even though it was against regulations to carry liquor on a military airplane. The copilot's injuries were not serious. Later, in the North African campaign, he was forced to parachute from a B-17 over the Sahara and finished the war as a prisoner in Germany.

There was speculation at the time about where the German aircraft came from. Some thought the B-17 had been picked up on radar from the continent, and there was also the theory that someone had talked too much in a pub. In addition to Lemnitzer and Doolittle, the plane's passengers included Col. Thomas J. Davis, a member of Eisenhower's staff, and eight British generals.

The real story came out after the war. A Lieutenant Molder of the Luftwaffe, his suspicions aroused by the activity at sea in connection with the "Torch" operation, had been leading a reconnaissance mission from a field in France. The flight of four Junkers was bound for home when the low-flying B-17 was spotted. Only because they were running short of fuel did they break off their attack on the B-17. By such a slender thread of fortune did this important group of British and American officers escape with their lives to help direct the campaign in Africa.

Our plane and three others arrived at Gibraltar on November 6. Summers's disabled plane got there the next day, just in time for the invasion, which started in the early morning hours of November 8.

We kept in touch with the landing operations through reports that were coming in from the beachheads at Casablanca and the Algerian coast. It was an awkward situation because we were invading the territory of our former ally, which was now technically neutral. We felt we were justified, however, because the neutrality had been imposed by German arms.

Matters were complicated by the fact that the ranking Vichy admiral, Jean François Darlan, happened to be in Algiers at the time and was in a position to countermand the orders of the friendly French military men on the scene. Furthermore, it turned out that General Henry Giraud, the respected French officer who had recently escaped Nazi imprisonment and stood ready to help us, did not have the following among his fellow officers that we had been led to expect.

Nevertheless, our landings at Casablanca, Oran, and Algiers came as a surprise to all except the handful of French officers whom we had taken into our confidence. There was some resistance and, although we didn't like the idea of having to overpower French defensive forces, the operation came off with a minimum of bloodshed.

The attacks began at 2:38 A.M. on D day. By 7:45 A.M., one force had by-passed Algiers and seized the nearby Maison Blanche air base. The city itself surrendered by 9:00 P.M.

General Clark got word to me that he wanted to get his staff into Algiers the next day. Once again, the *Red Gremlin* and the *Boomerang* would provide his transportation.

We flew low over the Mediterranean, this time with an escort of 13 Spitfires. General Clark stood by an open hatch and scanned the shore as we approached the coast where he had recently lost his trousers. It was a much faster trip than his submarine voyage two weeks before. We landed just as the Germans launched an air attack against the city. The JU-88s flew over the airport on their way to the harbor, now jammed with all sorts of landing craft.

As Clark was being driven away from our plane in a Bren gun carrier, a Spitfire made a pass at one of the Junkers and its bullets started a stream of black smoke from the enemy plane's engine. Another JU-88 was hit by anti-aircraft fire and spun toward the airport. Before it reached the ground, its bomb load exploded and the plane fluttered down in thousands of pieces. Just then, a stick of three bombs exploded only 100 feet from the *Red Gremlin*.

I climbed down through the hatch and dropped onto African soil, aware that I was in the middle of a shooting war. I had expected to return to Gibraltar and bring in Eisenhower as soon as our bridgeheads had widened a bit. As it turned out, that job would be done by another of our B-17s. My stint as a chauffeur for the top brass had ended. I could now go back to being a warrior.

16 Bombardment in Africa

In their excellent history of the army air forces in World War II, Professors W. F. Craven and J. L. Cate have this to say about Operation "Torch":

World War II was to see larger operations than the Anglo-American invasion of Northwest Africa, but none surpassed it in complexity, in daring—and the prominence of hazard involved—or in the degree of strategic surprise achieved. The most important attribute of Torch, however, is the most obvious. It was the first fruit of the combined strategy. Once it had been undertaken, other great operations followed as its corollaries; competing strategies receded or went into abeyance until its course had been run. In short, the Torch operation and the lessons learned in Africa, imposed a pattern on the war.

In spite of the experiences I had in England in the early bombing raids on the continent of Europe, my real introduction to warfare came in North Africa.

Here I was not only the bomber, but the bombed. I tasted the terror of aerial warfare from the disadvantage point of the person on the ground. I felt the forces of nature on a fighting army, the ability of mud and rain to grind everything to a halt. I saw the effect of war on the people of this land, saw the suffering of many, and also saw the spirit of "business as usual" for many others who could not have cared less who the combatants were and which side was winning.

Roman legions fought in North Africa and the ruins of their empire may still be seen in many places. I imagine that some day the remains of our airfields will be viewed in much the same way. And it wouldn't surprise me if the natives will be as impassive then as they were when we were there, or as their ancestors were to the invading Romans.

Having flown General Clark to Algiers on the day after the initial landings, I found myself in a situation that was new to me. The city, harbor, and Maison Blanche airport were under constant day and night attack from German planes for the next four days. We did not have air superiority, and the Nazis were striking us from bases in nearby Tunisia. Because Algiers was the easternmost point of the "Torch" operation, we were actually in the front lines in the sense that we were nearest to the existing enemy bases.

The Tommy gun I received when we were getting ready to leave the United States was used for the first time at Algiers. I aimed the .45 caliber weapon at the attacking dive bombers, hoping for a lucky hit that might bring one down with a slug in the engine or fuel line, or possibly by hitting the pilot.

I don't know that I even came close. A hand weapon of any kind is no match for an attacking plane, but small caliber guns were about all we had during those early days of invasion. There had not yet been time to set up anti-aircraft batteries. These came later as we consolidated our positions.

By this time, thanks to a deal worked out with Admiral Darlan, French resistance had ceased. Darlan, who was loyal to Pétain's Vichy government and was therefore viewed as an Axis collaborator, was brought into line only after an angry General Clark had served him with an ultimatum. Darlan was assassinated six weeks later in Algiers by a 22-year-old university student who was described as a Gaullist. The killer was promptly executed by the French.

My father, recalling his experience as a captain of infantry in World War I, once told me that a good commander had to be a leader who would never ask his men to do anything he wouldn't do himself. In a dangerous situation, he must do what was necessary to protect his troops before worrying about himself.

Bombardment in Africa   115

I remembered this as our situation became hazardous at Maison Blanche. We were using one of the hangars at the field as living quarters, and our dormitories were on the second and third floors. One day, a flight of German planes got to us without prior warning. The first thing we knew, they were flying down the hangar line, dropping antipersonnel bombs. And they were scoring hits.

Even though battle-tested in the air, my bomber crews had never been under this kind of attack. As the bombs fell, I stood in the doorway blowing a whistle and yelling at the top of my voice to keep these men—many were just boys—from falling into a state of panic. I got them down the steps in orderly fashion and out of the hangars before the enemy swung back for another bombing run. I stood there until the last one was safely out of the dormitory. Although there were many hits, none of my crewmen suffered injury. I credit my father's advice and the discipline I learned in military school for enabling me to cope with this and other emergencies throughout the war.

After finding out what it was like to be on the receiving end of a bombing raid, I decided—even considering the flak and enemy fighters—that it was better to fight a war from the pilot's seat of an airplane. It wasn't long before I got my chance to return to the air, where I felt more comfortable. My little force of five B-17s might not have much impact on the outcome of the war in Africa, but I felt we should be doing something.

I went to Air Marshal Sir William Welsh, commander of components of the Royal Air Force in North Africa and the man responsible for cooperating with the Eastern Assault Force and Eastern Task Force, and offered him the services of our men and planes. I'll never forget his response. He dug into a desk drawer and pulled out a road map on which he pointed to the seaport of Bizerte on the coast of Tunisia, 375 miles to the east. German reinforcements were pouring into Africa through that port, and these troops represented a serious threat to Allied strategy.

"If you chaps would go up there and harass them with a few bombs, it would be of inestimable service to us," he told me in his proper British way.

I was accustomed to getting orders for bomber strikes listing the number of aircraft, takeoff time, rendezvous points, altitudes, routes, initial points, bomb drop times, route of return to base.

Hours of planning and books of paper work. So I asked the air marshal when we should stage our attacks.

"Oh, just whenever you can do it," he replied. "Whenever you're ready, go."

That was all I needed. We had the airplanes and crews. However, we did lack a few other essentials for making war. We didn't have any fuel or ammunition or bombs. But ships were putting these supplies ashore, down at the docks.

I was able to commandeer a truck. We got aviation fuel in 5-gallon cans, loading them on the truck by hand, then driving to the air base where we unloaded them by hand and passed them up on the wing to be dumped into the tanks of the airplanes. I found out exactly how many 5-gallon cans were needed to fuel a B-17. It is a bit of information that I have now happily forgotten.

The bombs were British, which presented a problem. Putting a British bomb in an American airplane was like putting a two-shilling piece in an American slot machine. British bombs are equipped with one lug. American bombs have two. Fortunately, this was one of many problems that the planners had foreseen. Our airplanes were equipped with both kinds of bomb shackles.

We wrestled the bombs off the trucks, rolled them across the ground, and lowered the hoists out of the bomb bays. We worked so hard that we taxied out to run up the engines without even synchronizing our watches, something we normally did before a mission. We did everything wrong, but we hit the jackpot.

The date was November 16. I have no independent recollection of this date, but it has been noted by one of the historians of the war.

South of the hills that ring Bizerte was Sidi Ahmed Air Base. There the Germans based the airplanes that were to defend the city and its all-important port. Because they didn't expect us, we caught their planes on the ground.

In military talk, our first mission was to neutralize the enemy's air defenses. In plain English, we blew hell out of the place. It was lunchtime and everyone was in the mess hall. We got a direct hit on the mess hall and killed almost the entire squadron. We also destroyed some of their airplanes.

We hit them so hard that we had time to get back to Maison Blanche, take on a new load of gas and bombs from the docks, and return to Bizerte before the Germans had begun to resupply their fighter field.

The hills south of Bizerte were a little more than 3,000 feet high. We bombed the airfield from about 6,500 feet and swept over the hills and hit the docks. We had the element of surprise on our side and we remained relatively low. At this altitude, the anti-aircraft guns on the docks had trouble locking on and tracking us.

The Germans were using 88 millimeter anti-aircraft guns around Bizerte. It was a deadly and versatile weapon, even used as field artillery and as an antitank weapon. As an anti-aircraft gun, it could be fired at a rate of 40 rounds a minute.

We found out with experience that the best altitude for bombing Bizerte was around 14,000 to 20,000 feet. This height was particularly advantageous when we had built up our bombing fleet so that we could spare a few planes to go in first and take care of the German fighters, followed a few minutes later by the rest of the squadron to bomb the docks.

The 88s were most effective against planes flying at around 25,000 feet because, at this altitude, it was easier to track a formation. The gunners also had time to set the fuses more accurately.

On one mission, I saw first-hand and at close range just how deadly the 88 could be. The plane off my left wing was flown by Jesse Wikel of Birmingham, Alabama, a soft-voiced southerner who had been through a number of missions with me over Europe. His plane took an 88 in the bomb bay. The explosives in the shell and those in his bomb load let loose at the same time. One instant he was flying a short distance off my wing. There was a blinding flash. Then there was nothing there. No flying parts, no smoke. Nothing. His plane simply disintegrated. We continued our run with a hole in the formation. I was sad because I knew Wikel well and liked him very much. But as I mentioned before, I was learning to live with this kind of tragedy. With less luck, the hole in the formation might have been where the *Red Gremlin* had been flying.

In fact, an 88 almost ended my life over North Africa. The shell went through my wing spar. I'll never know why it didn't explode or how it missed the control cables or fuel lines. I didn't even lose a gallon of gasoline. Maybe mother had a gift of prophecy when she said, "I know you'll be all right, son."

The Germans also sent up smaller stuff. Close to the target, they had Bofors-type anti-aircraft weapons—about the size of our 37 millimeter. They weren't used to track an airplane; they simply put up a wall of exploding steel in your path. If they got into action before a low-flying airplane reached the target, they could be deadly.

From the time of its capture, Maison Blanche airport was under the control of the RAF. It soon became crowded as British Spitfires arrived, along with the many C-47s that were used to carry personnel and matériel needed at the front.

Next came the heavy bombers from the Eighth Air Force. The entire 97th and 301st groups were being transferred from England. There were those who accused Jimmy Doolittle of "castrating" the Eighth to get the forces he needed. But he knew the importance of the North African campaign to Allied strategy, which was designed to hit the Axis from as many directions as possible.

The overcrowding at the Algiers base was apparent to General Spaatz. He decided it wasn't suitable as a bomber base for other reasons. The B-17s there were too exposed. Although there were other airstrips in our part of North Africa, few had paved runways that were adequate to our needs. The one at Bone, east of Algiers, was even more exposed to enemy attack. Port Lyautey in Morocco was too far from our targets. It was decided to base our B-17s at Tafaraoui, near Oran. Even though it was 600 miles from Bizerte, it seemed ideal for our purposes.

Then the winter rains started.

Tafaraoui became the subject of a famous rhyme in which it was noted that the mud at Tafaraoui was "deep and gooey." The runways were paved, all right, but nothing else. When an airplane turned off the runway, it was on a clay surface which was fine in dry weather. When it rained, the clay became mud into which the airplanes sank deeper and deeper.

We tried to run a few missions after the rains started, but the situation was almost hopeless. We struggled to drag the airplanes through the mud to the runway but our task was slow and agonizing. Once a plane was on the concrete, the ground crews went to work with shovels and sticks, scraping the mud and slime off the wheels so they would roll freely and could be retracted without clogging up the wheel wells.

It soon became impossible to operate under these conditions, which were worse than we had in England with its rain and fog. When the need for an all-weather bomber base became obvious, Doolittle discovered Biskra, where, by enlarging an existing airstrip, adequate facilities were created. Biskra, home of the world-famous Biskra dates, is an oasis east of Oran and south of the Atlas Mountains at the northern edge of the Sahara Desert. Because it seldom rains there, it was an ideal bomber base. We ended up with a wide runway on which B-17s could take off three abreast. Our first airplanes arrived there on December 13.

In addition to the B-17s, a number of P-38 fighters were based at Biskra. The P-38 pilots didn't like it, however. Simply flying interference for a formation of bombers was beneath their dignity. They felt, perhaps correctly, that on some days it might be more important to strafe enemy tanks and trucks or to provide support for ground troops. The experiment of running fighters and bombers out of the same field and under the same commander worked well from the standpoint of the bomber pilots, but the idea wasn't widely adopted.

We had a supply problem at Biskra. There was one rail line through the mountains from the coast. The limit that could be moved from the docks to our oasis airport was 400 tons a day. Of this total, only 250 tons could be allocated for bombs and aviation fuel. The limitation naturally led to problems. Since the planning at this time wasn't the best, the matériel that came in wasn't always what we needed most.

Although it was in the Sahara, Biskra was no tropical paradise. In fact, it was often downright cold, especially at night. We received plenty of coffee from the coast, but no one bothered to send us sugar, cream, canned milk, or even powdered milk.

The early weeks in North Africa were hectic. I had very little sleep and seldom took time to eat a complete meal, but I did drink gallons of black coffee. I would dream of being able to sweeten the coffee with a couple of spoons of sugar and lighten it with rich, fresh cream. To my surprise, however, when I finally had these luxuries available, I discovered that I had learned to prefer my coffee black. To this day I drink it that way and give the blame—or credit—to my experience on the desert.

Our supply problem was finally solved with the start of an airlift from the coast, utilizing C-47s. It was one of the first uses of airplanes to carry supplies to an isolated base.

Colonel Hampton H. Atkinson, best known as "Hamp," was commander of the 97th during the time we were based at Biskra. A finer officer didn't exist, but he was suffering a period of poor health at the time, with the result that he delegated most of his duties to me. It was a valuable command experience.

As the end of the year approached, I was about to be transferred to the 12th Air Force headquarters in Algiers.

17 *Marauders in Algiers*

Moving to the 12th Air Force was a whole new life for me. My chief worry before had been the *Red Gremlin*. Now I was in an office in Algiers as General Doolittle's bombardment chief, with a whole squadron of gremlins to worry about.

I don't know when the word *snafu* came into the military jargon, but it applied to our situation in North Africa. Confusion was everywhere, due to the complexity and immensity of the operation and the haste with which it was put together.

My respect for Jimmy Doolittle multiplied during these weeks. He was all over the place trying to solve problems as they arose and trying to keep more from developing. He was no armchair general. He had his own personal Spitfire and used it to fly from one base to another in the war theater. He wanted to find out things for himself.

We shared one major problem: the B-26 bomber. We were losing these hot new two-engine planes at an alarming rate and the word was spreading that it was a jinxed and unsafe aircraft. Some of the B-26s were sent directly from the United States, and we lost more on crashes during the ferrying operation than you would expect to lose in missions against the enemy. The 319th Group was sent to North Africa from England. The flight was apparently picked up by German radar on the continent, and the group commander's plane was shot down by a German fighter off Cherbourg.

There were four different commanders during a seven-week

period. Colonel Claude Duncan took over on November 24. He was the brother of General Asa Duncan, who was killed on the B-17 flight from Hurn to Gibraltar. Claude was replaced on December 11 by Colonel Charles T. Phillips, who was killed in a B-26 crash four days later. Colonel Carlyle H. Ridenour came next. He lasted just two weeks. Finally Joe Cannon took command on January 1 and remained until February 18.

I was offered the B-26 command but declined. Although I wasn't afraid of the airplane, my combat background was in heavy bombers and I felt the role of the medium bomber would be limited as the war went on. The B-26 was a challenge, but not one that I was eager to tackle at this point in my career.

It was certainly the most controversial airplane of its time. Built by the Martin company, it was called the "Marauder." Four-bladed propellers turned by two Pratt and Whitney Double Wasp engines gave it 3700 horsepower and a speed of 315 miles an hour. This was a tremendous performance.

The plane demanded a lot of respect from the pilot because of its small wing which, with the pointed engine nacelles, offered little drag. There was also little lift until it reached relatively high speeds.

Our pilots had been trained in aircraft with large wings. The wing area of our B-17s was 1,486 square feet. By contrast, the B-26 had just 602 square feet of wing to lift 27,000 pounds of airplane and bombs. That meant a landing speed of 135 miles an hour, which compares with that of today's jet fighters. Our pilots were used to touching down at about 85.

Doolittle, a former racing pilot, was accustomed to this type of performance. Some of the racing craft he had been flying during the thirties were almost all engine and propeller. He knew what you could do with an airplane, how much performance could be milked out of it, and how far it could be pushed before the machine became master of the man in the cockpit. The Marauder was not frightening to a man who had horsed a B-25 off the deck of an aircraft carrier for a surprise raid on Tokyo.

I was with him when he flew the B-26 for what I thought was the first time. He didn't tell me that he had been assigned to evaluate the plane in the States at a time when some pilots were complaining that it was too hot to handle. Its reputation as a killer had followed the Marauder to North Africa.

Marauders in Algiers 123

Nothing was too hot for Jimmy. He strapped himself into the pilot's seat and pretended to be unfamiliar with the layout of the cockpit. I was beside him as copilot.

I had heard all the complaints about the B-26 and suspected some of the reasons for its troubles. For one thing, the generator switches were at the entrance as you came up through the fuselage. They had to be set as you got in. If you forgot, you were in for an unpleasant surprise.

Some accidents occurred because the pilot overlooked the switches. He would start the engines, turn on the radios, taxi out and take off. The batteries were not charging; instead, they were losing power. When they went dead, the electrically operated propellers went into flat pitch and lost their thrust. The plane lost flying speed and a crash became inevitable.

I should have suspected that Doolittle knew more about the B-26 than he admitted when he said, "It's just another airplane. Let's start it up and play with it."

That is exactly what we did. We got in the air and circled to 6,000 feet, remaining close enough to the field to reach the runway if we had trouble. But everything went smoothly.

Doolittle then shut down one of the engines and feathered the propeller. He got the plane trimmed and we did some flying on one engine, tuning both directions, climbing, making steep banks. The Marauder was a tame bird with Doolittle at the controls.

Suddenly he put the plane into a dive, built up excess speed and put it into a perfect loop—all with one engine dead. As we came to the bottom of the loop, he took the dead propeller out of feather and it started windmilling. When it was turning fast enough, he flipped on the magnetos and restarted the engine as we made a low pass over the airfield. We came around in a normal manner, dropped the gear and the flaps, and set the B-26 down smoothly on the runway.

The pilots and operations people who had been watching us were impressed. The flight was an important start toward convincing them that the B-26 was just another airplane. Doolittle later flew with the crews in this plane whenever he got a chance. He also took part in some of their combat operations.

Soon after settling in Algiers, I learned that an old friend, Bill Rice, had landed there with the invasion forces. I had met him in

Miami Beach, where we had attended officer training sessions during the early days of our entry into the war. The Air Corps had taken over several large hotels on the beach for this purpose.

I found that he was living at the Hotel Alletti, with a fifth-floor room and balcony overlooking the harbor. He invited me to move in as his roommate.

Almost every night, the Germans would send over a flight of JU-88s to attack shipping in the harbor. They would turn and start their dives just above the hotel. On the roof was a British anti-aircraft gun. The scream of the dive-bombers and the whoom-whoom of the ack-ack weapon created a deafening din.

When the nightly action started, Bill and I would go onto the balcony for a front-row view of the fireworks. The scene was spectacular. Every night was like the Fourth of July.

Then one night, the Germans cancelled our tickets to the show. Instead of going after the ships in the harbor, they apparently decided to silence the gun on the hotel roof. When we heard the first bomb explode nearby, Bill and I abandoned our balcony in a hurry, slammed the double french doors shut, and dived beneath the bed. We were not a second too soon.

There was a terrific blast. The glass doors, casings, and part of the wall were blown across the room, ripping the mattress and smashing against the opposite wall. That bomb tore up our sleeping quarters and dampened our enthusiasm for the harbor view we had thought so delightful.

"We'd better requisition a safer place to live," Bill said. I didn't know what he had in mind but he said he was going to the French authorities and demand an apartment elsewhere in the city.

Bill spoke French fluently and was assigned to accompany the invasion forces on that account. He was a member of a prominent Boston family and had been educated at Harvard, Cambridge, and the Sorbonne, studying economics and government. His primary task here was to serve as liaison between the English- and French-speaking forces.

By the time I was off duty the next day, he had four places lined up for us to look at. We finally decided on an apartment at 33 Rue Michelet. It was on the third floor of a four-story building. This time we had put plenty of space between us and the harbor.

We moved in and, to make a long story short, we had a ball. We were on British supplies and the British had a little more experience than the Americans in taking the harsh edges out of a war situation. They knew what was needed to get along and maintained a plentiful supply of aged Scotch, good gin, and such trading items as silk stockings. I remember the rich and creamy Cadbury chocolates, and although I don't really have a sweet tooth, I learned in a hurry that they could be exchanged for things that money couldn't buy. An officer could draw these supplies on the basis of the organization he had and the number of officers and sergeants in a unit. Bill and I quickly developed our own inflated reports.

Because he had to do a lot of shuttling back and forth between the commanders, Bill had a Buick that had been commandeered after arriving in Algiers. It was a sedan of 1936 vintage, in perfect running order. Our transportation was certainly a cut above that of the military personnel who had to get around in jeeps.

He would drive to the commissary once a week and pick up the goodies for our fictitious force. Jams, marmalade, all the things the British looked upon as part of the good life, were soon stored away in our apartment. These supplies paid for our laundry service, got our beds made and the apartment cleaned, and even got our cooking done for us whenever we decided to dine in, which wasn't often.

The Algerians were more bystanders than participants in this war. It might not be correct to call them innocent bystanders, because many of the natives took advantage of the wartime situation to live a little better than they had before.

Because of his command of French, and because he had traveled in Africa as a boy, Bill soon found his way around Algiers, including the Casbah, which proved to be much as it is portrayed in movies. We found restaurants of a quality one would not expect to find in such a city in the middle of a war. It was sometimes difficult to reach them in the nightly blackouts, but we somehow managed.

A majority of American and British officers never found these places, but there were many European business people and some we knew quite well to be German agents. You didn't have to check their ID cards to figure this out. They knew who we were because we were always in uniform. There was probably some mystery about what we were doing because of Bill's mastery of the French language and his ability to talk his way into almost anywhere.

There was a kind of unwritten truce. While we were enjoying the underground nightlife of Algiers, we didn't pretend to recognize the Germans and they didn't bother us. We were glad not many of our people patronized the places. If they had, the increased business would have driven the prices up.

As it was, we made our way to these restaurants over narrow blacked-out streets, and we lived like kings. Or sheiks, perhaps.

The good life ended all too soon, but I can't blame it on the Nazis. I left this pleasant scene because of an encounter with an ambitious American officer.

18 The Norstad Incident

Lauris Norstad was tall, handsome, and intelligent. He had what it takes to go places in the military. He also had political connections, which did him no harm.

Fate brought our paths together in North Africa in the winter of 1942–43, and the result was a clash of personalities that might have been avoided if he had been less arrogant and I had been a bit more tactful. Friends who knew us both have mentioned that I had a tendency to be a little abrasive, on occasions, in those days.

I was a 27-year-old lieutenant colonel full of confidence after leading many successful bombing missions over Europe and North Africa. General Spaatz had indicated that he considered me the most combat-experienced bomber pilot in the air force at the time. But Norstad, a 35-year-old full colonel, outranked me.

Although he had never flown in combat, he tried to tell me how to bomb Bizerte. This set the stage for an explosion during a mission planning session.

Friction between us dated from an earlier incident, however.

On Christmas Day, 1942, I led an 18-airplane attack on Bizerte. By this date, such a mission was so routine that we regarded it as a milk run. The Germans had to resupply their forces through Bizerte and we were committed to interrupt the operation of the port and airfield as fast as they could make repairs.

Word of the 97th's devastating raids against these objectives got back to President Roosevelt who, without knowing his name, ordered a promotion for the commander of the B-17s in North Africa. This was Colonel Hampton J. "Hamp" Atkinson, my group commander.

When he received the message announcing his promotion to brigadier general, Hamp was naturally pleased but somewhat embarrassed. It was a mark of the caliber of this fine officer that he said to me, "This belongs to you. You got it for me." He was referring to the fact that I had actually been doing his work while he was recovering from a prolonged illness.

Hamp had left England in poor health and the weather we had encountered in North Africa had not helped. He had a lung condition and for days at a time could not get out of bed. While he was in that shape, I took charge of my own accord and kept things running smoothly. Actually, I covered for him. Had his illness been known, he would have been sent to a hospital with the resultant loss of his command, causing bitter disappointment to him and to me. He was a proud career airman and believed he should be "fighting the war." I feared that, if he were replaced, we would get some incompetent bastard in command of the type I was seeing arrive with new outfits from the States. I did not want the 97th to suffer this fate if I could help it.

"Since I can't change this order, the rank that goes with it gives me the authority to give you a battlefield promotion," Hamp said, handing me a pair of his eagles.

It was soon after this that Jimmy Doolittle flew to Biskra. He wanted to congratulate Hamp in person, but from my standpoint, he had a more sinister purpose.

When Doolittle landed at Biskra, I was making another milk run to Bizerte. After my return and debriefing, one of the men told me that General Atkinson wanted to see me immediately. With him in his office was Doolittle, and it was obvious that they had been in serious conversation.

After a friendly greeting and a few questions about the mission, General Doolittle said, "I came to talk to Hamp and take you back to Algiers. We're getting operational there and since you're the most experienced bomber man in my command, I need you at headquarters."

I put up a protest but all I got was a friendly smile and the comment, "I've already heard all of those arguments from Hamp but the answer is still 'no.' Go pack your things. We're leaving in 30 minutes." Now after six months of flying with the best bomber outfit in that part of the world, I was being relegated to a desk to work for one of the most vain and egotistical officers I had ever met. I refer to Colonel Norstad, to whom I would report since he was General Doolittle's chief of operations.

Notice of my battlefield promotion arrived in Algiers on the first day I occupied my new office. To be official, such promotions have to be confirmed by a panel of officers constituting a "promotions board." If an officer on the board wants to blackball you, you've had it. I was told that Norstad killed my promotion with the comment, "There's only going to be one colonel in operations and I'm it." Consequently, my career as a full colonel was brief and it was another two years before I finally made that grade.

It had to be a case of jealousy. Certainly there was no personality clash between us at that time because we did not know each other. He had no doubt heard of my work as leader of the B-17 raids that had been widely praised by unbiased observers in the African theater and at home.

General Doolittle was too embarrassed by Norstad's petty reaction to break the news to me in person. He sent his executive officer, Colonel Ted Curtis, to explain things as tactfully as possible. "I'm sorry," Curtis said apologetically, "but we're getting so much flak over this that we won't be able to publish the confirming order."

I was puzzled and asked him what the difficulty was. Then, with some hesitation, he told me that Colonel Norstad was throwing his weight around. He filled in a few details.

The question in my mind was this: How could Norstad, a colonel, override the apparent wishes of Doolittle, a major general? I found out soon enough that Doolittle had the rank but not the power. The real influence in the 12th Air Force lay between Colonel Norstad and his crony, Hoyt Vandenberg, who had recently been promoted to brigadier general as Doolittle's chief of staff.

It wasn't long until I had my first face-to-face encounter with Norstad on an issue important enough to be worth risking my military future. That was my opinion at the time and it's my conviction today.

The scene was the starkly furnished and carpetless conference room in the 12th Air Force headquarters in downtown Algiers. The building that had been commandeered for this purpose had housed

Standard Oil's Algerian operations. Like most buildings in the city, it was of concrete block construction faced with beige stucco in the best Mediterranean tradition.

I was one of a half-dozen officers seated around a long conference table for the morning session, at which plans were to be laid for the next day's operation. Norstad presided, as usual. It was his habit to announce his plans with the expectation that the other officers would nod their agreement and limit their suggestions to a minor detail or two.

The subject of this session was the resumption of bombing attacks on Bizerte. The series of raids that I had led on that coastal seaport had been effective. We had knocked out most of the harbor installations and severely damaged the air base, but reconnaissance now showed that the Germans had been busy repairing docks and other installations. Bizerte was now ready for use once more as a resupply base for Axis forces in North Africa. More anti-aircraft batteries had been installed in the dock area.

Members of the staff were in unanimous agreement that the time was ripe for a new and devastating strike. On the record, I was the bomber expert and Norstad, having never flown a combat mission, was the novice. Nevertheless, he had worked out details for the next day's raid on Bizerte.

After designating the takeoff hour and the direction of the bomb runs over the target, he said, almost casually: "The B-17s will go in at 6,000 feet."

My response was a flat contradiction. "We can't send them in at 6,000 feet," I said. "We just can't do it."

My courage in speaking up so abruptly was born of earnest conviction based on my experience in raids over this target. In retrospect, I must admit that I might have made my point more tactfully.

Norstad's face reddened. He wasn't used to having a staff officer speak up in this manner. We were supposed to be rubber stamps.

"What do you mean, we can't do it?" he asked, obviously angry.

"I've been there," I replied. "I know if we send them in at 6,000 feet, they'll be wiped out."

Norstad's face froze in an expresion of contempt. He would now try to humiliate me. Addressing the other officers, he said: "It appears that Colonel Tibbets has been flying too much. He may be suffering from combat fatigue."

Something snapped in me at that moment. Whatever I had learned of discipline and self-control left me. This handsome desk jockey with the eagles on his shoulders was calling me a coward. Whatever my shortcomings, lack of guts was not one of them. I had flown enough bombing missions over Europe and North Africa to more than use up the odds in favor of getting back safely. Moreover, I had asked for more combat duty but had been brought into headquarters against my wishes to help make decisions of the kind we were discussing at that moment.

Our objective was to destroy enemy targets with as little loss as possible. We were prepared, in some cases, to accept losses of as high as 20 percent, but what Colonel Norstad was proposing would, in my opinion, mean a near wipe-out of our bombers.

I had an emotional as well as a military stake in preventing this invitation to disaster. Those fellows out there—the pilots and crewmen who would be flying tomorrow's mission to Bizerte—were friends of mine. As one of the official planners of the raid, I would have had their blood on my conscience if I had not spoken up to head off Norstad's plan.

With this in mind, and angered by Norstad's slur, I rose from my chair with fists clenched while the other officers in the room held their collective breath.

"I'll tell you what I'm prepared to do, colonel," I said in a voice that betrayed my agitation. "I'll lead that raid myself at 6,000 feet if you will come along as my copilot."

He promptly backed down under this challenge. Norstad wouldn't fly a combat mission over a heavily defended enemy target at that or any other altitude. I was flushed with a mixture of anger and conviction. It was my duty, I reasoned, to scuttle this ill-conceived scheme, whatever the consequences to my career. In all honesty, I should probably say that I was not thinking of the consequences at this time. We were in a wartime situation, not far from the battlefront, and the wrong decision could be costly.

Military blunders have cost many a life needlessly in the long history of warfare. There is more truth than poetry in Tennyson's "Charge of the Light Brigade." I didn't intend to be a party to a blunder at Bizerte.

Although I had blown my cool in this clash with a powerful superior, I retained enough self-control to make a convincing presentation once the smoke of anger had lifted. In a speech that was surprisingly restrained, I described in detail the layout of the harbor at Bizerte and the defense installations, and explained from personal experience the basis for my knowledge that a raid at the 6,000-foot level would be disastrous. This was an altitude, I said, at which enemy anti-aircraft fire would be most effective. It was true that my first raid on the German base was at such a low level, but this was a surprise attack for which the enemy was not prepared. In addition, the defenses had been strengthened.

Norstad had no choice but to hear me out. After all, these planning sessions were meant to be forums in which the opinions of the entire staff were weighted. Put on the spot, he was obliged to back down. If his plan were carried out, and the losses were as substantial as I had forecast, he would have been blamed for the disaster. And my warning would have been a matter of record.

The bombers flew to Bizerte the next day at 20,000 feet and the results were excellent. There were no losses, although anti-aircraft fire was heavy. The mission was carried out precisely as I had suggested. The B-17s were split into three groups. One attacked from the sea and another from the land, splitting the enemy defenses. The third group flew a diversionary mission.

Everyone seemed happy with the outcome, but Norstad, who should have been pleased that a debacle had been prevented, could not forget his personal defeat at the planning session. Unlike me, he had retained his cool at the meeting, but his agitation was more deep-rooted than I realized. I was soon to discover that he was a man of intense pride who knew how to harbor a grudge.

How deeply he resented my performance at the staff meeting soon became apparent. Relations were strained between us for the rest of the time I was stationed at Algiers. Colonel Curtis advised me to avoid Norstad wherever possible. A couple of weeks passed and the situation was growing intolerable. There were rumors that I would be punished somehow. The story of our showdown was widely circulated and it became an obsession with Norstad to save face.

One day, General Doolittle called me into his office. He was clearly agitated, for he and I had worked together and each of us respected the other. Doolittle remembered, of course, that he had brought me to headquarters against my will and, in a sense, felt a responsibility for having thrown me into an unpleasant situation. He was fully aware of the circumstances of our confrontation, and with his own considerable experience as a bomber pilot, I know that he agreed with my assessment of the Bizerte bombing problem. Now he was in an awkward position.

"Larry Norstad wants to court-martial you," he said, "and I can't stop him."

I wasn't surprised by the first half of his statement, but I couldn't understand the rest. When it appeared that I didn't believe that he was helpless to intervene, General Doolittle took pains to explain certain facts of military life. I was aware that politics existed in all branches of the service but hadn't thought it would hogtie a man of Doolittle's prestige and reputation, particularly in the middle of a war.

"I may be the commander here," he said confidentially, "but I don't have the power of Vandenberg and Norstad. They have the political influence and that's what counts."

General Vandenberg was the nephew of Senator Arthur Vandenberg, the influential Republican leader from Michigan whose support was essential to the Democratic administration of Franklin Roosevelt in the critical days before the U.S. was drawn into the war. Colonel Norstad, an intelligent opportunist, had fastened himself to the Vandenberg coattails, and together they moved up the military ladder. It was a push-pull operation. Norstad was constantly scheming to have Vandenberg promoted, and Vandenberg, in turn, would reach down and pull Norstad up after him. Both eventually reached the four-star summit. Doolittle understood what was happening and he didn't intend to involve himself in a showdown with Norstad on my account. I didn't blame him. But he did the next best thing, from my standpoint. He thwarted Norstad's plan to court-martial me by arranging my transfer to what he recognized as a very important assignment.

When he called me to his office, he had already made detailed plans for my departure from North Africa. "I've just received a message from Hap Arnold," he said. "He wants an experienced bombardment officer to come back to the States and help with the development of a big new bomber. I've recommended you for the job."

The big new bomber was the B-29, the superfortress then being developed by Boeing—the plane that was to win the war in the Pacific and the plane I was to fly to Hiroshima. Just as he had ordered me to pack my bags in a hurry at Biskra ten weeks before,

Doolittle now told me to pack at once and head for the United States. His own staff car was waiting outside to take me to my apartment and pick up my clothes, then speed me to Maison Blanche airport where a C-47 was standing by for the sole purpose of flying me down the coast to Liberia. On the long trip home, which included a flight across the South Atlantic and up the east coast of South America, I had time to reflect on many things, including the irony of a rescue operation in which I was involved on one of the first days of the African invasion.

It was a day of frantic activity along the African coast. As soon as the air base at Algiers was secured, I flew General Clark there and was on my way back to Gibraltar when a voice from the air base tower at Oran broke into the radio frequency on which we were tuned.

"Calling the B-17 passing north of Oran," the voice said. "Will you please answer?"

"Hey, that's us," said my navigator, Dutch Van Kirk.

Acknowledging the radio call, I identified our aircraft.

"A German airplane has two senior air force officers pinned down in a ditch at the far side of the base," said the tower. "Can you do anything to help them?"

Before responding, I sized up the situation as best I could from 5,000 feet. The landing strip at the south edge of the city was easy to locate. The rest of the field was literally covered with several hundred C-47s that had rendezvoused there after dropping paratroopers along the coast that morning. None of these twin-engine transports had the capability of taking off and attacking the German plane, which I could see circling at low altitude over the south side of the air base.

I made a left turn and started descending toward the field. To the Oran tower I replied: "I can land and pick them up. That's the best I can do."

My plane was well armed with .50 caliber machine guns and I was confident of our ability to deal with the Nazi aircraft even though, at that time, I was unable to spot the two American officers who had somehow wandered away from the newly established headquarters area.

To carry out the rescue mission, I ordered crewmen to their battle stations with guns ready for action if necessary against the enemy plane. We made a low pass over the field and the German pilot wisely moved out to a distance of about 3 miles, where he circled and watched our operation. He had apparently been having sport at the expense of the two officers, who we now saw waving at us from a ditch where they had found shelter from the strafing attack.

One more circle of the field and I landed on the hard-packed ground alongside the ravine. Van Kirk and my bombardier, Tom Ferebee, leaped out and helped the officers up the ladder and into the B-17. Meanwhile, the other crew members stood by with machine guns at the ready in case the German plane should return. However, the enemy pilot headed eastward, no doubt aware that the odds were against him.

I taxied back across the field and deposited the officers, both colonels, in front of base operations. I was busy with the controls of the plane and did not meet them. Although they expressed thanks, they did not identify themselves to members of my crew. Later, I was told that the officers I had rescued were Vandenberg and Norstad. I have no way of knowing if this was true for I never mentioned the incident to either of them. Nor, if it had been them, would they have known that I was the pilot of the rescue plane.

Only twice after Algiers did I meet Norstad.

A number of years after the war, I was serving in the requirements branch of air force headquarters at Bolling Field in Washington under Brig. Gen. Thomas S. Power. Norstad—by this time a major general—was transferred there as director of operations, U.S. Air Force.

On the Saturday morning when he was scheduled to arrive, all the senior officers were ordered to appear in uniform with shoes brightly polished because General Norstad was coming through each of the branches of the operations section to be introduced to his officers.

In the nonsensical fashion of the military, each of us was told in detail how the general was to be greeted. We were to step forward from the line as he came through our offices, then salute and say, "Sir, I'm Colonel Tibbets, and I do this," etc.

We had been at alert since 8:00 A.M., and by the time Norstad reached our offices it was almost noon. There were six or seven officers in our line and I was standing at the end.

When Tommy Powers introduced me, I said "Hello, Larry," and extended my hand instead of saluting. Norstad shook hands and said, "How are you, Paul? I haven't seen you in a long time."

Powers turned pale at the informality. He didn't know, of course, that our show of amiability concealed a long-standing mutual dislike. To this day I'm not sure why I impulsively greeted him this way instead of following instructions. We had been on a first-name basis in Algiers, and it seemed the only sensible way to greet an old acquaintance even if our relationship was strained.

Our paths crossed once more when I was in Paris as part of the military mission to NATO and Norstad was supreme allied commander in Europe, with headquarters also in Paris.

One day I was summoned to his office to explain some phase of the war plan, of which I had special knowledge. Accompanying me for the purposes of introduction was a two-star general who stood in obvious awe of the commander.

With an impressive show of formality, he addressed General Norstad and said, "Sir, I would like to present . . ."

At this point, Norstad interrupted him and said, "I know Colonel Tibbets." I nodded and this time said "general" instead of "Larry."

I have been in the same room with him a number of times since, at air force conventions and other military gatherings, but neither of us has taken the trouble to speak.

What I have said about Norstad is not meant to imply that he lacked qualities of leadership, for indeed he had an attractive personality that commanded admiration in the same manner that a movie star is admired. Although the word had not come into general use at that time, it might be said that he possessed "charisma."

The point should be made, however, that advancement in the military, as in politics, has often been based on such qualities rather than on competence as a soldier or statesman. It was in satirical reference to this fact that Gilbert and Sullivan offered their famous advice in song: "Stick close to your desks and never go to sea, and you all may be rulers of the Queen's na-vee."

19 Reunion

"You son of a bitch, put that down!"

The voice was mine, but I could hardly believe it. The scene was the U.S. customs shed at Homestead Air Force base south of Miami.

I had just pumped a live round into the chamber of my .45 automatic and was pointing the gun at a very surprised and officious customs officer who was trying to take $1,600 from me.

This was my return to the United States in February 1943, after eight months overseas. I was tired and run-down from months of combat flying and a strenuous seven-day trip home in slow-flying military transports. My weight was down to 155 pounds, 37 less than when I left for England the previous June.

Before I left Algiers, an old flying friend, Christopher Karis, had given me a little more than $800 to take to his parents back home. He had been helping to support them since he was in high school. When he gave me the money, he was on brief leave from his base in the desert, where there had been nowhere to spend the monthly pay he had been collecting. Although we were paid in Algerian francs, they could be converted to American dollars by a service man returning to the States.

I had taken Karis's money and my own to the finance officer and converted them into a little more than $1,600 in U.S. currency. This I put into a French-made Moroccan leather pouch that was a little larger than a billfold. Although it would fit in an inside jacket pocket, I put it in my B-4 bag, which was never out of my sight on the trip home.

My luggage consisted of the B-4 bag, which contained an automatic pistol, and a parachute bag in which was stowed an assortment of belongings, including my Thompson submachine gun.

I hoisted the bag onto a table and the customs agent started going through them. He saw the weapons and never said a word. When he came to the leather pouch, he asked, "What's this?"

"Money—about $1,600," I replied.

"Well, I have to take it."

That was when I exploded. Normally, my reaction would have been less violent, but the war and the long trip home had loaded the camel's back to the breaking point. I wasn't about to give up that money.

"You can't have that," the customs man said, looking nervously at the gun I was pointing at him.

"The hell I can't."

"Where did you get it?"

"I earned it fighting the war."

"Is it yours?"

"You're damned right it is."

I'm not sure what I would have done if the argument had continued much longer. Our heated conversation brought a man through the door immediately behind the customs officer. He calmly asked what the trouble was.

"This son of a bitch says I can't have the money," I told him.

"Is it your money?"

"Yes."

"Where did you get it?"

"I've just come back from North Africa. It's my pay and some money I'm bringing home for the parents of a friend of mine."

He took the pouch from the customs inspector and handed it to me.

"Take it," he said. "No problem. It's all right."

The man asked for my name and address, then returned to his office. I caught a taxi home at once.

I realize now, and I probably knew then, that there were some American servicemen profiteering from the war. They were selling supplies that were meant for the front, sending the money to bank accounts at home. It finally reached the point where a soldier was not permitted to send more home than he was paid in salary, even if—as many did—he claimed the money came from winnings at poker.

Despite the seriousness of the problem, I'm sure the Miami customs officer's solution wasn't the right one. His superior, who gave me back my money, confirmed my suspicions the following day when he called at my parents' home.

"I wouldn't have been very surprised if you had shot that inspector," he told me. "He's given us more trouble than he's worth."

He was fired and an investigation determined that he had seized a considerable amount of "contraband" that he never turned over to the government. It seemed all the people profiteering from the war were not in the supply dumps overseas.

I didn't realize until I arrived home how tightly my nerves had been wound by the war. Every time I heard a siren on the street, I would jump. In the middle of the night I would wake up, listening for airplanes. I was home, but part of my subconscious was still at war.

Lucy and young Paul came down from Columbus, Georgia. Mother did her best to restore the 37 pounds I had lost. I spent the time resting and eating mother's chocolate cream and banana cream pie.

But the war wasn't over. The loafing soon got to be old stuff and I became eager to learn more about this big new bomber, the B-29, that was being built. This was the project for which I had been sent home.

20 Flying Blind

In Washington, where I reported for assignment to the B-29 program, I found that the big bomber project was a shambles.

"I don't know whether we'll ever have a B-29," General Eugene Ewbank told me.

Only the week before, on February 18, Boeing's chief test pilot, Eddie Allen, and 10 top technicians had been killed at Seattle in the crash of a B-29 in a test flight. The tragedy had resulted from an engine fire that spread to the fuel tanks in the wing.

The project had been plagued by trouble, most of it due to the newly developed 3350 Wright engines, the four of which produced a total of 8,800 horsepower. It was the largest airplane engine built up to that time, and its difficulties stemmed from an effort to put it and the new airplane into operation before all the bugs had been worked out.

In any case, there was no B-29 program for me to join at the moment. Although a decision was made soon to go ahead with the building of this aircraft, it would be several months before I would be involved.

For a while, I played the old military game of "hurry up and wait." I was sent to Orlando to the Air Corps School of Applied Tactics, working there for a fine two-star general, Gordon Seville. Gordon was in the tactical evaluation business but at this time he didn't have anything to evaluate. Along with most of his staff, I spent a large share of my time there loafing and playing cards. "Hearts" was our favorite game.

Since I was eager to get back into flying, Gordon and I figured a way that I could get some time in the new Douglas four-engine transport, the DC-4. There was much I could learn from this plane that would be helpful in flying the big bombers. The DC-4 was suitable for long over-water flights and would be a good training aircraft for such things as cruise control and over-water navigation.

C. R. Smith had just come back from North Africa to take charge of American Overseas Airline, which handled the civilian branch of the Air Transport Command. C. R. and American Airlines, of which he later became president, were the driving force behind American Overseas, operating out of New York's LaGuardia airport.

General Seville called C. R. and arranged for me to be attached to the 19th Transport Group in Milwaukee for advanced instrument flight training.

Even though Jimmy Doolittle had made the first completely "blind" flight several years before, sophisticated instrument flying was still in its early development stage. There were high-ranking Air Corps pilots with thousands of hours in the air who did not have much instrument flying capability.

As a 28-year-old lieutenant colonel with almost 3,000 hours of flying time, I understood the basics of instrument flight but was a long way from knowing all of the rapidly advancing techniques that enable a pilot to get from one place to another by reference only to instruments. To a modern airline passenger accustomed to jet flights in all kinds of weather, this may seem simple. Not so in those days.

Many a pilot, flying through clouds, has gone into a "graveyard spiral" and lost his life because the balancing mechanism of his inner ear gave him the false impression that he was in level flight. The secret of successful flight under conditions where you cannot see the ground is to trust your instruments.

With the help of an artificial horizon on the instrument panel, a pilot can tell if his plane is level even though he can't see the ground. Then there is a turn-and-bank indicator to show if the plane is turning and at what rate. A gyro compass shows direction and the air-speed indicator is a right good barometer of whether the nose is high or low.

I was well acquainted with these basic instruments, as I had to be for foul-weather flights such as the one from England to Gibraltar with General Eisenhower. But there was more that I wanted to learn about the use of newly developed instruments and techniques.

The idea of instrument training is to react in the worst of weather conditions—fog, clouds, rain, or snow—with the same ease and confidence as if you were on a sightseeing flight over familiar territory on a sunny day. Believe me, everyone in the 19th Transport Group could do just that. The junior birdman of the outfit when I arrived was a 35-year-old airline pilot with 5,000 hours of flying experience. The group commander had 26,000 hours to his credit, and his executive officer, 19,000.

My instructor was Maynard Cowan, who had the air force rank of captain. He had been a pilot for United Airlines, flying DC-3s between Seattle and San Francisco, and on to Salt Lake City. These flights were over some of the roughest terrain and through some of the most unpredictable weather the United States had to offer.

The training schedule was rigorous. We flew each morning from 8:00 A.M. until noon and, after lunch, from 1:00 to 4:00. Our plane was a twin-engine Lockhead Lodestar, fast but not very large.

My first lesson was a blind takeoff during which I was under the hood, a device that prevented me from seeing anything outside the cockpit. I had to maintain my runway heading by reference to the gyro compass, at the same time applying a bit of right rudder to compensate for the inevitable torque produced by the propellers. This, however, was not new to me, for I had made such takeoffs before.

Until now, such takeoffs were made with some trepidation. After a few days of practice with Cowan, it was ducksoup. In the air he put me through all types of flying maneuvers, strictly on instruments.

On the first flight, he switched off one engine and feathered the propeller. When that happens, the good engine tends to turn the plane in the direction of the one that's dead. The pilot keeps it straight with the rudder and then adds power on the engine that's running to maintain flying speed. He then trims the controls so as to fly on one engine without compensating pressure on the rudder or elevator.

I had the airplane well trimmed and was flying straight and level with the right engine shut down, when he shocked me by saying "Make a 60 degree bank to the right."

I didn't respond. Just sat there as if I didn't hear.

He lifted the hood and looked at me.

"What's the matter?" he asked. "Isn't the damned interphone working?"

"It's working," I replied.

"Then why didn't you turn?"

"Because you're not supposed to turn into a dead engine." I was repeating a warning given to me when I started multi-engine training four years earlier.

"Where the hell did you get that idea?" he demanded. "Do you know what makes an airplane fly?"

"Airspeed."

"And what gives you airspeed?"

"A throttle and an engine."

"So if you keep up your airspeed, why won't the airplane fly no matter what happens to one engine?"

I had no answer for that.

"Look," he said, "I'm an older man than you are. I've got a family. I'm not going to do anything that would kill us. Now make that damned turn."

I banked the airplane up on its right wing, pushed the left throttle forward, and hauled the yoke back to keep the nose up. The Lodestar slowed a little but I kept sufficient airspeed and didn't lose altitude. We hung right there in that 60 degree bank until I rolled out of the turn.

That exercise gave me all the faith in the world in everything Cowan told me after that. In eight days of constant flying, he taught me to fly an airplane on instruments in a way I never knew it could be done.

Next we practiced emergency landing procedures. He pointed out that the loss of an engine from carburetor icing wasn't unusual. In these exercises, It seemed we were flying the airplane more often than not on a single engine. We had one emergency after another.

Airway navigation facilities were primitive by today's standards. There were range stations whose constant broadcasts advised you if you were on the "beam." On one side of the beam, you heard the letter "A," a dot and a dash in Morse code, and on the other side the letter "N," a dash and a dot. When you were on the beam, there was one continuous tone.

Since one beam of the range station was aligned with the airport runway, it was possible to land under difficult weather conditions by keeping the plane in the center of the radio signal, which became narrower as you approached.

For the final test of my skill as an instrument pilot, Cowan said, "Tomorrow we're going up and we're going to go through everything. And then we're going to make three approaches to the range. You will have to make three successive approaches so that you can land on the runway without more than a 10 degree bank to correct yourself."

I had no trouble with all of the maneuvers until we came to the runway approaches. The first two were about perfect, but I missed the runway the third time by almost 100 yards.

"No good," said Cowan. "You've got to start all over and make three in a row."

This time there was no problem. On the third, I landed with one propeller feathered. My instructor was pleased.

"That's fine," he said. "You graduate."

He took me at once to the commander's office and they did all the necessary paperwork on the spot. I was given an instrument card that indicated, under my name, that I had met all the army requirements for instrument flying. I was particularly proud of an endorsement, typewritten on the back of the card, which said: "This officer has not only met but surpassed the requirements and, in accordance with the authority granted the 19th Transport Group, may fly an airplane any time under his own authority."

I walked out of that office feeling like Mr. God.

No one other than pilots of the 19th had such personal clearance authority. I could now take off under zero-zero conditions, if I wished, and no base operations officer could stop me. I was fortunate to have learned about instruments from such an excellent instructor.

From Milwaukee, I went to New York and reported to the chief pilot of American Overseas at LaGuardia. He assigned me to an all-civilian crew and said, "Tomorrow we're going to take off for North Africa, and I'm going along to give you and another pilot a route check."

Our plane was a DC-4. We flew first to Newfoundland and then to Prestwick, Scotland, before heading south for Marrakech, Morocco. I soon got to know that route well, flying it regularly for the next three months, transporting supplies for our troops in North Africa. During this period, I was literally in the role of an airline captain with a civilian crew and an American Overseas plane. It was useful flying experience.

Returning from one of these trips in July, I received word from Washington directing me to report to Wichita, Kansas, where B-29s would soon be rolling off the production line at Boeing's new plant. I had another job to do.

21 Testing the Super Fortress

Upon arrival at "Boeing Wichita," I found four or five of the "Y" models on the flight line with full-scale production of the big new bomber under way. In those days, it was customary to build an "X" model for experimental purposes, then the "Y" for service testing. Thus the designation YB-29.

After the Seattle crash, mentioned in the last chapter, the entire program was reevaluated. Some of the early problems with this airplane and its engines seemed insurmountable, but the need for a bomber of this size and range was such that it was decided to go ahead on the theory that the difficulties could be ironed out concurrently with production. The plane was needed in the Pacific and 1,664 were on order. They were to be built at the Boeing plants in Renton, Washington, and Wichita; at the Martin plant in Omaha, Nebraska, and the Bell aircraft factory in Marietta, Georgia.

Plans for the B-29 were on the drawing board as early as 1940. Although designed as a replacement for the B-17, and built by the same company, it was much more than an overgrown version of the Fortress. It contained many innovations, including a fire control system that would permit mounted guns outside the airplane to be fired by a gunner who had no manual contact with the weapons. As a result, one man could control more than one of the five guns.

A pneumatic bomb-bay door device opened the doors in less than a second and closed them in three seconds, thus reducing the time the open doors could act to slow the plane down while on the bomb run.

The B-29 was also pressurized, enabling the crew to get to the target in shirtsleeve environment, reducing the fatigue on long missions. For me, it meant that I could puff on my pipe during the flight instead of having to wear an oxygen mask at high altitudes.

In addition to carrying more and larger bombs, the B-29 could fly higher, faster, and farther than the B-17. These qualities were urgently needed if we were to wage a devastating aerial war against Japan. It was also the only plane capable of carrying a terrible new weapon, still under development, about which I had not yet heard.

The front crew section of the plane was pressurized and was linked by a crawl-through tube to the midsection. which was also pressurized. There was also pressure in the tail gunner's compartment, but he had no tube to crawl through, so that he was isolated from the rest of the crew after the plane reached the higher altitudes.

A tricycle landing gear made it easier to handle this plane on the ground and also improved forward visibility for the pilot while taxiing. Consequently, the fuselage was level instead of sloping as in the case of the B-17, which was a tail-dragger.

At Wichita, I found no experienced pilot on hand to check me out on the B-29. Fortunately there was a flight engineer who had flown with Allen in early tests. With another officer as copilot and the experienced engineer on board, I took one of the planes out on the runway to get the feel of it. With its wing span of 141 feet and length of 93 feet, it was a giant compared with the B-17, which had corresponding measurements of 103 and 75 feet, respectively.

We started with speed runs in which, after lifting a few feet off the runway, I would cut the power and let the plane settle back on the surface. This procedure gave me the feel of handling the world's largest airplane. After three such high-speed taxi runs, I decided it was just another flying machine with characteristics that were not too different from those with which I was familiar. It was time to take off.

On the next run, I gave it full power, pulled the gear up, and retracted those big flaps. Once in the air I felt the thrill of handling an airplane considerably larger than any I had expected to fly when I joined the Air Corps in 1937.

There was plenty of open prairie around Wichita, and I didn't think it possible to get into serious trouble even if the plane developed one of the flaws for which it had already become famous. It would be easy to belly it in and walk back for another one and keep on testing. The flaws diminished during the next few months and I like to think that my experimental flights, along with others that were being made from the same field, helped to spot the troubles and lead to their correction.

Production still wasn't up to what the air force desired. Chiang Kai-shek had promised to have secret fields ready in China from which to launch mass bombing attacks on Japan. President Roosevelt had made arrangements with Great Britain and India to deliver the B-29s to China and to supply the new bases by flights "over the Hump," as the high-altitude crossing of the Himalaya Mountains was called. The Pacific islands from which we would eventually carry out most of our bombing raids on the enemy homeland had not yet been captured from the Japanese.

General K. B. Wolfe was made responsible for devising the plan to get the airplanes to China and to train the combat crews to take them there. Wolfe was made commander of the 58th Bomb Wing, which was the first operational organization of the 20th Bomber Command. It was eventually decided to station 150 B-29s in the Calcutta area to serve as flying transports for the support of a 100-plane strike force in China. This move was carried out with the understanding that the bombing fleet would be transferred to the Mariana Islands as soon as they came into our hands.

The first crews that would be going to China started training at Smoky Hill airfield near Salina, Kansas, and I was assigned to assist with this program. There is a legitimate question as to whether they got all the training they needed for combat in this new airplane, but our orders were to shove them through as rapidly as possible and start them on their way to war.

Soon I was assigned to Grand Island, Nebraska, to start a school that would train B-29 flight instructors. The new assignment brought me back in touch with Frank Armstrong, my old commander at Polebrook, who had been placed in charge of the Grand

Island school. He asked me to be his director of operations, but before I could settle into that job a new and very important assignment came along.

I was ordered to go to the army airfield at Alamogordo, New Mexico, to collaborate with Dr. E. J. Workman, a distinguished University of New Mexico physics professor who had been involved in a theoretical study of the B-29's vulnerability to attack by enemy fighter planes. It was my job to work with him and put his theories to a test through simulated combat.

One thing we learned in this test program was the difficulty of maintaining control of the airplane while flying in the thin air that exists at high altitudes. I found that flying at 30,000 feet was an entirely different ball game from flying at lower altitudes. A too-steep bank or a sudden movement of the controls might cause the plane to stall. We came to realize that it would be almost impossible to fly the B-29 at high altitude in the tight formations we had used with the Fortress in raids over Europe.

Without a tight formation, would the B-29s be sitting ducks for Japanese fighters? The answer could be calculated theoretically, but actual test experience was needed to be sure.

We had one Japanese Zero that had been captured and rebuilt, but most of my work was done by pitting the Republic P-47 Thunderbolt fighter against the big bomber. I flew the B-29 in these test maneuvers and began to have doubts about the survivability of my plane against a skillfully flown fighter at extreme altitudes.

The B-29 assigned to me for these tests was fully equipped, including a full complement of weapons and armor plating. Then one day when this airplane was down for maintenance, and we had some tests that needed to be accomplished in a hurry, I borrowed an aircraft from Grand Island. It came equipped only with tail guns and no armament.

Without the armament, the plane was 7,000 pounds lighter. And what a difference it made in performance! It would climb higher and handle much better. The difference proved to be an important though unexpected payoff in its defense against fighter aircraft.

I found that, at between 30 and 35 thousand feet, I could turn in a shorter radius than the attacking P-47. When he tried to get on my tail for a shot, I simply turned inside of him. When he tried to tighten his turn and keep on my tail, he would stall out and lose altitude, which he could not regain in time to keep me from running away.

We never developed these experiments to the point where we had sufficient evidence to persuade authorities to have the armament removed from all the B-29s that were going to the Pacific. I did not remain in the assignment long enough to follow through, but I was convinced to the extent that I was able to use this knowledge to good advantage a couple of months later.

My interesting experimental work at Alamogordo came to an end one day with an unexpected telephone call from Colorado Springs.

22 My Secret Air Force

After the excitement of combat over Europe and North Africa, my assignment in the States had been an emotional letdown. The war, which had been a day-to-day reality, now seemed remote. Wichita, Salina, and Grand Island were safe havens in a world that was being torn apart.

To the people I met on the streets of America, war was the inconvenience of gasoline rationing and sugar scarcity—hardships that many were crafty enough to circumvent. The shock of Pearl Harbor and early setbacks had given way to optimism as the tide turned in our favor in the Pacific, North Africa, and Europe.

Despite the good news from the war fronts that came in daily newspaper headlines and nightly radio reports from H. V. Kaltenborn, Lowell Thomas, and Gabriel Heater, my own recent battle experience told me there was still a need for all-out effort. My contribution to this effort consisted of working 16 hours a day testing B-29s and training crews to fly the big new planes.

Because this bomber was being built for action in the Pacific, I was obliged to reorient my thoughts about the priorities in this global war. In Europe, it was easy to conclude that here was the primary theater of action. In a sense it was, but President Roosevelt and his war planners had the vision and good sense to understand that we had to fight simultaneously on two fronts.

In the Pacific, the strategy was to reconquer the islands seized by the Japanese in the early days of the war, and to be ready for a massive assault on the enemy's homeland as soon as victory had been won in Europe.

This was the grand design, but there was an even grander plan in the making, one which only a few people knew about. It started with a capital "A" and the key word was Atom.

On the first day of September in 1944 as I packed my bags and pointed my B-29 toward Colorado Springs, I had no idea that fate had laid her unpredictable hand on me for an important role in a supersecret program designed to bring a swift end to the war.

My flight to Colorado was in response to an urgent telephone call the day before from General Uzal G. Ent, commander of the Second Air Force. I knew it was urgent because he told me to pack my bags, since I would not be returning to Alamogordo. There was something cryptic in the way he spoke of my new job, which, he confided in answer to my question, would eventually take me overseas.

Overseas? I was sure this meant the Pacific because of my work with the B-29.

Arriving at Colorado Springs, I reported to General Ent's office shortly before the appointed hour of 10 o'clock. I was not prepared for the reception that awaited me.

In an outer office, I was met by an officer wearing the insignia of the Army Corps of Engineers, which puzzled me even though I had learned long ago that the unexpected is quite normal in time of war. After introducing himself as Lt. Col. Jack Lansdale, he ushered me into a small side room and said, "I'd like to ask you a couple of questions before we go in to see General Ent."

Without explaining his purpose, he began talking about my personal history, my record as an officer and, before that, my civilian life.

His "couple of questions" stretched into an interrogation from which I soon discovered that he knew more about me than I could remember about myself. I began to suspect that the new assignment which General Ent had mentioned on the phone was considerably more important than I had imagined.

Some of the questions were highly personal. I was surprised that the Air Corps had gone to the trouble to learn so much about my past. Suddenly I realized the meaning of a phone call I had received two weeks before from my father in Miami.

"Are you in some kind of trouble, son?" he asked.

"Not that I know of," I replied. "What makes you think so?"

"Well," he said, hesitating, "I hear some investigators—I think they were from the FBI—have been down here asking questions about you."

Dad had been tipped off by a couple of family friends who had been questioned. I passed off the matter as a routine check. Now, in the presence of Jack Lansdale, I knew it had something to do with my new assignment.

The penetrating nature of Lansdale's questions baffled me but, however embarrassing, I knew that tough questions called for honest answers. I made my replies as straightforward as I could, even though some of the incidents he mentioned had all but escaped my memory.

One question related to some critical comments I had made to friends in Cincinnati, after my return from overseas, regarding certain aspects of military strategy in Europe. Part of what I said had been distorted and I had no trouble setting the record straight.

His last question startled me.

"Have you ever been arrested?" he asked.

I had never forgotten the traumatic experience when, as a college student of 19, I was interrupted by a nosy policeman with a flashlight during a love-making episode while parked in a secluded spot on the beach at Surfside, Florida. Since it was obvious that my questioner knew about this, I promptly acknowledged the incident, which was the nearest I ever came to acquiring a criminal record.

Lansdale now rose from his chair and indicated that our conversation was over. It had been informal and reasonably pleasant.

"Now let's go see General Ent," he said, leading the way into the commander's office where, to my surprise, two other people were waiting. One was in the uniform of a navy captain and the other was a civilian. Behind the general's desk were the customary emblems of his office: an American flag on a staff on one side and the banner of his Second Air Force command on the other.

By now I was completely puzzled. There had been the brief but pointed questioning. Now a reception committee. Obviously, I was to become involved in something very sensitive from a security standpoint.

How sensitive I could never have imagined! Before that morning was over, I was transported into a strange new world in which the most incredible miracles of science replaced all the realities of my military experience.

After making me welcome, General Ent introduced the others. The naval officer was Captain William Parsons and the civilian was Dr. Norman Ramsey, a Columbia University professor. My interrogator, Colonel Lansdale, was then identified as a security officer for the Manhattan District, U.S. Army Corps of Engineers.

"I'm well satisfied with Colonel Tibbets," Lansdale said to General Ent.

"That's good," said Ent, who had known me and my record. "I felt sure you would be."

The general then explained that I had been chosen for a task that was both important and highly secret. Before supplying the details, he impressed me with the need to conceal the nature of my work from everyone, including my family and—this just about floored me—even the people I would be working with.

I would be expected to organize a combat force of my own to deliver a new-type explosive so powerful that its full potential was still unknown. In fact, General Ent said, it hadn't yet been devised, but such progress was being made that success seemed quite certain.

After this preliminary and intentionally vague explanation, he turned to Professor Ramsey and said, "Now you take over and explain the whole thing to Paul."

It turned out that the professor was involved in our meeting because of his ability to simplify a complex scientific subject. Before the war he had been a successful classroom teacher of physics. Some science professors are born for research, others for teaching. Ramsey was a happy combination of both.

He started out by asking me, "Did you ever hear of atomic energy?"

I remembered enough from my college science courses to answer that I understood the subject in a general but nontechnical way. I had also read newspaper predictions, a few years before, that the atom might some day be harnessed as an energy source.

Professor Ramsey went into a brief explanation of what had happened in the field of atomic science during the past few years. He explained that the United States had become secretly committed to a crash program to develop a bomb, using the principle of atomic fission, that would have an explosive power equal to that of several thousand tons of TNT. He touched upon things that were going on at laboratories in Los Alamos, New Mexico, and at factories in Hanford, Washington, and Oak Ridge, Tennessee.

General Ent picked up the conversation at this point and explained my role in the atomic warfare that the United States was preparing to introduce sometime next year to an unsuspecting world. Development of the weapon had reached a point, he said, where the problem of delivering it on target now needed urgent attention. It was one thing to build an atomic bomb of incredible destructive power. It was quite another to drop it safely. What would be the explosion's effect on the bomb-carrying plane and its crew? There would be tremendous shock waves, as well as the new phenomenon known as radiation. Ours was not a nation with a kamikaze mentality. When our bombers took off, the odds had to favor their safe return by at least ten to one.

The discussion that morning touched on a number of details, although it was explained that I would have broad authority to work out technical problems as they developed. One B-29 had already been made available to the Manhattan Project, as the atomic enterprise was known, and some experimental flying had been done, but there had been no agreement on delivery technique. That would be left to an experienced combat pilot, which is where I came into the picture.

Even though the first bomb might not be ready for almost a year, my task was given high priority. I would have the airplanes—15 B-29s—and the support personnel, numbering approximately 1,800 men. The organization was to be completely self-contained with its own engineering, maintenance, and technical units, ordnance squadron, troop transport aircraft, military police, and a medical unit with specialists in the field of radiology.

There had been nothing like it in this or any other war. Some were to call it "Tibbets's Individual Air Force" because I was given the authority to requisition anything needed to carry out my assignment.

We would operate under the name of the 509th Composite Group, a designation that would confuse other military people and arouse their unconcealed curiosity in the months to come. If I ran into trouble, such as a refusal to make available some needed service or equipment, I was authorized to break the impasse by use of a code word, "Silverplate," which would be recognized even by those who had no knowledge of the project with which it was associated.

My job, in brief, was to wage atomic war. It didn't matter that I was not a scientist and had very little understanding of the strange world of neutrons, protons, electrons, and gamma rays. In the months ahead, I was to learn somewhat more than the average layman about uranium, plutonium, and chain reaction, because I would be in regular contact with scientists who were working with those terms on a daily basis. I had to be told of the explosive power of the weapon that was being developed, and the dangers inherent in the device, including such hazards as radioactivity.

The question that worried General Ent and others, and which now became my problem, was how to drop a bomb of such magnitude without risking damage to or destruction of the airplane that made the delivery.

What made the matter so difficult was the fact that there was no precise agreement among the scientists on the size of the explosion they proposed to set off. There were formulas which indicated that, if it were 100 percent efficient, the resulting explosion might crack the earth's crust. It was assumed, however, that such efficiency could not be attained. Then there was the matter of radiation. What about the fallout from the atomic cloud?

In our discussion in General Ent's office, it was quickly agreed that conventional methods of bombing a target would not work. In order to escape destruction, the bombing plane would have to put as much distance as possible between itself and the point of the blast.

"What do you consider a safe distance?" I asked.

Captain Parsons, a balding Naval Academy graduate who was an associate director of the Los Alamos bomb laboratory in charge of atomic bomb ballistics, undertook to answer.

"We're not sure," he confessed, "but our best calculations

indicate that an airplane should be able to withstand the shock waves at a distance of 8 miles."

Closer than that, he implied, the bomber might suffer structural damage or even be thrown out of control.

This brought up another question. "How much will the bomb weigh?" I asked.

Although it was still to be built, Parsons said it was expected to weigh in the neighborhood of 9,000 or 10,000 pounds. This was approximately the same as the bomb load carried by B-29s on a typical mission.

With some effort, a plane carrying such a load with enough fuel to return to its base could attain an altitude of 30,000 feet over the target, or a little less than 6 miles above the ground. It would be my job to find a way to increase the distance between blast and bomber to 8 miles.

Our conversation touched briefly on other matters pertaining to the project. For one thing, Parsons said, the bomb bays of the B-29s assigned to my command would have to be modified to accommodate the pumpkinlike shape of the bomb that was being developed. I would be given the responsibility of selecting a training site for my atomic air fleet. It would have to be in an isolated location—the farther from civilization the better—in order to maintain all possible secrecy. The matter of security would be another of my responsibilities.

General Ent said I would have a choice from among three bases that were available: Wendover, Utah: Great Bend, Kansas: and Mountain Home at Boise, Idaho.

Although I was to have broad authority to recruit the most competent personnel available in the air force, the general had already taken steps to provide me with the nucleus of my special air force. He mentioned that there were three B-29 squadrons of the 504th Group in training at Harvard, Nebraska.

"These squadrons are combat-ready," he said, and suggested that I visit Harvard at once and check them out. He had already earmarked the 393rd bomb squadron there for detachment from their parent wing, subject to my approval.

I soon got the idea that my new job would be a back-breaker. There was more that could go wrong than right. Although it represented an honor, it carried such a burden of responsibility that I viewed the assignment with mixed feelings. I was about to acquire an exciting headache. Fortunately, the excitement of the next 10 months made the headache endurable.

I have been asked how I happened to be chosen to organize and command this important operation. I'm not sure, but from what I've been told, and from what has been written about the enterprise, I have reached some conclusions.

First, it was obvious that the commander must have had considerable combat experience. I qualified on this score. Having been involved from the start of the air battle against Hitler-held Europe, I had demonstrated the ability of leadership.

A second requirement was familiarity with the airplane that was to be used for the mission, the new B-29. Here I was probably the most qualified pilot available, since I had been involved in the testing of this aircraft for almost a year, working out the inevitable bugs and making recommendations that developed it into the best heavy bomber ever built.

Add to this the fact that I had gained a reputation as an independent type of operator. In the European theater, I was called on to do things for which no formula or standards had been established. Maybe I had simply "lucked out," but whether it was luck or good sense, I had written the book, so to speak, on many of the bombing techniques that were now being applied successfully in the air war against the enemy,

I had been given the responsibility of launching daylight bombing raids when our British allies, with their prior experience in this war, had told us they would be suicidal. The tactics I devised and carried out in those early days of air war against the Germans continued to be the pattern with which U.S. bomber squadrons were destroying Hitler's ability to make war.

If this seems an immodest self-appraisal, let me pass along the opinions of others. One book on the subject of the atomic attacks on Japan mentioned my "calm efficiency" and described me as "one of America's finest bomber pilots. Another said I "gave a reassuring impression of stability and reliability."

Although I did not know it at the time of the interview in

General Ent's headquarters, I learned later that I was one of three candidates given serious consideration for the task of organizing the atomic bomber fleet.

At 29, I was the youngest of the three, one of whom was a brigadier general and the other a full colonel. I was a lieutenant colonel and did not win my eagles until January 1945.

The brigadier was Frank Armstrong, a competent officer whom I had served in England in 1942. At the time of our first encounter at Polebrook, he had not flown a B-17. Consequently, he gave me full responsibility for planning the bombing missions over Europe. General Ent was aware of this and had no trouble recommending me over Armstrong when our names came up for consideration.

The other candidate was Colonel Roscoe "Bim" Wilson, who was later to attain three-star rank and is now retired. Colonel Wilson was already involved in the secret project as General H. H. "Hap" Arnold's personal representative to the Manhattan District. After my appointment, he was responsible for making sure that I was given all the men and matériel necessary to carry out my mission.

In view of the Norstad incident at Algiers, and the fact that that officer had inserted derogatory information about me in my record file, it may seem strange that I was chosen over such senior officers as General Armstrong and Colonel Wilson. If Arnold and Ent were aware of the incident, and I'm sure they were, it is likely that they recognized it for what it was: a display of pettishness by an ambitious officer. At this time, Norstad held the rank of brigadier general and was chief of staff of the 20th Air Force (rear)—that is, in Washington, D. C., not out in the islands where the going was rough. It was to be more than four months before he learned of the atomic project.

In the busy days to come, I was given details of our atomic undertaking. The so-called Manhattan Project, in charge of producing the bomb, was under the command of Major General Leslie R. Groves, an engineering officer of bulldozing efficiency. From his office in the Pentagon, he managed a complex program that was carried on in complete secrecy not only from the enemy but from the American public, even though it involved the expenditure of two billion dollars and the employment of more than a hundred thousand workers and scientists in factories and laboratories scattered around the country. Incredibly, most of the factory workers were not aware of what their labors would produce.

The largest concentration of scientists, including a number of Nobel Prize winners, was at a secret laboratory on a mesa at Los Alamos, New Mexico, not far from Santa Fe. Their director was a brilliant nuclear physicist, J. Robert Oppenheimer, who came to the project from the University of California at Berkeley.

Inspiration for the program came from a letter that Albert Einstein wrote to President Roosevelt in 1939, describing the possibility of developing an "extremely powerful" bomb. A study was authorized, but the decision to devote full energy to the production of the bomb was not made until December 6, 1941—coincidentally, the day before the Japanese attack on Pearl Harbor.

The most important milestone in the bomb's development came on December 2, 1942, when the first controlled chain reaction was achieved in a pile of uranium and graphite on a squash court beneath the stands of old Stagg Field at the University of Chicago.

As Captain Parsons briefed me that day in General Ent's office, he explained that the scientists were confident of success, but the first bomb would not be ready until the following summer. Where it would be used depended on the war situation at that time. My job was to organize and train a bombing force.

We would be organized for the purpose of dropping a bomb that hadn't been built on a target that hadn't been chosen.

Two-year-old Paul Tibbets, Jr. with his father, a World War I captain.

Paul Tibbets, Jr. at age 8.

This picture of Cadet Tibbets appeared in the 1933 yearbook of Western Military Academy.

Lt. Paul Tibbets after winning wings at Kelly Field, San Antonio, in 1938.

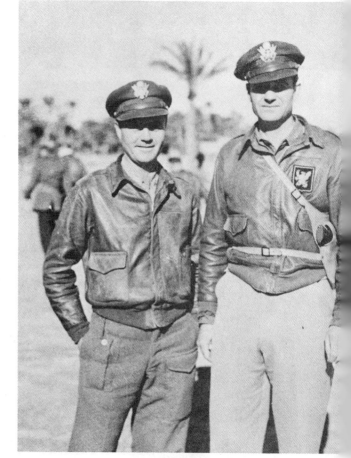

Colonel Tibbets (left) with General "Hamp" Atkinson at Biskra, North Africa, in December, 1942.

The crew of the B-17 *Red Gremlin* at Polebrook air base in England. Standing (left to right) are Col. Paul Tibbets, Lts. Dutch Van Kirk, Gene Lockhart, Tom Ferebee, and Sergeants Fitzgerald and Walker. Kneeling: Sergeants Rich, Hughes, and William Titsworth.

After a successful raid on enemy targets in France, Maj. Gen. Carl Spaatz decorates the crews. Colonel Tibbets is second from right. The officer at the right was his copilot, Lt. Gene Lockhart, whose left hand was shattered by a shell that exploded in the cockpit.

Views of the 509th Composite Group's headquarters and living area on Tinian.

The crew of *Enola Gay* before takeoff for Hiroshima. Left to right, standing: Lt. Col. John Porter, ground maintenance officer; Capt. Theodore J. Van Kirk, navigator; Maj. Thomas Ferebee, bombadier; Col. Paul W. Tibbets, pilot and commanding officer, 509th Group; Capt. Robert A. Lewis, copilot; and Lt. Jacob Beser, radar countermeasure officer. Kneeling: Sgt. Joseph Stiborik, radar operator; S-Sgt. George R. Caron, tail gunner; Pfc. Richard H. Nelson, radio operator; Sgt. Robert H. Shumard, assistant engineer; and S-Sgt. Wyatt Duzenbury, flight engineer. Colonel Porter did not make the flight. Not pictured are the ordnance officers: Navy Capt. William S. Parsons and Army Air Corps Lt. Morris R. Jeppson.

The atomic burst 20,000 feet over Hiroshima.—U.S. Air Force photo

A fire bomb raid on Tokyo—e
more deadly than the atomic bo
—U.S. Air Force ph

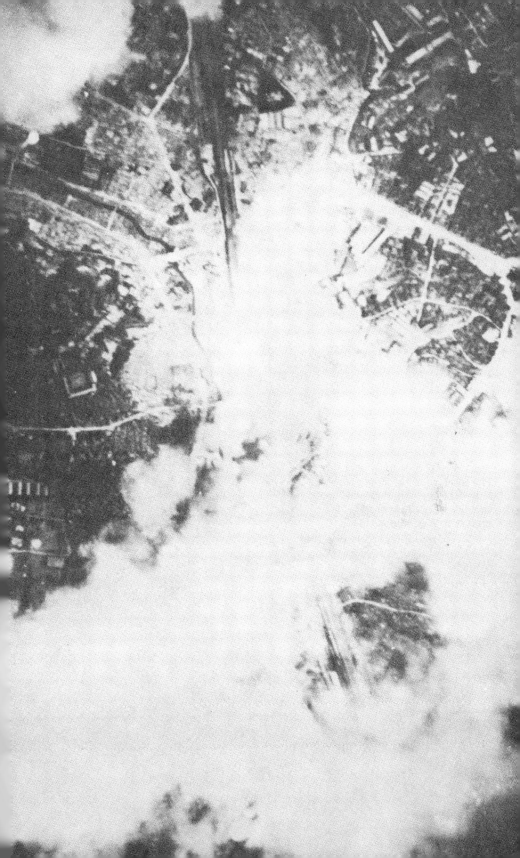

The *Enola Gay* was turned over to the Smithsonian Institution in 1949 in Chicago, where a convention of the Air Force Association was in progress. Left to right are Carl Mitman, representing the Smithsonian; Colonel Tibbets, who flew the plane to Chicago; Maj. Thomas Ferebee, and Maj. Gen. Emmett "Rosie" O'Donnell.
—Photo by Joseph Minardi

The fuselage of the *Enola Gay* rests today in a Smithsonian warehouse in a Maryland suburb of Washington, D.C.

Colonel Tibbets as test pilot of new six-jet B-47 bomber in 1951.

Paul Tibbets, Sr. and Enola Gay Tibbets, after whom the plane was named.

Paul Tibbets

23 The Air Base at the End of Nowhere

Although I came out of General Ent's office flattered by the importance of my new assignment, it wasn't until the next day that I became fully conscious of the terrible responsibility that was now mine.

At the age of 29, I had been entrusted with the successful delivery of the most frightful weapon ever devised, one that had been developed at a cost of two billion dollars in a program that involved the nation's best scientific brains and the secret mobilization of its industrial capacity.

Even as this all began to sink in, it never occurred to me that I might not succeed. Although the weapon was beyond my comprehension, there was nothing about flying an airplane that I did not understand. If this bomb could be carried in an airplane, I could do the job.

In the next few months, I discovered that I had a great deal to learn. There would be no room for error. Then there was the matter of secrecy that I would have to enforce.

My first job was to find a home for the outfit that I still had to organize. Of the three bases General Ent had offered me, I flew first to Wendover in northwestern Utah on the Nevada border.

As I approached Wendover from the air, I liked what I saw. It was remote in the truest sense. Except for the nearby village of Wendover, with a population of a little more than 100, that part of

Utah was virtually uninhabited. Surrounding the field were miles and miles of salt flats. There would be few security problems, for there was no place nearby for fun-loving men with six-hour passes to get into trouble and possibly leak information. The runways were adequate to handle the B-29, and my inspection on the ground showed that hangar and maintenance facilities were in good shape. I was so well satisfied with what I saw that I didn't even examine the other two bases.

The isolated location of Wendover, which would bring cries of horror from my men and the label "Leftover Field" from Bob Hope when he visited it that winter, was precisely the feature that made it attractive to me. We had a lot of work to do in a short time, and the fewer distractions the better for this purpose and for security. The only drawback was substandard housing, but I figured shabby living quarters were a small price to pay for a few months in return for the other advantages that the place offered.

Wendover had been used for P-47 fighter training, an activity that was being phased out. There was only one plane left on the field. The base commander and a few of his men were still there, but they would be leaving in a few days—without regrets, no doubt.

With the base selected, my next task was to round up the necessary personnel. I went over to Harvard, Nebraska, to take a look at the 393rd Bomb Squadron, which General Ent had offered me as the nucleus of my outfit. I was pleased with what I found. I don't know how the men of this squadron were impressed with me, but they must have wondered how a lieutenant colonel could suddenly show up and grab off a combat-ready squadron that was about to be sent overseas.

The squadron commander, Lt. Col. Tom Classen, turned out to be my kind of airman. He became my deputy commander and was a great help in the months ahead, taking care of much essential work while I was away, as I frequently was, on flights to Albuquerque, Washington, and elsewhere.

I set up headquarters at Wendover on September 8, just one week after being given my assignment. The 393rd squadron personnel arrived with their airplanes three days later. They consisted of the flight and ground crews for 15 B-29s.

With authority to draw upon the best available men in the air force, I set out to surround myself with people whose superior skills

I recognized. From my old B-17 crew in Europe I summoned Tom Ferebee, the best bombardier who ever looked through the eyepiece of a Norden bomb sight; Staff Sergeant George Caron, my old tail-gunner; Dutch Van Kirk, navigator; and Staff Sergeant Wyatt Duzenbury, flight engineer. They would be assigned to my plane in the squadron and would be in charge of training their counterparts in the other aircraft.

I also called on Bob Lewis, who had been involved with me in B-29 testing and would serve as my copilot, often becoming commander of my aircraft when other duties prevented me from flying. In fact, he would fly the plane so often that he came to consider it his.

Other key people brought into the outfit, on the recommendation of those whose judgment I respected, included bombardier Kermit Beahan, navigator James van Pelt, radar specialist Jacob Beser, and pilots Charles Sweeney and Don Albury.

Although we began training flights almost at once, a couple of months went by before our entire organization was complete. It was on December 17, 1944—by coincidence the 41st anniversary of the Wright Brothers' first flight in a powered aircraft at Kitty Hawk—that the 509th Composite Group was officially activated.

Meanwhile, one of our most important tasks was related to security. It was necessary to impress upon every man as he joined our outfit that he must not discuss the nature of our operation with anyone. We put the screws on very tight. It was awkward to explain to our people that they must not talk to outsiders about our mission. They themselves were in the dark, so how could they give away information they didn't possess? We explained that we didn't want them even to speculate or to give out a hint that our operation was different from any other in the military.

Not all our men took these warnings seriously. With some we had to get tough, with the help of an efficient security organization attached to our group by the Manhattan District. It was commanded by William "Bud" Uanna, who had been sent to us by General Groves. He was accompanied by a small army of special agents, about 30 in number, whose job it would be to infiltrate every phase of our operation and literally spy on our people to be sure there was no information leakage.

As soon as he arrived, I sat down with Uanna to plan our

strategy. We went over the records of key personnel, checking for clues that would indicate instability or a tendency to shoot off their mouths. Claude Eatherly, one of the pilots who had joined us with the 393rd, gave us some concern. He had been in trouble with his superiors occasionally and had a reputation for unpredictable behavior. But he was a first-rate pilot, the kind we needed. I decided to let him stay.

We worked out a plan to monitor the mail, the phone calls, and even the off-duty conversations of our men. In peacetime civilian life, this would have been an unthinkable invasion of privacy. In the military, and particularly in our supersecret operation, it was an essential precaution.

The trouble with trying to impress a soldier with the need for security is that he has been hearing this sort of thing, routinely, ever since entering service. Everywhere on military bases were posters warning that "A slip of the lip can sink a ship" and other catchy slogans.

We had such signs all over the place. One read, "What You Hear Here, What You See Here, When You Leave Here, Let It Stay Here." There were also "restricted areas" where only certain technical personnel were allowed to enter. There was barbed wire everywhere.

Everyone knew that when an outfit was shipping out from one of the hundreds of training bases in the United States, the girls at the local USO club often seemed to get the word before the local commanders. Americans had treasured freedom of speech for so long that it wasn't easy to keep them silent. And when you're one of millions of Americans in uniform, it's hard to believe that you might have some bit of information that is unknown to the enemy, or that might help prolong the war.

The 509th was different, and I had to make the men aware of the difference.

Shortly after the outfit was activated, I surprised almost everyone by granting a large number of Christmas leaves. Because of the urgency of our training program, General Groves was fit to be tied until I told him the reason. The home-for-Christmas caper was an important part of my security check.

There were only a few ways the men could get out of Wendover to go home for Christmas. The routes were through the airport, the train or bus stations at Salt Lake City, or the bus depot at Elko,

The Air Base at the End of Nowhere 165

Nevada. The friendly civilian who struck up a conversation in one of these places, or who offered to buy a serviceman a drink while he waited for his train or bus, was most likely one of Uanna's trained security agents.

As the men headed home, the reports started coming into my office. Just as I feared, many had failed to take seriously my warnings about the need for secrecy.

Even though they had only a vague idea of our mission, there was the danger that they would give away some information that a trained espionage agent might find useful.

Because of remarks they had made to our anonymous security men, a considerable number of our people found their holiday leaves interrupted by telegrams ordering them to return immediately to base.

When they arrived, I called them to my office, one at a time. A typical conversation, and one that I remember because it involved a sergeant for whose ability I had considerable respect, went like this:

"Why didn't you keep your mouth shut?" I demanded in a voice calculated to scare him out of his wits.

He stammered and his face reddened. It was clear he didn't know what I was talking about.

"We warned you not to talk about what we do here," I continued. "You violated security."

When he protested that he had not talked, I picked up a sheet of paper from my desk and read off the time and place and exactly what he had said to the friendly stranger in the bar next to the Salt Lake City bus station.

He was stunned. The conversation had been comparatively harmless, but my security agent had managed to find out where he was stationed, and that we were flying the new B-29 bombers.

"You're under arrest," I told him sternly. "You will be confined to quarters under military police guard until we decide on further action."

Twenty-four hours later—sometimes they were kept for 48 hours—I would call the offenders back to my office.

This time I would say:

"Look, it will cause me a lot of trouble if we go through a court-martial now. I'm willing to forget this one, but it's going into your record. We've got one strike on you. If you talk too much again, it's going to be rough on you."

The house arrest and the threat of future action were enough to throw the fear of God into just about everyone. No one knew how we kept tabs on security leaks, but the word soon got around the barracks that talking wasn't healthy. Some suspected that I had a personal gestapo watching their every move. And this supposition came close to being true.

The security checks didn't stop with the Christmas leave operation. We read mail and monitored phone calls through the base switchboard and from pay phones on the base. If a sergeant's wife told him on the phone that she was pregnant, I'd make a point of having someone congratulate him. He didn't know how the other soldier knew about his wife's condition, but he and everyone else in the outfit became aware that they were being watched.

Fiendish in some aspects, perhaps, but our methods were effective. In all of the postwar revelations about the stealing of atomic secrets and the leaking of information that got into enemy hands, not one single leak was ever traced to a member of the 509th. There was never a hint that any enemy agent obtained information, even indirectly, from any of my men.

We did arrange transfers for a few men who talked too much. For the most part, these were men who just couldn't keep a secret. Some people are compulsive talkers and can't resist the opportunity to boast of their work in order to appear important. Several found themselves assigned to Alaska, where they could talk to their heart's content to any polar bear or walrus they found willing to listen.

It would be unfair to say that our strict security measures were totally responsible for our good record. Almost all our men were good soldiers and patriotic Americans who were ready to observe the rules when convinced that security was really important.

I knew the men were dying to know what our mission was all about, and why they were being subjected to such tight security that Wendover was being likened, in their minds and private conversation, to Alcatraz.

I decided to give them a hint.

At a meeting of the entire outfit in the base auditorium, I said; "You have been brought here to work on a very special mission. Those of you who stay will be going overseas. You are going to take part in an effort that could end the war."

This brought a stunned reaction. When the meaning of my little speech sank in, the men began to understand why they were being subjected to such security.

Recognizing that there was a natural curiosity about certain things on the base, such as the fenced-off technical area, I said, "Stop being curious." Then I warned them not to mention the nature of the base to anyone, including their families.

For morale purposes, we decided to let the married men bring their families to Wendover. I think this was a good thing for most of the men, but it put a serious strain on my own marriage. As the one man who knew everything about our mission, I found it necessary to lie to Lucy on frequent occasions. Sometimes, when she exercised a natural curiosity about some of the things that were taking up 16 hours a day of my time I had to tell her it was none of her business.

Then there were the numerous times that I had to leave the base for meetings with the scientists at Los Alamos and the military planners in Washington. I spent little time in our living quarters, just outside the gates of the base. By now we were a family of four. Our second son, Gene, was less than a year old, and little Paul was four.

Lucy and the two children must have had a difficult time in this remote base on the desert, because my involvement with the project was consuming my thoughts, my time, and my energy. Army life is often a strain on domestic relationships, and this period held more than the usual difficulties.

There were a number of civilian scientists on the base at times. To explain the presence of these people in civilian clothes, I told Lucy they were sanitary engineers. When I came home one day, I found that she had called one of them to unplug a stopped-up bathroom drain. This Ph.D. didn't understand how he came to be asked to do the job, but he was a good sport and took care of the problem, for which his advanced degree in physics did not necessarily qualify him.

He and I laughed about it later.

24 Escaping the Shock Wave

My experience with the B-29 at Wichita, Grand Island, and Alamogordo gave me a knowledge of the strengths and weaknesses of this newest and largest of all bombing planes.

Although it would fly high and carry a heavy load, its engines had a tendency to overheat on a long flight at high altitudes. Also, in the thin upper air, the controls behaved badly when the plane was heavily loaded. Under those conditions, the B-29 was sluggish: it lacked maneuverability. These were serious problems since our mission to deliver the atomic bomb called for a long flight at high altitude, climaxed by a maneuver that required exacting control response.

The scientists had warned that it would be unsafe to drop the bomb from an altitude of less than 30,000 feet. Because of the combined weight of the bomb and the fuel required for the 14-hour round-trip flight, the plane had to operate beyond its design specifications.

The solution seemed obvious to me. I remembered my experience at Alamogordo with the bomber that came to us without armament. Why not fly it with only the tail guns? To do so would immediately save more than 7,000 pounds of installed weight, increase its operating altitude, and relieve some of the strain on the engines.

But how about flying over enemy territory with so little protection? So little firepower in case of attack?

Escaping the Shock Wave 169

At 30,000 feet, we would be above the effective range of most anti-aircraft fire. As for any fighters that might be sent up, our practice against the P-47s had shown that, without heavy armament, we could turn in a shorter radius than the smaller planes and get into position to fight them off with our tail guns alone.

My authority was so broad that I didn't need permission to strip the planes of the superfluous weapons and armor plating. Although some of the pilots were not sold on the idea at first, they came to agree with me after finding how the flying qualities of the planes were improved.

Word of what I was doing soon got back to Colorado Springs, where my old friend General Frank Armstrong was commander of the 315th Bomb Wing. Theoretically, the 509th was a part of his command structure, even though he had no knowledge of our mission. It was a strange situation, one of many involving our outfit.

"How can those people expect to fight a war without guns?" Armstrong demanded of Colonel Roscoe "Bim" Wilson, who was commander of the 316th. Paradoxically, Wilson knew of our mission by virtue of having been General "Hap" Arnold's personal representative to the Manhattan District. Arnold was chief of staff of the U.S. Army Air Force.

When Armstrong announced that he was going to Wendover the next day to find out what was going on and "straighten things out," Wilson didn't know what to say. A few minutes later, when he was alone, he phoned General Groves at the Pentagon and reported the problem. He asked what he should do, since he was only a colonel and Armstrong was a general.

Groves told Wilson to use "the formula"—in other words, that Armstrong must keep hands off the 509th and that, if he needed confirmation, he should call Hap Arnold in Washington.

Armstrong was understandably puzzled when Wilson walked into his office and told him that he must not go to Wendover, but that he couldn't give him the reason. Nonetheless, the general accepted the ultimatum from the colonel without taking up his challenge to phone Arnold. So far as I know, he didn't find out the reason until after the atom bomb was dropped.

With our newly modified airplanes, we began intensive training at once over the vast open spaces of the western desert from Utah and Nevada to California.

My first concern was for accuracy in dropping the bomb, and my next, for a maneuver that would put us as far as possible from the point of explosion.

Although the 393rd Squadron came to Wendover with its own airplanes, these were later replaced with newer models direct from the production line but modified to my specifications.

Since the potential power of the atomic weapon was only theoretical at the time, and its consequences open to speculation even by the most knowledgeable scientists, there was no assurance that we could escape the violent shock wave that would be created by the explosion. Survival demanded a solution.

The scientists had told me that the minimum distance at which we could expect to survive would be 8 miles. It takes a B-29 two minutes to fly 8 miles, whereas it would take the bomb only 43 seconds from the moment it left our airplane, flying at 31,000 feet, to the point of detonation less than 2,000 feet above the ground. The shock wave would race toward us at the speed of sound—about 1,100 feet a second—which meant that it would take approximately 40 seconds to travel 8 miles.

It was obviously impossible to reach a point over the earth 8 miles from the explosion in 1 minute and 23 seconds. However, we would be almost 6 miles away, vertically, at the time we released the bomb; hence a slant-line distance of 8 miles from the detonation to the plane at the time the shock waves reached us could be achieved by flying only a little more than 5 miles in the opposite direction after bomb release.

My strategy, then, was to make a tight turn that, when completed, would have our plane flying almost directly away from the aiming point. Calculations convinced me that the most effective maneuver would be a sharp turn of 155 degrees. This would put considerable strain on the airplane and would require a degree of precision flying unfamiliar to bomber pilots. Nevertheless, it seemed our best bet for survival.

Once I had decided on this unorthodox maneuver, the next requirement was to practice. I worked on this tactic before the new planes began to arrive. My immediate goal was to train all our pilots in the techniques required to make a fast diving turn of 155 degrees the moment their bombardiers released the practice bombs.

As for the bombardiers, their task was to drop the bomb from

30,000 feet onto a target on the ground that consisted of a circle 400 feet in diameter. We would accept a miss of no more than 200 feet from the aiming point.

A lot of nonsense was written during the war about the pickle-barrel accuracy of the Norden bomb sight. Many had the idea that a bomb could be dropped into a pickle barrel through the use of the sight. This was a figure of speech, of course, and the Norden sight was miraculously superior to any other that had ever been invented, but a miss of several hundred feet from high altitudes, where the wind factor could not be determined as accurately as we would have liked, was not unusual.

To begin with, we used conventional practice bombs. With the extreme accuracy essential to our mission, it soon became apparent that we should have a supply of dummy bombs the same size, shape, and weight as the real thing. Practicing with them would be useful in determining the ballistics. We wanted no aerodynamic surprises when the real one was dropped.

General Groves saw no need for the dummy bombs. He considered them a waste of time and money. I was supported by a number of the scientists, however, particularly Dr. Ernest O. Lawrence of the University of Southern California's radiation laboratory. Lawrence wanted to check their ballistic trajectory, just as I did, and we finally won out.

Because of the bulbous shape of the plutonium bomb, made necessary by its complicated firing mechanism, our practice shapes became known as "pumpkins." Altogether, we received about 200 of these dummies. Eventually, a few were filled with conventional explosive material for use against a number of selected objectives in Japan.

In addition to dropping bombs and practicing the difficult getaway maneuver, our training also involved intensive navigational exercises. There was one problem that bothered me, however. It was the transition between flying over water and flying over land.

We were aware that crews on long over-water flights sometimes made mistakes after reaching land. The methods of navigation were entirely different. Once a crew sighted land, there was a tendency to navigate by landmarks. We got the idea that some of them tried to switch over to this type of navigation before they had really verified their positions. We also knew that the rate at which a plane appears to close on a target is different over water and land. I didn't want these differences to jeopardize our mission.

Classroom work and lectures were helpful, but I was convinced that the crews wouldn't really understand and conquer the problem except by experience. Accordingly, I asked for and received permission to send crews to Batista Field near Havana, Cuba, where we could use the whole Caribbean for flying practice missions. There were dozens of islands of all sizes on which to make simulated bomb runs while practicing the transition from over-water to over-land flying. We sent five airplanes at a time to Cuba for 10 days of training.

Quite by coincidence, the training exercise in Cuba gave me an opportunity to take my mother for a flight in one of our C-54 support aircraft, a four-engine plane used for the transport of cargo and personnel. It was the military counterpart of the well-known DC-4 commercial airliner.

Mother had agreed to come to Wendover for Gene's first birthday in March. She made the trip from Miami to Salt Lake City by scheduled airlines, changing planes at Chicago's Midway airport. There she boarded a United Airlines DC-3 for a flight that involved several stops.

I had been summoned to Washington and was returning to Wendover on the day of mother's flight. Since she had never before made a trip by air, I arranged to stop in Chicago at the time she would be changing planes. I met her in the airport terminal to make sure that she checked in at the right gate.

From the air force I had obtained approval to pick her up in Salt Lake City and fly her to Wendover. It would have made more sense, of course, to take her all the way from Chicago, but I was reluctant to make such a request.

When the United plane took off from Chicago for its first stop at Des Moines, I followed it off the runway and flew about 200 yards off its left wing in a position where the captain could see me, but far enough away that he wouldn't be alarmed.

Making a position report to the nearest Civil Aeronautics

Administration flight station, I asked them to relay word to the United captain that my mother was on his airplane and that I would be following him all way to Salt Lake City.

Mother told me later that, as soon as the captain got the word, he had the stewardess come back and tell her that I was in the other plane. Of course, she already suspected it. Meanwhile, the captain waved to me to indicate that he had received the message from CAA.

I accompanied the airliner for the entire trip. When it landed, I simply circled the field until it took off again. In addition to Des Moines, he stopped at Omaha and Cheyenne. From Salt Lake City, mother rode in the cockpit with me to Wendover.

Conveniently, her visit ended at about the time I was scheduled to fly a C-54 to Cuba to check on our training operations. This time I was a little bolder than before, and talked with General Bob Williams of the Second Air Force, who told me it would be all right to take mother with me to Miami, saving her the inconvenience of a long and tiring trip across the country with many stops and a change of planes. The airlines were booked up on almost every flight in this wartime period, when many civilian passengers were being bumped to make room for military personnel with priorities.

I shall never forget that flight. We put mother in the folding "jump seat" between me and the copilot. She had told me she was uneasy on the airline flight to Utah, so I didn't know what to expect now. But I shouldn't have worried. She was completely thrilled with the trip, watching everything that went on. I explained to her what the instruments were for and what we were doing.

It was not an ideal flight. We ran into icing conditions soon after takeoff, and chunks of ice would thump against the fuselage when they were dislodged by the alcohol in the propeller de-icing system. We flew first to Oklahoma City and then down to Houston to refuel. Crossing the Gulf of Mexico, we encountered a series of thunderstorms.

After being tossed around by the turbulence, we arrived over Florida and ran into a spectacular display of St. Elmo's fire, a phenomenon well known to airplane pilots. It was dancing up and down the windshield as I had never seen before. The propellers were turned into luminous discs. Most novice air travelers would have been scared out of their wits, but mom took it all in stride. She was sitting on the edge of her seat, not through fear but from excitement. She enjoyed every hair-raising minute of the flight.

I sensed that her confidence arose from the same kind of faith she had shown in me when I announced my plans to enlist in the flying service. Her faith, I must confess, sometimes exceeded my own. Frankly, the turbulent trip to Miami bothered me more than it did mother.

When she got home, she told all her friends about her enjoyable trip. I was happy for the chance to give her that ride, because I knew we were approaching the time when I would have to head overseas.

25 The Green Hornet Line

Because of the need for almost constant communication between my headquarters at Wendover and the atomic laboratory at Los Alamos, we maintained an air shuttle for personnel and cargo. Most of the passengers were scientists who were working with ordnance experts to perfect the shape of the bomb and to design the intricate fusing mechanism. The importance of fusing cannot be overstated because, even though the bomb was to be set off at a predetermined altitude above the ground, safeguards had to be taken to prevent a premature explosion.

I made frequent trips to Los Alamos by way of Kirtland Air Force base at Albuquerque. Often, Bob Lewis or Chuck Sweeney would come along as copilot. Sometimes they would wait at Kirtland for me to return; frequently, however, they would fly on to Oklahoma City or some other base to pick up engine parts or other equipment we needed at Wendover.

I usually went to Los Alamos in the morning and returned that evening. A couple of times I stayed overnight, once at Captain Parson's house and the other time at the Officers' Club.

For some reason, great pains were taken to disguise the fact that air force personnel were at Los Alamos. The purpose may have been to keep from ruffling the sensitive feathers of a few scientists who didn't mind making a bomb but who were appalled by the thought that it might actually be used. These touchy types knew they were working for the military, but only for a nonfighting branch of the service: the Manhattan Engineering District. They chose to ignore the fact that there were military people who were actually engaged in the ugly business of dropping bombs.

When I went to Los Alamos, I was met by a staff car at Kirtland Air Force base and whisked off to the secret laboratory 60 miles to the north, in the mountains beyond Santa Fe. First, however, I removed all Air Corps insignia from my uniform and substituted the gold castle emblem of the U.S. Army Engineers. Sometimes I would even change shirts so that the pinholes for the wings did not show, although I always wondered if those Ph.D.'s were knowledgeable or interested enough in military matters to make the necessary deductions.

To keep the charade going at both ends of the line, I was met by one car at the air base and driven to the security office on the outskirts of the base, where I would get into a civilian car, ride a short distance, and then transfer to a staff car bearing the distinctive registration emblem of the Los Alamos laboratory. Only a car with such an emblem was permitted to pass through the gates of this secret 45,000-acre installation, the heart of which stood on a mesa with rugged mountains in the distance. It was a setting of breathtaking scenic beauty.

When I look back, the secrecy seems a bit overdone, but it must be conceded that the operation was effective. The atom bomb was probably the best-kept military secret since a handful of Greek soldiers got inside the gates of Troy in the belly of a wooden horse.

Unlike the few who had misgivings about the actual use of the bomb, there were many scientists at Los Alamos who were closely involved with the Air Corps in the development of the weapon. I became acquainted with many of them. They shuttled back and forth between the laboratory and our base to work out, with our ordnance people, the many perplexing problems that arose. We called our air shuttle the "Green Hornet Line," after a popular radio program of that period.

Piloting many of these flights, in the C-54s attached to our unit, were two of the most competent multi-engine pilots I ever hope to meet. The fact that they were women was a plus factor from my viewpoint. Their names were Dora Dougherty and Helen Gosnell.

I liked to assign them to the shuttle flights and other missions because they were more dependable than the men. By that I mean that they always returned from a mission when they were supposed to. It was a well-known trick among male pilots, and one that was often winked at by their superiors, to find something mechanically wrong with their airplanes during a trip to a base that happened to be located near a city which had interesting sights to see and an exciting nightlife to enjoy. The probability of a "malfunction" increased in almost exact proportion to the number of bars, nightclubs, and available females that a city was known to have. Crewmen have even been known to disable an airplane in some minor way as as excuse to stay overnight, or perhaps for a weekend, if their visit offered opportunities for purposeful entertainment. With Dora or Helen in command of an airplane, I didn't have that problem.

On my frequent flying trips to Los Alamos, I became acquainted with a number of the world's leading scientists—men whose understanding of the elementary forces of the universe was so profound that I was actually awed in their presence.

I soon discovered that a majority of them were warm and friendly. Although some did indeed have their heads in the clouds, others had the same interests as the normal everyday citizen, as I would classify myself. On becoming acquainted with these scientists, I lost much of the feeling of inferiority that overwhelmed me at the start. Awe was replaced by admiration as friendships developed, and I found that the people who were harnessing the atom had equal respect for my own special skills as an airplane pilot and an organizer of aerial attack strategy. If their language in the area of nuclear physics was unintelligible to me, my own field of expertise was equally foreign to them.

I was most impressed, as were all who met him, by the trigger-quick mind of J. Robert Oppenheimer. A pleasant man and unpretentious, he had a way of making a nonacademic layman like myself feel at ease. In size, he was a wisp of a man, very slender and seemingly fragile. He was highly nervous, a chain-smoker who talked so rapidly one had to concentrate to catch all the words. One had the feeling that, when he was talking to you, he was thinking of two other things at the same time. I felt that here was a man whose brain was divided into several remarkable parts from which he could extract bits of knowledge, on demand, in the same way that a computer spits out stored-up information.

I met his wife, Katherine, who waited on him hand and foot.

Because he sometimes became so immersed in a problem that he was oblivious to all that was going on around him, she frequently had to remind him when it was time to eat or take a drink of water, or even—I suspected—go to the bathroom.

The mental strain of his intense concentration created stomach problems that required frequent medicine, administered dutifully by Katherine, who was both maid and nurse to this frail genius without whom the United States might never have succeeded in its atomic endeavor.

I didn't know until much later that Katherine, like Oppenheimer's first wife, Jean, had a background of sympathy for Communist causes. But although Oppenheimer was frequently surrounded by pro-Communists during his academic life before coming to Los Alamos, and even contributed to their causes, I have never believed that he deserved the stigma that was attached to him in later years when he was deprived of his top-secret clearance. It should be mentioned that he was publicly cleared, before his death, when President Johnson bestowed on him a singular honor for his wartime achievement.

I was given an impressive example of his mathematical brilliance one day when we were walking together through one of the narrow corridors of a building at Los Alamos that housed offices and classrooms for the scientists. Many of the rooms were designed in classroom fashion, with blackboards on the walls so that a group of specialists could work together on a single problem.

As we passed an open door, Oppenheimer glanced inside at a blackboard filled with mathematical equations and formulas. Seated in a chair, staring at the figures, was the man who had written them on the blackboard.

After proceeding a few steps beyond the door, Oppenheimer stopped, wheeled, and returned to the room we had just passed. He walked to the blackboard and, with the palm of his hand, erased one of the many figures. Then he picked up a piece of chalk and made a correction.

The man who was seated there rose from his chair and exclaimed, "My God, how did you do it? I've been looking for that mistake for three days."

The scientist, I learned later, was Leo Szilard, one of the world's leading nuclear experts, who later became the leader of a group that tried unsuccessfully to persuade President Truman not to use the atomic bomb against Japan unless it was preceded by a message of warning.

It seems worth mentioning, in view of the later controversy over his loyalty, that I never heard Oppenheimer express a reservation about the use of the bomb. Quite the contrary, he gave the impression that he was in full accord with the purpose of the project; namely, to end the war as swiftly as possible.

The winter was coming to an end and I knew we would have to be in place and ready to go long before the bomb was ready. The first and only test was scheduled for July, and plans called for us to drop the first bomb on an enemy target in early August.

When the 509th was organized, we had assumed that the outfit would be divided, with one unit going to Europe and the other to the Pacific. Now it seemed a foregone conclusion that Germany would throw in the sponge before the A-bomb was ready. By summer, our lone enemy would be Japan.

Los Alamos was playing percentage games by this time. The complicated implosion-type plutonium bomb, for which the pumpkin shapes had been fabricated, was presenting problems. On the other hand, the scientists were sure that they could create a nuclear explosion by the less-sophisticated method of firing one slug of uranium into another. This alternative involved a long, comparatively slender bomb, whose mechanism would be like that of a gun barrel, with a conventional explosive charge to drive one cylindrical piece of uranium through a shaft to the other end of the bomb, where it would impact with a cup-shaped piece of uranium. The instant they came together, an explosion with the force of 20,000 tons of TNT would occur.

The firing mechanism was so simple that the scientists calculated the chances of failure were only one in ten thousand. Yet some of the purists in the Los Alamos community felt that the odds should be lengthened to a million to one. I was involved in several discussions on the subject and soon got fed up with the endless hassling.

"Hell, nothing is that certain," I told them in a moment of exasperation. "I'll take ten thousand to one any day." I noted that the acceptable odds for survival on our bombing raids in Europe had been ten to one.

The month of April found us still hogtied by petty bickering. I knew that, if we were to get our Pacific base in operation in time for the scheduled use of the bomb in early August, we would have to get moving.

I had just passed my 30th birthday and now wore the eagles of a full colonel on my uniform. A load of responsibility had been thrown on my shoulders and I decided to exercise the authority that went with it. Without asking anyone's advice or consent, I transmitted to Washington the code word that said, in effect, "Issue the orders for the 509th to be processed for overseas movement."

Getting to war wasn't as simple as the two or three days it would require to fly our bombers to the Pacific. Even with our high priority, there wasn't enough airlift available to get my entire personnel of almost 1,800 men to the Pacific by air. Many of the men, and a considerable quantity of supplies, would have to go by ship.

Knowing the interminable discussions that would result if I went through the routine channels, I had deliberately avoided mentioning my plans to the higher-ups.

Then all sorts of things began to hit the fan, as I had anticipated.

Geveral Groves summoned me to Washington. When I walked into his Pentagon office, he kept me standing at attention while he gave me a thorough chewing-out, complete with profanity. He said my unilateral decision bordered on insubordination. Before he was through, I began to see myself as the oldest second lieutenant in the Air Corps, ferrying worn-out airplanes back from the war zones.

As he finished, I noticed a twinkle in his eye. His lecture had been intended to put me in my place. But it was now evident that he agreed with me and was glad that I had taken it upon myself to make the decision. His message, loud and clear, was that I should have let him know in advance. He disliked surprises. Nevertheless, he was privately pleased.

"Dammit," he said, "you've got us moving." By leaving for the Pacific, I would be putting pressure on the scientists to quit quibbling over the odds and finish the job of getting the bomb ready.

26 Manhattan in the Pacific

Tinian Island became known as Manhattan in the Pacific, New York without subways. The nickname originated when a New York member of the Engineering Corps, laying out streets for our military installation, observed with a little imagination that the island bore a geographical resemblance to Manhattan.

Accordingly, he named the streets he was creating for some of the best known in the Big Apple. Broadway and Forty-second Street, for instance, was our most important crossroads on the base. Then there were Park Avenue, Madison Avenue, and Riverside Drive. The section reserved for our 509th Composite Group was in the "Columbia University district."

Tinian had been captured from the Japanese in July of the previous year after a nine-day battle in which casualties were light compared with those sustained three weeks earlier on nearby Saipan. Both are islands of the Marianas group, which also includes Guam.

Within two weeks after I sent word that we were ready to go overseas, two-thirds of our group were on their way. A troopship, the S.S. *Cape Victory*, which had been standing by at Seattle, sailed on May 6 with 1,200 of our people. They reached their destination on May 29.

Meanwhile, our advance air echelon, consisting of transport planes and other support aircraft, arrived on May 18 on Tinian, where their quarters were in the final stages of construction. Our 18 B-29 bombers—we had added three to the original 15—made the flight during the first week of June.

By this time, the 509th was a self-contained unit consisting of the 393rd Bomber squadron, the 320th Troop Carrier squadron, the 390th Air Service group, the 603rd Air Engineering squadron, and the 1027th Air Matériel squadron. In addition, there was a newly arrived special unit, the First Ordnance squadron, consisting mostly of highly skilled specialists in charge of handling the atom bombs when they arrived.

Eager to see the facility from which we would be operating, I flew to Tinian in mid-May for a personal inspection and for talks with General LeMay and Admiral Nimitz. LeMay, then commander of the 20th Air Force, would soon become deputy to General Carl Spaatz when the latter was named chief of the Strategic Air Forces in the Pacific. Nimitz was commander in chief of our Pacific fleet.

I found Tinian ideally suited to our purposes. The 509th would live in relative isolation near North Field, one of two air bases on the island. Since the Japs had been driven out, the four runways of North Field had been extended to a length of 8,500 feet. They were said to be the longest operational runways in the world at the time, but not too long considering the heavy loads of bombs and fuel that were being carried nightly on the 12-hour round-trip flights to the enemy homeland.

My first view of Tinian as I approached it from the air confirmed my preconceived notion of an island in the southern Pacific, a part of the world I was seeing for the first time. Except for our military installations in the north and west, and some cultivated land in the south, there was considerable jungle vegetation over the island's 12-mile length and 6-mile width. Near the northwest coast was a high plateau culminating in a 500-foot hill called Mount Lasso.

Because the war in Europe had just ended, Americans were enjoying a period of exhilaration. V-E day, May 8, was important to my group because the end of fighting on the other side of the world freed an enormous battle-hardened army for transfer to the Pacific to carry out the scheduled invasion of the Japanese home islands.

By mid-June, plans were being drawn up secretly in Washington for two operations that would involve two million American soldiers. The initial invasion, under the code name "Olympic," would put more than 800,000 troops ashore on the southern part of the island of Kyushu in early November. A second amphibious landing, called "Coronet," would take place in April 1946, on the island of Honshu near Tokyo.

Only a few of us knew that these elaborate invasion plans would probably not be carried out. Our small force of 1,800 men and 18 bombing planes would do the work of two million soldiers! We were confident that we would end the war and save hundreds of thousands of lives, both American and Japanese.

The months of May, June, and July were among the most frenzied of my military career. So many problems came up, requiring my attention, that I found myself torn between frustration and exhaustion. Complications developed so fast that it was a rare night in which I managed to get five hours of sleep.

There were confrontations brought about, in part, because of the secrecy which surrounded our operations. Even the high-ranking officers who had to be briefed in a general way did not seem to understand that our mission was quite different from the routine bombing strikes with which they were familiar.

My first hassle was with Brig. Gen. John Davies, commander of the 313th bombardment wing, which was already operating on Tinian when we got there. He had not been let in on the atomic secret and resented the fact that I declined to answer his questions about our mission.

Because his crews had experience over Japan, he thought my flight people should attend classes in which his most proficient officers would conduct briefings. Rather than argue the point, I sent three of my crews to one of his indoctrination sessions.

That afternoon, he summoned me to his office.

"Are all of your crews like the ones you sent here this morning?" he asked.

"Yes, they are," I replied.

"Goddamn it," he shot back. "They're demoralizing my whole school. They know more about airplanes and navigation and everything else than my instructors know."

That disposed of the class requirement, but I soon had another quarrel on my hands, this time with Bill Ervine, General LeMay's director of matériel. He had centralized maintenance for all of the several hundred B-29s on the island, and he didn't see why our outfit should have its own maintenance facilities. So far as he was concerned, a B-29 was a B-29; and he insisted that we pool our maintenance people with his and send our airplanes to central maintenance for such things as tune-ups and repair. Actually, the concept of a central facility for repairing airplanes made sense, but I didn't want anyone but my own mechanics fooling around with my airplanes. I told him so, without success, whereupon our argument was carried to LeMay, who backed me up. Another problem solved.

Between May and mid-July, I made three round-trips to the States to attend conferences and work out problems as they arose. Twice I went to the Pentagon for the purpose of discussing target selection.

I was fortunate during this hectic period to have an officer as capable as Colonel Classen as my chief deputy. He ran the final training operations in exactly the manner that I would have done it if I had been on the scene full-time.

Flying one of our C-54 four-engine transport planes, I made two of these trips to the States and back in 76 hours, including the time it took for the meetings.

At our first target discussion, preference was expressed for Kyoto, Hiroshima, Yokohama, and Kokura, in that order. They were chosen because of their importance as war industry and military centers.

Two weeks later, Secretary of State Henry Stimson struck Kyoto from the list, although it was the target most favored by General Groves at our previous meeting. Stimson, an expert on the Far East, pointed out that Kyoto was a city of great historical significance and that it contained many shrines that the Japanese held in deep reverence. By this time, as the result of a more detailed study, Niigata had replaced Kokura on the target list, and finally Nagasaki was substituted for Kyoto.

At a June meeting in General Arnold's Pentagon office, it was disclosed that some of the scientists who had been involved in the bomb's development were having qualms about its actual use. Their attitude was just one more factor that wrapped a cloud of uncertainty about the mission we had been assigned to carry out.

The decision to use the bomb was made jointly by President Truman and Prime Minister Churchill after listening to alternate proposals by scientists and others. Among the ideas was to conduct a preannounced demonstration bomb drop at sea off the coast of Japan as a means of convincing the enemy that further resistance was futile.

Oppenheimer was asked about this possibility and expressed doubt that such a demonstration would be convincing. The sight of a fireball and a towering cloud at sea might not be impressive when viewed from a distance. It would afford no way of showing the weapon's destructive capability.

Moreover, an advance announcement would certainly invite the Japanese to destroy the bomb-carrying plane if they wished. Then there was always the possibility that the demonstration bomb might prove to be an embarrassing "dud."

Ironically, scientist Leo Szilard, one of those who had helped persuade President Roosevelt to authorize the bomb's development when he thought it would be used against Hitler's Germany, was now among those who had second thoughts.

A similar overture in the name of humanity had been made in 1944 to President Roosevelt, who had listened patiently but had chosen to ignore it. Roosevelt, like Truman and Churchill later, correctly read the mood of a war-weary world that wanted nothing more than to finish the conflict as quickly as possible.

During the second week of July, I was in Washington for a meeting, intending to stop in New Mexico to witness the first test-firing of an atomic bomb at Alamogordo on July 16. My plans were suddenly changed, however, upon receipt of an urgent message from Tom Ferebee on Tinian, advising me to return there at once. I had great respect for Ferebee, my bombardier and longtime friend, who had served with me in Europe and North Africa. So I left Washington the same day, stopping at Cincinnati overnight for a brief visit with my old friends Dr. and Mrs. Harry Crum.

Landing my C-54 at old Lunken airport along the Ohio River brought back memories of my early flying days there while a medical student. My abortive stab in the direction of a doctoring career seemed an almost-forgotten page out of a misty past, even though it was less than nine years before. So much had happened in those nine years.

After a stop at Wendover, where we still maintained a housekeeping unit, I left for Tinian by way of Hickam field adjacent to Pearl Harbor, reflecting as I landed that here was the site where the war had begun for the United States on December 7, 1941. I reached Tinian, as I remember it, on July 16.

I was met by Ferebee, who gave me what he called "the bad news." He said there was a move afoot to switch the atomic mission to an outfit other than the 509th.

It turned out that General LeMay, for whom I had great respect and whom I regarded as a friend, had demonstrated that he didn't understand the complete nature of our operation. Nor was he aware of the reasoning that went into the formation of our self-contained unit. His attitude was, no doubt, partly due to the fact that he had not been made privy to the atomic secret until recently, when he was given only the basic facts. The rule was to divulge such information only on a "need to know" basis. And no one thought LeMay needed to know more than the mere fact that the weapon existed and was soon to be used. Because of his position with our strategic forces, the actual operation would be under his general command.

Because of this, LeMay had been authorized to disclose the atomic secret to his operations officer, Colonel William "Butch" Blanchard, who was cagey enough to sense that the atom bomb, if successful, would bring credit for ending the war to an obscure outfit that had just moved into the Pacific.

Blanchard was clearly jealous of our scheduled role in what was to be the greatest single event in the history of warfare. With an island full of B-29 pilots who had flown many missions to Japan, he proceeded to belabor LeMay with his notion that we, as newcomers with no comparable experience in that part of the world, were not qualified for the job.

He did not understand, nor apparently did LeMay, that we had been training since the previous September in the special techniques required for delivery of the weapon and that we had 18 pilots infinitely better skilled at this specific job than any that were then under LeMay's command. I did not know at the time that LeMay had already had a losing quarrel with general Groves on the question of who would have actual control of the atomic bombs when they arrived in his area.

The next morning, when I flew to the island of Guam for my confrontation with General LeMay, I was in no mood to let him or anyone else take over the task for which our people had been preparing for almost 11 months.

The whole thing was silly, of course, because I had only to get in touch with General Arnold in Washington to set things straight. Arnold would have acquainted LeMay and Blanchard with the facts of life in this dawning atomic age, even though the confrontation might have been unpleasant for him.

Although I was doing a slow burn inside, I had no desire to put Arnold in a position where he would be obliged to side with me against one of his most famous generals. Nor would it have helped my future relations with LeMay to have gone over his head without first exhausting every other alternative.

The first alternative was a face-to-face showdown in LeMay's office. When he confirmed Blanchard's suggestion that the job should be done by a more experienced crew, I might have been excused for blowing my top. That I didn't may be credited to the fact that I had matured considerably since my belligerent encounter with Lauris Norstad in Algiers three years before. I had won the battle with Norstad at possible cost to my future military career. I answered politely but firmly that I intended to fly the mission myself and that the 509th must be allowed to operate, as intended when it was formed, without outside interference.

Then I suggested that if Blanchard or anyone else on LeMay's staff wished to check our proficiency, he would be welcome to come along on one of our practice flights.

I took no risks in the challenge. It was better to do it this way than to go over LeMay's head. The result, I was confident, would be the same.

Blanchard was assigned to join us the next day on a training flight to the nearby island of Rota, which was still in the hands of the Japanese. We would drop a practice "pumpkin" on one of their installations.

I was in the pilot's seat and Bob Lewis was the copilot. Blanchard was in the "jump seat" just behind us. We gave him a ride he would not soon forget. It was all "by the book"—his 20th Air Force book.

We arrived over our aiming point at the exact time that

navigator Van Kirk had estimated. Then Ferebee dropped the bomb and it landed squarely on target. At that moment, I went into the 155-degree diving turn, as we were supposed to do, and Blanchard was almost paralyzed as the G-forces pinned him to his seat. He hadn't expected this.

"That's enough," he said, his face pale. "I'm satisfied." For extra measure, I gave him some idea of our plane's improved performance. Then we returned to Tinian and landed within 15 seconds of the time that Van Kirk had estimated. Blanchard was so glad to scramble out of the airplane that I heard no more from him or LeMay or anyone else about our qualifications to carry the bomb to Japan.

I think that LeMay was rather pleased that I had proved my point. Once before, I had given him some advice that he was reluctant to accept but for which he later gave me credit. The incident had occurred at Grand Island, Nebraska, where Frank Armstrong was in charge of the B-29 training school and I was director of operations. We had a barbecue one Saturday night at Armstrong's country home, and LeMay, who had come to Grand Island to get his first look at the B-29, was among those present.

It was there that he found out that the B-29 was not an overgrown B-17, as he had supposed. I explained to him that it would not fly successfully in formation at high altitudes, as he had planned to use it for the same kind of daylight mass bombings of Japanese cities that he had employed so successfully against German targets.

"If that's the case," he said, "I don't know what I'm going to do with that airplane."

I took the opportunity to make a gratuitous suggestion, based on an experience at Eglin field, where I had watched the testing of fire bombs. To LeMay, I said, "I'd load the B-29s with fire bombs for low altitude attacks of the kind the British employed against Germany." I pointed out that many Japanese buildings were constructed of flammable material. Paper houses, we called them.

"All you need to do is 'area bomb' these cities," I said.

He didn't seem impressed with my argument, and when he went to the Pacific with his 20th Air Force, he insisted on using the high-altitude bombing tactics that paid off in Europe. He encountered the troubles I had predicted. The heavily loaded B-29s refused to stay in close formation at 30,000 feet. The engines overheated on long flights with the power settings required for this kind of operation. The strong winds that prevailed in that part of the world caused the bombs to miss their mark, sometimes by a wide margin.

On my first trip to the western Pacific in May, I had lunch with him and his staff at his headquarters. I sat next to him at the table, and as we finished eating he said, "Come with me, I want to show you something."

We went to his briefing room where, dramatically displayed, were aerial photographs of the cities LeMay's B-29s had burned out with fire bombs. After pointing to a number of the pictures he said, "You were right, Paul." He told of the several unsuccessful missions that were flown when he first arrived in the Pacific. "Then I remembered your advice about the fire bombs." he said.

He tried the plan I had suggested and sent in his B-29s at night, flying at 6,000 to 8,000 feet, heavily loaded with incendiaries. With this tactic, one after another Japanese city was virtually destroyed.

Tokyo was laid waste on one memorable night when 325 bombers, each loaded with 7 tons of fire bombs, destroyed an area of 16 square miles and took one hundred thousand lives. I have often mentioned that episode when people have spoken of the horror of the atom bomb.

On the day of my showdown with LeMay over the role of the 509th on Tinian, I received a coded message from General Groves advising me that the Alamogordo test had been successful.

Until now, the whole project had been theoretical. Two billion dollars had been spent on faith that the scientists and their equations and formulas were correct. Now the atomic bomb was a reality. Whatever skepticism might have found a place in the back of my mind had disappeared.

27 Taunts and Jibes

July was a nerve-shattering month for the men of the 509th, particularly those with thin skins. To other outfits on Tinian, we were a bunch of pampered dandies. While they were flying hazardous bombing missions, from which some did not return, our crews were making training flights with an occasional sortie into the enemy skies to drop a single bomb from high altitude.

We had our own quarters and seemed to be living a bit high, thanks to priorities that brought speedy response to our every requisition. To all questions about what the hell we were doing in this war, our people invented devious and certainly unsatisfactory answers. Inevitably, the word got around the island that we were involved in something special. But when days passed and nothing happened, we came under suspicion.

Our men were soon the object of taunts and jibes. Sometimes, when a jeep passed in the night, we would be awakened by the rattle of rocks thrown on one of our tin roofs as a token of the contempt in which we were held. It was an understandable case of jealousy.

In self-defense, some of our people no doubt responded to their tormentors with language that conveyed the idea that we were there to win the war. It was a fact, of course, but no one believed it. An anonymous headquarters clerk in one of the other outfits was inspired to write a sarcastic poem entitled "Nobody Knows," which was mimeographed and widely circulated on the island. The verses follow:

> Into the air the secret rose,
> Where they're going, nobody knows.
> Tomorrow they'll return again,
> But we'll never know where they've been.
> Don't ask us about results or such,
> Unless you want to get in Dutch.
> But take it from one who is sure of the score,
> The 509th is winning the war.
>
> When the other groups are ready to go,
> We have a program on the whole damned show.
> And when Halsey's Fifth shells Nippon's shore,
> Why shucks, we hear about it the day before.
> And MacArthur and Doolittle give out in advance,
> But with this new bunch we haven't a chance.
> We should have been home a month or more,
> For the 509th is winning the war.

Even the Japanese radio poked fun at us, and Tokyo Rose referred to the distinctive arrows on the tails of our B-29s. How the enemy learned so much about what was happening on Tinian was a mystery, although Japanese soldiers were known to be still hiding in the dense jungles around us, holed up in caves in the hills. It may have been that they had a low-power radio transmitter that was capable of being heard as far away as Rota, a Japanese-held island not far away to the south.

Almost every night, a patrol would be formed to go into the hills and flush out enemy soldiers. Many were rounded up in this fashion, but the Japanese also displayed cunning and sometimes penetrated our installations at night to steal food and supplies they needed for survival.

For the first two or three weeks after arriving on Tinian, our crews engaged in routine training or familiarization flights, dropping conventional bombs on islands that were still in enemy hands. Then, during July, we started sharpening our skills for the atomic missions by carrying the pumpkin-shaped high-explosive bombs to selected targets in Japan. These flights gave our pilots, navigators, and bombardiers the type of experience they would need when it came time to drop our nuclear weapon.

The simulated atom bombs were filled with black powder or torpex. They were destructive, and they made an explosion that was easy to spot from the air. The missions over Japan proved something I knew all the time: all our crews were competent. They could find their way around this part of the world, and they could put their bombs on target.

I worked out a deal with General LeMay to have some pinpoint targets to work on. Precision bombing would not only be good training for our men, but it would accustom the Japanese to seeing daylight flights of two or three bombers over their target. Since the single bomb dropped from each of these planes would not cause the sort of widespread damage inflicted by the mass attacks, we hoped they would be lulled into ignoring us, when we came to deliver the real thing. We did avoid striking the cities that had been placed on the reserved list for possible atomic attack: Hiroshima, Niigata, Kokura, and Nagasaki.

Indeed, our strange tactics served to confuse the enemy. Although air raid sirens would sound when we came overhead, fighter planes were seldom sent up, and anti-aircraft artillery was unable to reach our 30,000-foot altitude.

I did not participate in any of these flights. Because I knew more about the atomic bomb and our plans for using it than any officer in the Air Force, I had been ordered not to fly over enemy territory in advance of my nuclear mission. It was decided in Washington that I must not risk falling into enemy hands. LeMay warned me that he was enforcing that order.

One incident during this period of hit-and-run raids nearly created a sensation. Claude Eatherly, in one of the impulsive moments for which he was famous, decided to drop his bomb on Emperor Hirohito's palace in Tokyo. The target to which he was assigned had been obscured by clouds, so he and his fellow crewmen decided it would be a lark to head for the capital and surprise the emperor.

The weather was also unfavorable over Tokyo, no one on the plane was quite sure of the palace's location, and the bomb missed its mark. The miss was no doubt fortunate since Hirohito, a moderate compared with some of his ministers, was worshipped by his people and turned out to be a stabilizing influence for his war-sick country after the signing of the peace treaty. His example of cooperation eased the work of our occupation authorities in the years following the war.

When Eatherly's plane returned and I found out about his quixotic attempt to bomb the palace, I gave the pilot one of the most X-rated chewing-outs I ever delivered. Accustomed to reprimands, he said he was sorry, as he always did. This irrepressible pilot was one of the few in my outfit whose behavior was impossible to predict.

It was ironic that when the scientists were preoccupied with the chances of a successful atomic explosion, the fusing mechanism was the real headache.

We had two cases of premature explosions, one on a flight out of Wendover and the other over the Pacific. Had such a mishap occurred with the atomic bomb, I would not be around to tell about it.

The proximity fuse was a sensitive device designed to set off the bomb at an altitude of 1,890 feet above the ground. On the two occasions when it failed, the "pumpkin" filled with conventional gunpowder went off soon after it left the plane. No harm was done, but the misbehavior of the fusing mechanism gave us cause for serious concern.

During the last half of July, our planes made 12 strikes with "pumpkins" on Japanese cities. The weather was not always cooperative during this period, and some of the bombs had to be dropped by radar sighting, even though it had been decided that when the time came, the atomic bomb would be released only under visual conditions. We learned that cloudy weather was typical for the Japanese islands during July, but long-range forecasts led us to expect some clear days soon after the first of August.

Even though we were working hard to perfect our methods of operation, and were under the unpleasant pressure that the security of our mission imposed, it would be a mistake to say that all was serious work among the 509th personnel on Tinian. Our people found time for recreation and just plain fun.

For one thing, there was a hospital staffed with pretty nurses.

194 THE TIBBETS STORY

And then there was the beautiful Pacific Ocean. The Seabees had used bulldozers to plow away some of the coral along one stretch of shoreline to create a good beach for swimming. We also had a recreation area with ball diamonds. There were some lively games involving teams from various outfits.

We were billeted about 2½ miles from the beach. There was a great deal of swimming in the daytime, and the beach was also popular at night.

I recall one evening when a couple of our popular nonflying officers used one of our jeeps to take two nurses to the beach, picking up enough food at the mess hall for a picnic. As darkness came, Ferebee, Van Kirk, Behan, and I decided to investigate and perhaps indulge in some harmless mischief.

We found the jeep parked in an isolated spot. On the front seat were two sets of uniforms: two of the Army Air Corps and two of the Army Nurse Corps. Naturally, we didn't wish to disturb the swimmers, but we took the rotor out of the jeep's distributor. Then we took the uniforms back to camp as a precaution against having them fall into unauthorized hands.

It was almost dawn when the two officers got back to quarters. It turned out that they didn't even have bathing suits, and every time a car came along the road they had to leap into the weeds and wait for it to pass. The underbrush and the coral of the road were not kind to their bare skin and the soles of their feet. We never did find out how the nurses got back to the hospital. We were afraid to ask. Such incidents relieved the tensions that were building up as time for our mission approached.

At my July meeting in Washington, it was agreed that everything would be ready for our bomb drop during the first week in August, weather permitting. We had the bomb casings, but the ingredients were still to come from that mysterious center of secret sorcery known as Los Alamos (or Site-Y, as it was called by the Manhattan district people).

Then on the morning of July 26, the cruiser *Indianapolis* dropped anchor about a half-mile off shore and unloaded a 15 foot wooden crate onto the deck of an LST. Two men left the ship by ladder, struggling with a heavy lead bucket as they stepped into a waiting motor launch.

The crate, containing the firing mechanism for the bomb, and the bucket, with a slug of uranium (U-235), were taken to the bomb assembly hut, where they would be fitted into one of the three casings that had previously been supplied.

The men who had accompanied the precious shipment on the 10-day voyage from San Francisco were Major Robert R. Furman, an engineer, and Col. James F. Nolan, a physician and radiology officer, both attached to the Manhattan Project. During the trip, they took turns guarding the bucket, actually a cylinder made of lead to prevent the escape of radiation.

Still needed to complete the explosive elements of the bomb was a second slug of uranium. This was put aboard a B-29 at Hamilton Air Force base in California on the day that the cruiser delivered its cargo on Tinian. Two other B-29s, with plutonium for the second bomb, left at the same time.

Four days after departing Tinian en route to the Philippines, the *Indianapolis* was sunk by a Japanese submarine. Only a few of the 900 crewmen survived.

Now we were ready. Since we were to drop the bomb only by visual sighting rather than by radar, the weather was an important element. Rather than rely on long-distance analysis, I hit upon the idea of sending three weather planes ahead of our flight to report on conditions over the primary target and two alternates.

In all, seven planes would be taking part in the mission. Two would accompany me, one with scientific instruments to measure the intensity of the blast and another with photographic equipment to make a pictorial record of the event. Then there would be a standby plane, which would land at Iwo Jima for use in case the bomb-carrying plane ran into mechanical trouble.

General Spaatz arrived on Guam on July 29 to take command of the Strategic Forces in the Pacific. With him he brought an order that had been drafted in Washington by General Groves, authorizing the dropping of "the first special bomb" on one of four cities: Hiroshima, Kokura, Niigata, or Nagasaki. No specific date was set, except to indicate that the mission would take place after August 3.

At a meeting with Spaatz and others in LeMay's office, I assured them that we were ready and that the bomb had been assembled, minus the two small slugs of uranium that were being kept under guard in the ordnance area.

Ever since examining aerial photos of the four cities on the reserved list, I had favored Hiroshima as the primary target. It was important industrially and militarily and had been spared from previous attack only because it was one of several that were being saved for atomic destruction.

Several additional considerations went into the final decision. One was the report that prisoner-of-war camps might be located in two or three of the cities, but none was known to exist at Hiroshima. Not until after the war was it learned that 23 fliers who had been shot down in the area were housed in Hiroshima castle.

On the basis of the order received from Groves, I drafted a more detailed one and sent it to LeMay. On August 3 it came back in approximately the same form over his signature as the official order for Special Bombing Mission No. 13, designating Hiroshima as the target. In case the primary was clouded over, the secondary target was to be Kokura; the third, Nagasaki. The 12 previous "special missions" had been our flights to Japan with the nonatomic "pumpkins."

With the decision now made, Tom Ferebee and I studied a huge airphoto of the city and surrounding area. From this, he chose a geographical feature east of the city as the Initial Point, from which we would start our bomb run. As the Aiming Point, he put his finger on a T-shaped bridge near the heart of the city. There were many bridges across the deltaic branches of the Ota River, which divided the city into many sections, but this one stood out because of a ramp in the center that gave it the shape of the letter "T." To Hiroshimans, it was known as the Aioi bridge.

Since a code word seems necessary to describe any important military operation, ours was "Centerboard." LeMay's order established August 6 as the date for "Centerboard" to be carried out.

As the time approached for the Hiroshima mission, I gave serious thought to a name for my plane. Considering the historical importance of the event, it seemed hardly fitting to announce that the world's first atomic bomb had been dropped from an unnamed B-29 bearing the number 82.

The B-17 I flew in Europe and North Africa was named the *Red Gremlin*. Most of the planes in the 509th had been given names such as Claude Eatherly's *Straight Flush*, Chuck Sweeney's *Great Artiste*, and Frederick Bock's *Bock's Car*.

My thoughts turned at this moment to my courageous red-haired mother, whose quiet confidence had been a source of strength to me since boyhood, and particularly during the soul-searching period when I decided to give up a medical career to become a military pilot. At a time when dad thought I had lost my marbles, she had taken my side and said, "I know you will be all right, son."

I remembered the excitement she displayed on our rough flight through the thunderstorms from Wendover to Miami. From that flight, she had come to understand and even share some of the thrills of flying that had led me into my present career.

Her name, Enola Gay, was pleasing to the ear. It was also unique, for I had never heard of anyone else named Enola. It would be a fine name for my plane: *Enola Gay*.

I had mentioned it to several of my crew members, including Tom Ferebee and Dutch Van Kirk, who had become acquainted with mother on her visit to Wendover. They gave hearty approval.

I looked upon this airplane as one of the best B-29s ever produced. I remember picking it out of the production line at the Martin factory in Omaha with the help of a couple of foremen. When it was completed and modified to specifications, I sent Bob Lewis to the factory to pick it up.

Because I was away quite often on trips to Washington, Los Alamos and elsewhere, Lewis piloted this B-29 so often that he came to look upon it as his plane. It has even been represented in recent years that he expected to be in command of the atomic flight.

This was nonsense, of course. He and everyone else among the flying crews of the 509th knew that I would fly the plane and would choose the best qualified men in the outfit, namely Tom Ferebee and Dutch Van Kirk, as my bombardier and navigator, respectively. Bob didn't know for sure that he would be making the flight until three days before it was scheduled. I chose him as my copilot for that mission because I regarded him as competent and dependable.

28 Last-Minute Preparations

The word came Sunday morning, August 5. After three days of uncertainty, the clouds that had hung over the Japanese islands for the past week were beginning to break up. Conditions were "go" and tomorrow was the day.

Aside from lettering the name on the nose of my plane, which took less than a half-hour of a painter's time, there were other last-minute chores to be done. Most important, of course, was the loading of the bomb aboard the *Enola Gay*.

In order to sort out the day's responsibilities and tie up all the loose ends, the so-called Tinian "joint chiefs" had a meeting before noon. This committee of top officers and scientists included, aside from myself, General Thomas F. Farrell, the Manhattan District's ranking officer on the scene: Admiral William R. Purnell; Navy Captain William S. "Deak" Parsons, who would be the weaponeer on the flight; Commander Frederick L. Ashworth, another weaponeer; Professor Norman F. Ramsey, whom I first met in General Ent's office the previous September; and Professor Robert Brode.

General Farrell sent a message in code to General Groves in Washington who, in turn, passed the word of our scheduled 2:45 A.M. takeoff time to General Marshall. The tension in the Pentagon must have equaled that on Tinian.

In the messages that flew back and forth across the Pacific during our period of preparations, there were code names for everything

Last-Minute Preparations   199

and everyone. I was "Yoke," Deak Parsons was "Judge," General Farrell was "Scale," and General LeMay was "Cannon." The recent atomic test in New Mexico was "Trinity," atom was "Top," atomic was "Topic," and uranium fission was "Urchin Fashion."

At this morning's meeting, Captain Parsons startled us all by expressing concern over our plans to take off with a live atomic explosive in the bomb bay. In the few days since he had arrived on the island, he had witnessed a number of fiery crashes as overloaded B-29s failed to become airborne. Four crashes had occurred the night before with thunderous explosions of bombs, torpedoes, and incendiaries that lit up the sky and cost the lives of all crewmen aboard.

Deak Parsons, who knew just about all there was to know about the workings of our bomb, having participated in its development, was blunt and convincing as he spoke of the risks.

"If we crack up and the plane catches fire," he said, "there is danger of an atomic explosion that could wipe out half of this island."

General Farrell winced at the thought and suggested that we would all have to pray that such a thing would not happen. But Deak had an idea that seemed more feasible than the combined prayers of our committee. His motive may not have been so much a lack of faith in the Lord as it was a fear that He might not get the message from men who might have neglected to keep open their channels of communication with Him.

The navy man proposed that he be permitted to make the final assembly of the bomb during the early stages of our flight. In other words, he would insert one of the uranium slugs and the explosive charge into the bomb casing after takeoff. That way, if we crashed, we would lose only the airplane and crew, himself included. The island would be saved.

"Are you sure you can do it?" Farrell asked.

"No," Parsons replied, "but I've got all day to learn."

We were all concerned about the difficulty of working on the sensitive mechanism of the weapon in the cramped quarters of the bomb bay while the plane was in flight.

What we did not know was that Parsons himself had sided with General Groves and Robert Oppenheimer in vetoing the very same idea when Lt. Commander Francis Birch, Parsons' ordnance deputy, had suggested it at Los Alamos two months earlier. Birch had developed a double-plug system for the bomb that, he contended, made it feasible to complete the assembly in flight.

The decision having been made, I went to the hard stand where my plane was waiting to be towed to the loading area. I looked with pride at the newly painted *Enola Gay* on the left side of the nose beneath the cockpit, and noted that the painter had also carried out my instructions to replace the arrow and circle on the tail with a big black letter "R," also inside a circle.

This was probably an unnecessary precaution, but my purpose was to make the plane conform in marking with several hundred others based on Tinian. The 509th's arrow insignia had set our planes apart, and it now occurred to me that to look special might not be wise. The same change was made on the other six planes that were to take part in tomorrow's historic mission. There was no sense identifying ourselves in distinctive fashion for any Japanese interceptors that might come close enough to make such an observation.

Shortly after noon, the tarpaulin-covered bomb was taken by trailer from the assembly hut to the loading pit. I watched every step of the operation as the *Enola Gay* was towed into position above the bomb.

As I stood there during the loading, I reflected that it seemed incredible that a single bomb should have the explosive force of 20,000 tons of TNT, as the scientists predicted. Forty million pounds—surely the scientists were exaggerating. This would be equal to 200,000 of the 200-pound bombs which I carried over Europe and Africa three years before.

Despite a temptation to skepticism, I was compelled to accept the estimate. In 11 months of association with Dr. Oppenheimer and the other wizards at Los Alamos, I had acquired a great respect for them. Even so, I could sympathize with the disbelief of Admiral Leahy, President Roosevelt's military adviser, who said quite positively (to his eventual regret) that such a bomb would never explode.

Looking at the huge bomb with its blunt nose and four tail fins, I wondered why we were calling it "Little Boy." It was not little by any standard. It was a monster compared with any bomb that I had ever dropped. "Little Boy" was 28 inches in diameter and 12 feet long. Its weight was a little more than 9,000 pounds. With its coat of dull gunmetal paint, it was an ugly monster. I watched as it was hoisted slowly into the bomb bay, which, like the other B-29s in our outfit, had been modified to accept this superweapon.

It did not matter that this was the only bomb of its type that would ever be dropped. If we had to use more than one, any future bomb would be of a more bulbous shape. That's why we called the next one "Fat Man." Its pumpkinlike shape was familiar to all of our crews.

A number of our people stopped by to scrawl messages on the side of the bomb. One, addressed to Emperor Hirohito, was signed "From the Boys of the Indianapolis," implying revenge for the loss of those aboard the cruiser that had been sunk after delivering the material for this bomb.

The weapon was no sooner in place than Deak Parsons arrived to begin his experiment of arming the weapon in flight. He climbed aboard and dropped into the bomb bay, where for the next two hours he practiced the delicate task of inserting the explosive material into the bomb, utilizing Commander Birch's "double-plug" system.

It was a hot day and the temperature inside the bomb bay, where he worked in cramped quarters, was well over 100 degrees. He finally emerged, dripping with perspiration, his hands and overalls blackened by the graphite that lubricated the movable parts of the weapon, and his fingers bleeding from cuts caused by the sharp edges of the finely tooled steel. He was confident, however, that the task could be done in flight.

During this busy afternoon, I was introduced to William L. Laurence, a *New York Times* science writer who had been given leave of absence from his newspaper to work for the government and write the official history of the atomic development. The secrets of the atom were no great mystery to Bill Laurence even in the prewar days. For *The Saturday Evening Post* of September 7, 1940, he had written an article, "The Atom Gives Up," based on successful atom-splitting experiments overseas. His interpretive releases, some prepared well in advance, would be given to the world press when it was determined that our bombing mission had been successful.

Laurence had just arrived on Tinian that morning, having been delayed three days by misadventures on his flight from the West Coast. He had hoped to accompany us on the Hiroshima flight, but it was now too late to squeeze him into one of the planes.

Shortly after evening mess, the seven crews that would be taking part in the mission gathered for a preflight briefing in the assembly hut. The briefing was routine, involving such things as the route to be followed and the altitudes for each segment of the flight, the radio frequencies to be used, and the latest information on weather en route.

Two deviations from our normal procedures were pointed out. First, I had changed our radio call signal from Victor to Dimples in order to confuse any enemy listening post that might have been monitoring our calls. Second, the first leg of our flight was to be at an altitude of less than 5,000 feet, the purpose being to allow time for Deak Parsons to arm the bomb in the unpressurized bomb bay.

Air rescue capabilities were also described. For this mission, submarines and surface ships would be spaced along the 1,700-mile route from Tinian to the south coast of Japan.

When the briefing was over, I returned with Tom Ferebee, Dutch Van Kirk, and my supply officer, John Porter, to the Quonset hut which we shared. We intended to snatch a few hours of sleep, but somehow our tightly wound nerves vetoed this idea. Instead, we passed the time by playing blackjack, a favorite pastime at which the stakes were never excessive.

At 11:00 came the final briefing for the three crews that would be making the 13-hour trip together. I soon found that the tension that had been building up within me was shared by almost everyone else in the room. This was no dry run. It was the real thing for which we had been preparing since the previous autumn.

The word "atom" had never been spoken in our nearly one year of training. Nor was it in this briefing. Yet, many of our people had the intelligence to suspect the nature of our mission. Knowing that we would be carrying a weapon of tremendous power, some no doubt had enough scientific knowledge to suspect that atomic fission was involved.

On the platform with me at the final briefing were Captain Parsons and Professor Ramsey. I had not prepared a written statement in advance but Bill Laurence, who took notes has quoted me as follows:

"Tonight is the night we have all been waiting for. Our long months of training are to be put to the test. We will soon know if we have been successful or failed. Upon our efforts tonight it is possible that history will be made. We are going on a mission to drop a bomb different from any you have ever seen or heard about. This bomb contains a destructive force equivalent to twenty thousand tons of TNT."

The mention of this figure made an impression. The men sat there in shocked disbelief. Even though they had seen the Alamogordo pictures the night before, they were unable to imagine a single bomb with such explosive force. Frankly, neither could I, even though I had been exposed to detailed explanations by the scientists ever since being placed in command of the 509th.

I concluded with a rundown of our operational plans, including the oft-rehearsed maneuvers after bomb release. I would immediately begin a diving turn of 155 degrees to the right, while Chuck Sweeney in *The Great Artiste* would make a similar sharp turn to the left after releasing the instrument packages that would be dropped by parachute to record such things as shock effect and radioactivity. George Marquardt's photo plane would lag far enough behind to be out of the radius of immediate danger.

Deak Parsons and Professor Ramsey then spoke briefly, both confirming my statement about the bomb's tremendous explosive capability.

Anyone who was still skeptical must have been given pause when goggles of the type used by welders, with adjustable Polaroid lenses, were passed out to each member of the three crews. All were warned to have the goggles ready for use as soon as the bomb was released in order to protect their eyes from a flash far brighter than the sun.

The briefing closed with a prayer for our safe return and a rapid end of the war by Chaplain William B. Downey, who, before entering service, had been pastor of the Hope Lutheran Church at Minneapolis.

From the briefing room, we trooped to the nearby mess hall, sometimes called "Dogpatch Inn," for the preflight breakfast. It was 12:30 A.M. and our mess sergeant, Elliott Easterly, had gone all-out for what he recognized as a historic occasion. He had decorated the walls with paper pumpkins and fixed up mimeographed menus decorated with his own drawings and humorous comments on the food.

For this pre-takeoff breakfast, or late supper as some called it, he had put together a menu of "real eggs" and sausage, which he spelled "sassage," as well as rolled oats and apple butter, with milk or coffee to drink.

I ate lightly, even though we would have to subsist on box lunches during our 13-hour flight. However, I drank several cups of black coffee as we sat around the table and tried to make small talk and pretended to be perfectly calm.

When we arrived in the mess hall, the crews of the three weather planes, *Straight Flush, Jabbitt III* and *Full House,* were finishing their meal. They left, after receiving our best wishes. Their takeoff time was to be more than an hour ahead of ours. Each was to fly to one of the designated target cities and let us know by radio if weather conditions were suitable for a visual bomb drop.

When we were about to leave the mess hall, flight surgeon Don Young came to my table and slipped me a small cardboard pillbox.

"I hope you don't have to use these," he said, trying to be cheerful.

"Don't worry. The odds are in our favor," I replied, slipping the box into a pocket of my coveralls.

However casual we tried to be, the subject was grim. The pillbox contained 12 cyanide capsules, one for each member of the *Enola Gay*'s crew.

Except for Deak Parsons and myself, no one on our flight knew about the suicide preparations. Nor would they know unless an emergency would occur forcing us to bail out over enemy territory.

The subject had come up a few days before when Parsons and I, in a private conversation, discussed all the aspects of the mission, including the hazards.

There had been many reports, some of them documented, about the fate of airmen who fell into Japanese hands. Some of the atrocity stories were no doubt propaganda, but it was reliably reported that a few of our fliers had been stoned and beaten to death by angry mobs of Japanese civilians, infuriated by our fire-bombing of their cities. To avoid such a fate, the pilots of disabled American bombing planes tried desperately to reach the sea where friendly submarines, called "dumbos," were waiting to pick up survivors.

There was a further hazard connected with our mission. Assuming that we were forced to bail out after dropping the bomb, and escaped death at the hands of angry mobs, we would no doubt be subjected to intensive questioning and possible torture to wrest from us the secrets of our new weapon.

"What do we do if we're shot down?" Parsons asked me. "I'll be goddamned if I want to fall into their hands."

Confident of a successful flight—overconfident, perhaps—I had not given the matter much thought. Now I had to be realistic. It was a fact of war that we could be shot down.

"I've got a .45 and I might be inclined to use it if I was about to be captured," I said.

Dr. Young joined us about this time and took part in the conversation. A couple of days later, he came around to me and said, "I've been thinking about what you and Deak were saying. I hope it's something that never comes up but—just in case—it would be easier to swallow a pill or capsule than to blow your brains out with a pistol shot."

As a good friend, he found it difficult to discuss the subject, but as an experienced doctor, he considered it his duty to give us advice. He assured me that, with cyanide, there would be no pain.

I slipped one of the pills to Parsons, who put it in a match-box. The others would be passed out only if an emergency occurred, and the crewmen would be told that their use was a matter of discretion. No one was ordering or even urging them to commit suicide to avoid capture.

It was shortly after one o'clock when we left "Dogpatch Inn" and returned to our quarters long enough to pick up our flying gear. I had to gather my smoking equipment which, for a 12-hour flight, consisted of cigars, cigarettes, pipe tobacco, and pipes. Then the four of us jumped in a jeep and headed for the flight line, where a surprise awaited us.

There stood the *Enola Gay*, bathed in floodlights like the star of a Hollywood movie. Motion picture cameras were set up and still photographers were standing by with their equipment. Any Japanese lurking in the surrounding hills—and there were still some who had escaped capture—had to know that something very special was going on.

I had known, of course, that there would be some routine picture-taking before departure, but I was unprepared for this. For the next 20 minutes, we were put through a photo routine to which none of us was accustomed. These were official army photographers, of course, assigned to take pictures for the record of this most important bombing mission of the war.

The entire crew was photographed together beside the plane, and separately for use in hometown newspapers when announcement of the bombing would be made to the press. I was photographed waving from the cockpit, and I think the picture-taking would have continued all night if I hadn't called a halt shortly before two o'clock in order to complete preparations for takeoff.

The weather planes had already taxied away. Their takeoff was at 1:37 A.M.

General Farrell was among those on hand to wish us well. We shook hands and he gave me a few words of encouragement.

Meanwhile, I personally made all the external preflight checks. Although I don't remember the entire checklist today, I made sure that there were no open pieces of cowling, no pitot covers left hanging, and that the tires were inflated and in good condition. I also checked the pavement for telltale evidence of hydraulic leaks and looked into the bottom of the engine cowlings with a flashlight to be sure there was no excessive oil drip.

Twelve of us climbed into the B-29 for the historic flight. The others were Captain Robert A. Lewis of Ridgefield Park, New Jersey, the copilot; Major Thomas W. Ferebee, Mocksville, North Carolina, bombardier; Captain Theodore J. Van Kirk, Northumberland, Pennsylvania, navigator; Lt. Jacob Beser, Baltimore, Maryland, radar countermeasures officer; Navy Captain William S. Parsons, Santa Fe, New Mexico, weaponeer and ordnance officer; Second Lt. Maurice Jeppson, Carson City, Nevada, assistant weaponeer; Sgt. Joe Stiborik, Taylor, Texas, radar operator; Staff Sgt. George R. Caron, Lynbrook, New York, tail gunner; Sgt. Robert H. Shumard, Detroit, Michigan, assistant flight engineer;

Pfc. Richard H. Nelson, Los Angeles, California, radio operator, and Tech. Sgt. Wyatt E. Duzenbury, Lansing, Michigan, flight engineer.

It is interesting that almost every part of the country—both coasts, the Midwest and the South were represented. All of us wore the loose-fitting belted coveralls that were customary for bomber flight crews. With two exceptions, we wore the standard long-peaked flight caps. George Caron was wearing the Brooklyn Dodger cap that had become his trademark. He was a fanatical Dodger fan. A preflight picture shows Dutch Van Kirk in an ordinary overseas cap.

Each of us was equipped with a standard service pistol. When Deak Parsons arrived at the plane without his weapon, he borrowed one from Nick Del Genio, a security officer. Our other gear, which we kept handy to wear only if needed, included parachute harnesses and the heavy flak suits that we kept within reach to wear only if there were signs of anti-aircraft fire when we approached our target.

Once aboard, I settled in the left-hand seat beside Bob Lewis and began to run through the checklist, with Lewis verifying each item. We checked all the instruments and radio equipment and turned on the auxiliary power unit to check the electrical system. Now it was time to start the engines.

First, it was our practice to have a ground crewman pull the engines through by hand. This meant that he turned each of the four propellers through 12 blades, or three revolutions.

I signaled for Duzenbury to start No. 3, the inboard engine on the right side. We always started it first because it was opposite from the side which anyone would approach the plane. Moreover, the two inboard engines were fitted with hydraulic pressure pumps.

Duzenbury ran the engine through 12 blades with the starter before switching on the ignition. It caught immediately, with the customary tongue of flame spitting into the darkness. Next engine to be started was Number 4, the right outboard, then 1 and 2.

With all engines running smoothly, I checked the rise in oil pressure and made sure the fuel pressure was steady, also that the RPM gauges showed all performing at full efficiency. The entire checkout and starting procedure required about 35 minutes, and it was now 2:30. Making sure that the brakes were set, I signaled with both thumbs pointing outward for the ground crewmen to remove the wheel chocks. We were ready to taxi.

Waving to the crowd of almost a hundred well-wishers who were standing by, I gunned the engines and began our taxi jaunt of more than a mile to the southwest end of the runway from which we would take off. Behind me, having followed the same procedures, were Sweeney's *Great Artiste* and Marquardt's No. 91, a plane with a number instead of a name. Following them was McKnight's standby plane, which would fly with us as far as Iwo Jima.

General Farrell and a number of observers climbed into jeeps and headed for the tower to watch the takeoff. Among them was reporter Bill Laurence, disappointed that he could not go along.

The tropical night was warm—and dark. It would be another hour or more before the moon would appear as we flew north. I was confident of a successful takeoff, despite the concern of Parsons and others that had led to the decision to arm the bomb after we became airborne.

The possibility of mechanical trouble in takeoff is never completely outside the subconscious thoughts of a pilot, particularly when handling an airplane that is loaded considerably beyond its design limit, as ours was that night. Nevertheless, my insistence on thorough maintenance minimized my worry as I turned the *Enola Gay* into the runway and prepared for the final warm-up before releasing the brakes for takeoff. Destination: Hiroshima.

29 Using Every Inch of the Runway

More than a mile and a half of chipped coral runway stretched out before me in the darkness. At full warm-up power, the four 2,200-horsepower Wright Cyclones roared in a deafening rhythm that told me they were well tuned for this, their most important mission. The plane trembled and shuddered during the engine run-up. We were heavily loaded, with 7,000 gallons of gasoline and the 9,000-pound bomb.

Some of our people were uneasy because of the many accidents that had occurred on takeoffs from this runway. The blackened skeletons of the four B-29s that had crashed the night before had not yet been cleared away.

I like to think that my reputation for keeping cool in moments such as this was deserved. That's why I was given the assignment. But now I found myself gripping the controls with a nervous tension I hadn't experienced since that first combat mission from Polebrook in 1942.

"Look, Paul," I told myself, "this is just another takeoff. You've done it many times before. No sweat." But there was sweat. I had the moisture in my palms to prove it.

I glanced at my wristwatch. It was 2:45 A.M. I remembered the bombs I had carried to Rouen on my first mission over Europe. Their combined weight was 2,200 pounds, slightly more than a ton. Now I thought of the single four-and-one-half-ton bomb that was cradled in the belly of this much larger plane, behind and below my seat. The explosive material in this bomb weighed less than 50 pounds—yet I had been told that it had the power of 40 million pounds of TNT.

These thoughts tumbled through my mind. Of the crashes that had occurred here recently, none had involved planes of the 509th, largely because I insisted on painstaking inspection of aircraft and engines before and after every flight. If an engine wasn't performing perfectly, the plane didn't leave the ground until the trouble was found and corrected. We were fortunate to have one of the best maintenance units in the whole air force, and it paid off.

Now had come the moment of truth. After 11 months of planning and practice, it was showdown time. Making a quick check to make sure that all the crewmen were at their posts, I called the tower.

"Dimples Eight Two to North Tinian Tower. Ready for takeoff on Runway Able."

The Tower replied promptly. "Dimples Eight Two. Dimples Eight Two. Cleared for takeoff."

The brakes were released and Eighty-Two, now named *Enola Gay*, began its run toward the sea at the end of almost 2 miles of runway.

Special Bombing Mission Number 13 was on its way. We were not consciously superstitious, but for those who may have given it some thought, the bad luck traditionally associated with the number 13 was assumed to be reserved for the enemy.

As always when you are piloting a heavily loaded aircraft, the takeoff run was slow at first. Gradually we picked up speed—75, 100, 125 miles an hour. The end of the runway was approaching fast and the lights on both sides of the paved surface were running out. Instinct told me to ease back on the wheel, but experience had taught me to wait a little longer.

I learned later that my delay caused some uneasy moments among the watchers in the control tower, including Tom Farrell. "I never saw a plane use that much runway," Farrell was quoted as saying. "I thought Tibbets was never going to pull it off." Someone else remarked that I was using "every inch of the runway." Well, not quite—but almost!

Even Bob Lewis, beside me in the cockpit, became concerned, although we had flown together many times and he was familiar with my practice of holding a plane on the runway until it had attained 10 or 12 miles an hour more speed than necessary for

Using Every Inch of the Runway 211

takeoff. He started to ease back on the yoke, but I held firm until we were little more than 100 feet from the end of the pavement.

Thanks to our extra speed—we were at 155 miles an hour—the plane lifted off easily and climbed steadily. Had I yielded to the temptation to struggle into the air the moment we attained minimum flying speed, we would have risked settling back on the runway at the very time we should have started our climb. I was glad to have this cushion of safety in case, by some chance, we had lost an engine at this moment of maximum strain on the four powerplants, all straining at full throttle.

As soon as we were off the ground, navigator Dutch Van Kirk made his first notation in what was to become a historic log. In the space beside "Time Takeoff" he wrote "0245."

His next notation was made ten minutes later. By this time we had passed over nearby Saipan and attained our initial cruising altitude of 4,700 feet. He misspelled the island's name as "Siapan" and correctly listed our heading as 338 degrees, which is almost precisely at the compass point of north northwest. Our indicated airspeed at the time he listed at 213 knots (247 mph). He noted the temperature outside the cabin was 22 degrees Centigrade (72 degrees Fahrenheit).

It was a pleasant tropical night, warm with a light breeze. Around us were cream-puff clouds, their edges outlined by the faint glow of a crescent moon that had just appeared above the horizon to the east.

We were very comfortable inside the plane and the monotonous drone of the engines made me drowsy, for I hadn't had time to steal a wink of sleep on this memorable night. In fact, with all the planning, briefing, and detail work for this mission, sleep had somehow been in short supply for several nights. On a long flight such as this, there would be opportunity to relax, even to doze, but first there were important matters that needed my attention. Back on Tinian, General Farrell was waiting for my radio report on Captain Parsons' difficult task of arming the bomb.

We were only eight minutes off the ground when Parsons and Morris Jeppson lowered themselves into the bomb bay to insert a slug of uranium and the conventional explosive charge into the core of the strange-looking weapon called "Little Boy." Jeppson held the flashlight while Parsons struggled with the mechanism of the bomb, inserting the explosive charge that would send one block of uranium flying into the other to set off the instant chain reaction that would create the atomic explosion.

Working in cramped quarters and handling tooled steel so sharp that it sometimes cut his fingers, as it had in practice the afternoon before, Parsons managed to put the incredible weapon in working order in just 25 minutes.

Through an intercom system that had been extended into the bomb bay, Parsons kept me advised of his progress and I passed the word along to General Farrell, using a prearranged code to describe each stage of his work. Farrell and the scientists who were with him in the communications shack on Tinian were thus able to follow every step of the delicate task that Parson was performing. Every step, that is, until just before the last one.

Static made communication on our low-frequency radio difficult as the distance lengthened between us, and contact was lost just before the job was finished. The progress was such by this time, however, that they had no doubt of Parsons' success.

We were not alone in the sky. Taking off behind us, at two-minute intervals, were *The Great Artiste,* piloted by Chuck Sweeney, and an unnamed B-29 bearing only the number "91," with George Marquardt at the controls. These planes carried no bombs and, being comparatively light, were off the runway without a struggle. In addition to instruments for measuring the effects of the blast, Sweeney's plane carried a number of scientists. Marquardt's photographic plane also had scientists aboard.

A third plane following us was Chuck McKnight's *Top Secret,* the standby aircraft that would land at Iwo Jima, remaining there as a spare in case *Enola Gay* should encounter trouble en route. This possibility was so unlikely that I didn't give it a second thought. If mechanical difficulty had occurred, however, I would have landed at Iwo and transferred, with members of my crew and the bomb to *Top Secret* for the flight to Japan.

On this first stage of the flight no attempt was made to achieve any sort of formation. The other planes were a few miles behind. It was our plan to rendezvous over Iwo Jima and complete the final leg of the mission together.

With the bomb armed, tensions eased among our crew as we settled down for the long flight so familiar to other B-29 men on Tinian, who every night had been carrying incendiaries and bombs from the Marianas to the Japanese home islands. Jake Beser made his way aft, curled up on the deck, and soon fell asleep. I checked by radio with Sweeney, Marquardt and McKnight to make sure that all was well in the other planes.

Before taking a catnap, I decided to check on the men who were assigned to comparative isolation in the back of the plane. To reach them, I had to crawl 30 feet through a tunnel that was only 20 inches in diameter. It was not difficult, for at the age of 30 I was' slender and agile.

At the end of the tunnel, I found Stiborik and Shumard, as well as Bob Caron, who had come forward to the waist from his lonely tail turret station.

"Have you figured out what we're doing?" I asked Caron. All the crewmen had seen the picture of the Nevada test explosion, and knew we were carrying a bomb of great explosive force, but the word "atom" had never been mentioned.

"Hell, colonel, I'd probably get in trouble with the security around here," Caron replied. "I don't want to think."

Like all members of the 509th, he was conscious of the airtight secrecy that had been imposed. No one had been permitted to forget the hush-hush nature of our assignment.

"We're on our way now. You can guess anything you want," I replied.

"Is it a chemist's nightmare?" he asked, recalling a newspaper item he had read a couple of years before about British experiments with a superweapon.

"Not exactly, but you're warm," I said.

We chatted a little longer and I started back through the tunnel, only to feel a tug at my foot. It was Caron.

"Are we splitting atoms today, colonel?" the tail-gunner asked with a twinkle in his eye.

"That's about it," I said, observing to myself that the brighter men in the outfit—and Caron was a sharp one—had managed to figure out the secret in advance. You couldn't live as long as we had in the shadow of the atom without getting an inkling of what we were preparing to do. It was a tribute to the personnel of this well-disciplined organization that, even though they possessed all the evidence they needed to solve the mystery, there was never a clue that anyone had leaked a word of what they correctly assumed our mission to be.

Back in the cockpit, I found it a good time to catch some sleep.

Parsons and Jeppson were hovering over their black box, connected with the bomb, which gave them word on the operational condition of all the weapon's circuitry. Green lights were glowing, which meant that everything was in order.

Now for a brief rest. I had no wish to withdraw even briefly from the excitement of this important flight, but a bone-weariness told me I needed to relax, if only briefly, in order to be reasonably sharp for the work ahead. Having had little sleep in the past 48 hours, I sensed that I was operating on nervous energy alone.

Normally, on long flights in this airplane, it had been my practice to stretch out in the tunnel leading to the rear compartments. This time, however, I felt the need to remain near the controls. I managed to make myself comfortable with the help of my life jacket and a parachute pack that enabled me to stretch out in my seat to a semireclining position. I can't say that I really slept, but I did doze off after a fashion for the better part of an hour. There is nothing better to induce drowsiness than the rhythmical throbbing of four airplane engines.

With my permission, copilot Bob Lewis had taken on the task of jotting down occasional notes on our flight for the benefit of *New York Times* reporter Bill Laurence. I did not look over Bob's shoulder as he penciled his unofficial log on the lined pages of a small notebook, but I was later to learn its contents from a book Laurence wrote.

The first notation was made soon after the bomb assembly had been completed and we were flying smoothly at an altitude of 4,600 feet. He wrote:

"At 45 minutes out of our base everyone is at work. Colonel Tibbets has been hard at work with the usual tasks that belong to the pilot of a B-29. Captain Van Kirk, navigator, and Sergeant Stiborik, radar operator, are in continuous conversation (on the interphone), as they are shooting bearings on the northern Marianas and making radar wind runs."

As I stretched out in the cockpit for my nap, Lewis wrote:

"The colonel, better known as 'Old Bull,' shows signs of a tough day, with all he had to do to get this mission off. He is deserving of a few winks, so I'll have a bite to eat and look after 'George' (the automatic pilot)."

Other members of the crew were also taking catnaps, as is customary on long over-water flights when boredom or weariness have to be conquered. Anyone who has made a nonstop flight of 12 hours will understand the feeling.

I have been asked by friends who read Laurence's book if I was aware of the nickname "Old Bull." Or was it a handle that the men used only behind my back?

I was not only aware of it but was responsible for it. The nickname dates back to a conversation between us regarding Bob's eager-beaver pursuit of female companionship whenever we landed at a new base.

Bob was young, rambunctious, and unmarried, and whenever we made an overnight stop, he would head for the brightest lights in the neighborhood and start searching for girls.

"You remind me of a young bull," I told him one day.

"And what do you mean by that?" he replied.

So I told him a parable.

"There were a young bull and an old bull that had been kept shut up in a farmer's barn all winter. Spring came and the farmer turned them loose. When he opened the door, the young bull leaped outside, pranced around a bit and, looking to the far side of a nearby pasture, saw a whole herd of cows.

"He turned to the old bull and said, 'Come on, let's run over there and make a cow.'

"The old bull, wiser and more experienced, replied: 'Son, let's take it easy and walk over there and make all of them.'"

From then on, I was the "Old Bull" to Bob Lewis.

The casual atmosphere aboard the plane on this flight came as a surprise to Parsons' helper, Lieutenant Jeppson, who was to remark later on the lack of tension during what he knew to be history's most significant bombing mission. Although an air force officer, Jeppson had not flown in combat—he was a technical type—and doubtless expected something quite different, with crewmen nervously sitting on the edge of their seats and perhaps biting their fingernails. That pilots, bombardiers, and radar operators could sleep on their way to the target, particularly this one, taxed his power of comprehension.

After less than an hour of fitful but useful slumber, I was back at the controls. I had told Bob Lewis to awaken me before the time to start our climb as we approached Iwo Jima, but his call wasn't necessary. The knowledge of a task to be done called me from the sack in plenty of time. It was shortly after five o'clock, and the first light of dawn had begun to appear in the east.

In the half hour after I resumed control of the plane, we ascended gradually from 4,600 to 5,500 feet. Then, at 5:34, I began our climb in earnest. Twenty minutes later, we reached our new cruising altitude of 9,300 feet.

Through broken clouds ahead, the island of Iwo Jima came into view. Iwo Jima! The name had already come to signify a historic milestone in America's relentless island-hopping march toward victory in the Pacific.

Iwo was a relative newcomer to the world's geography. Thrown up from the bottom of the sea by a great volcanic upheaval, it had been home for a mere 1,000 Japanese in the years before the war. They made their living mining sulfur.

Two features stood out on the island's treeless landscape as we approached: Meatgrinder Hill and Mount Suribachi, the now extinct volcano. The capture of these elevations had accounted for most of the 5,000 lives lost by Marines in their conquest of Iwo Jima six months before. The 509th had still been in the States when this battle occurred, and we had been thrilled by Joe Rosenthal's widely published photograph of five Marines raising the American flag on Suribachi's 550-foot summit.

Now below us was the island for which so much blood had been shed. More than 100,000 soldiers—82,000 American invaders and 26,000 Japanese defenders—had struggled for more than a month over this 8 square miles of volcanic soil. For the Japanese, dug into caves from which they were routed or incinerated by flamethrowers, the toll was 25,000 dead, with 1,000 taken prisoner, many of them wounded.

Why was such a small and remote piece of real estate worth the toll of 5,500 American dead and 20,000 wounded? To understand the strategic importance of Iwo Jima, one need only look at a map of the western Pacific. The island, which had become Japan's prime defensive outpost, lay directly on the route our bombers flew on their missions from the Marianas to Tokyo and other cities in the enemy homeland. Without it, our own mission would have been considerably more difficult. The Japanese had built two runways and were constructing a third at the time the Marines made their amphibious attack on the morning of February 19. With these in our possession, our planes were spared the need of fighting off interceptor planes on their way to and from Japan. Moreover, many American bombers that had been crippled in combat over Japan were saved through emergency landings on Iwo. By the end of the war, 2,400 B-29s had found haven there.

Iwo Jima had special importance for me this day because it was the rendezvous point with Sweeney and Marquardt, who were about 10 miles behind the *Enola Gay*. I decided to circle Mount Suribachi at about 9,300 feet. I was never good at remembering names, particularly those of foreign origin, so I got on the microphone and gave instructions, as I remember them, something like this:

"I'm going to come in and go over that thing and I'm going to make a left turn at slow cruise. I want you guys to come in by the time I make a 360 degree turn and I want you to slide into position on my wings. Then we'll set a course to our target."

At this point, we were precisely on schedule. I made my circle, and by the time I got around both of the other planes were in position. Van Kirk noted in his official log that we arrived at Iwo at 5:55 and departed at 6:07 after circling for our rendezvous. Bob Lewis made another entry in his log for the benefit of Bill Laurence and the world press. He mentioned our new altitude and observed that we would maintain it "until we are about one hour away from the Empire" (the word we used to designate the enemy's home islands).

While we were circling, Chuck McKnight took leave of us and dropped down for a landing on one of Iwo's long runways. His was the standby plane, needed only if we encountered difficulty. But there was no problem. Our engines were behaving perfectly and McKnight, with his crew, was destined to spend the next few hours on the ground, awaiting word that our mission had succeeded.

As we took leave of Iwo Jima, we were slightly more than three hours away from our target.

Our target? We weren't sure at this time where we were going or on what unlucky city our atomic lighting would strike. It would be one of three: Hiroshima, Kokura, or Nagasaki.

30 "My God, What Have We Done?"

The sun flamed red above the eastern horizon almost at the moment we completed our Iwo Jima rendezvous. We had viewed the island through the half-light of predawn and now we were winging toward Japan, surrounded by scattered clouds that were edged with reddish gold from the slanting light of the newly risen sun.

Our course changed leftward by 14 degrees until we were at a compass heading of 322–325, or almost northwest. This would bring us to the island of Shikoku, beyond which lay the city of Hiroshima near the southern tip of Japan's main island of Honshu. Whether this industrial city would become our target depended on the word we would soon receive from our three weather planes, which had taken off from Tinian a little more than an hour ahead of us.

These were *Straight Flush*, piloted by Major Claude Eatherly, which headed for Hiroshima; *Jabbitt III*, commanded by Major John Wilson, en route to the secondary target, Kokura; and *Full House*, Major Ralph Taylor's plane, which had been assigned to check the weather over Nagasaki.

If the first priority target was found to be obscured by clouds, we would turn westward to Kokura or Nagasaki on the coast of Kyushu, a somewhat smaller island to the southwest.

We began to have some misgivings when a thin layer of clouds appeared beneath us. Our orders were for a visual bombing run.

Even though radar sighting had proved accurate throughout the war, it had been decided that this bomb should be dropped only if the target was clearly visible. If weather conditions proved unfavorable over all three designated targets we would return with the bomb, but only after it had been disarmed by Deak Parsons.

On this stage of the flight, I was smoking my pipe with a little more intensity than usual. The popular notion of a pipe smoker is that of a person not easily upset or flustered. I like to think this impression is correct, for I smoked pipes for years with considerable pleasure.

Perhaps the patience required to keep a pipe fired up contributes to the belief that the smoker must be phlegmatic and unflappable. On the Hiroshima flight, I kept the fire going in my Kaywoodie briar most of the way. There's something relaxing about a long flight when you prop your feet up and puff away while surrounding yourself with the smoke from an aromatic tobacco. My favorite Bond Street brand was hard to find in the Pacific, and when it did show up it was sometimes moldy, but I smoked it anyway. It came in a can, like Prince Albert, and one can would usually last a full day.

I was a chimney in those days. I would start in the morning, as soon as I climbed out of bed, with a cup of coffee and a half-dozen cigarettes. After that, I turned to the pipe and kept it going most of the day. After dinner in the evening, I would switch to cigars. Don't ask why this triple-nicotine habit didn't wreck my health, but it didn't.

I had bought a supply of cigars, sufficient to last several months, while we were training in Cuba. I kept them fresh by storing them in the refrigerator, which usually contained more cigars than food.

At 7:30, Deak Parsons made some adjustments on the console that controlled the bomb's intricate circuitry. He informed us that the bomb was armed and ready. Bob Lewis wrote on his tablet: "The bomb is now alive. It is a funny feeling knowing it is right in back of you. Knock wood."

Bob expressed the fear that we might encounter weather of such turbulence en route that it would set off the bomb. If so, there wouldn't have been a scrap of aluminum left or a fragment of humanity. The airplane and all of us who were in it would have been atomized. I had no such unpleasant concerns because, even though the mechanics of nuclear fission were a mystery to me, I was aware through briefings at Los Alamos that the system could not be triggered except by the firing of a powerful explosive within the bomb itself.

The next hour was one of suspense as we droned toward the enemy homeland. Without waiting for the weather word, I climbed slowly toward what was to be our bombing altitude of 30,700 feet.

We were almost at this level when, at 8:30, the awaited message came in code from Eatherly's *Straight Flush*, high over Hiroshima. As tapped out by Sgt. Pasquale Baldasaro aboard that plane, and taken down on his pad by our radio operator, Dick Nelson, the message consisted of these cryptic letter-figure combinations: "Y-3, Q-3, B-2, C-1."

Bending over Nelson as he wrote, I translated the message to mean that the cloud cover was less than three-tenths at all altitudes. "C-1" was advice, quite unnecessary under the circumstances, to bomb the primary target.

After acknowledging the message, I returned to the controls and strained for the first sight of land ahead. Sweeney and Marquardt, whose planes were accompanying the *Enola Gay* in formation, also received the message and there was no need to break the radio silence that our little group had maintained.

Over the intercom, I gave the word to members of our crew. "It's Hiroshima," I said.

Within a few minutes, the island of Shikoku came into view. It was 8:30 when we arrived over the shoreline. Our recent tactic of sending flights of one, two, or three planes into the area without dropping bombs was paying dividends. The Japanese had become indifferent toward American aircraft flying at high altitudes on missions they did not understand. They saw no need to waste scarce ammunition, or fuel for interceptor planes, on these apparently harmless visitors.

We flew across Shikoku toward a narrow body of water called the Iyo Sea. Our destination lay just beyond.

Dutch Van Kirk's navigation had been accurate. The airplane was functioning well and, from the green lights on the black box over which Parsons and Jeppson hovered, it was apparent that the bomb circuitry was in order. Parsons tested it frequently.

Below were the scattered clouds that the weather plane had

reported—not enough to hinder a visual bomb drop. We were glad that we didn't have to accept an alternate because this was the target for which we had prepared exhaustively for the past week. We had studied maps and aerial photographs of the approach path and the city of Hiroshima. We knew every feature of the terrain over which we would be flying. And now the Japanese landscape was unfolding below us just as the pictures had promised.

We were eight minutes away from the scheduled time of bomb release when the city came into view. The early morning sunlight glistened off the white buildings in the distance. Although I was sure this was our target, there were other cities in the area and I wanted my judgment corroborated. I remembered a pharmacist of my acquaintance who always required an assistant to verify the label on every bottle before mixing a prescription. "Do you all agree that's Hiroshima?" I asked the other crewmen. They promptly concurred.

Now it became our task to find that geographical position on the ground from which the actual bomb run was to begin. This was the Initial Point, or I.P., as it is known to the bombardier. Our I.P., an easily identifiable landmark that stood out in the aerial photos, was 15½ miles east of the point in the heart of the city which was to be our target.

Just south and west of the I.P., which we spotted without difficulty, I made a leftward turn of 60 degrees and came over the point at a heading of 264 degrees, flying almost due west. The reason for this approach, and the reason we had chosen an I.P. to the east of our target, was that the prevailing winds in this area were known to be from the west. It was desirable, from the standpoint of accuracy, to make a bomb run against the wind.

On this important morning, however, the wind was from the south at 10 miles an hour. This was an unpredictable variance, of course. In our planning, we had played the odds and lost.

But Tom Ferebee was an old hand at dropping bombs with the wind, against it, or in a crosswind. From long experience, he knew what a falling bomb would do under almost any condition, and he knew how to crank all the right information into his Norden bomb sight. It made little difference to him that we were delivering a bomb of tremendous size, unlike any that had ever been dropped in warfare. Its shape was even unlike the "pumpkins" with which we had practiced over the Utah desert. As I have explained, it had been decided that the first bomb would be as foolproof as possible. Thus the more slender uranium "Little Boy" was chosen over the more complicated plutonium "Fat Man," which was to be used against Nagasaki later the same week.

Although by now we were all concentrating on the bomb run, Dutch Van Kirk found time to note in the plane's log that eight large ships were anchored in a nearby harbor. We were relieved, of course, that no enemy planes had come up to challenge us and that no flak was visible, although frankly, from the experience of our reconaissance flights into the area, we had expected none.

As we zeroed in on the target ahead, I took the microphone and reminded all the crewmen to put on their goggles. They were to keep them poised on their foreheads until the bomb was released, at which time the heavy dark Polaroids were to be slipped over their eyes to protect them from the blinding glare of the bomb blast, which was calculated to have the intensity of 10 suns. In Sweeney's *Great Artiste* and Marquardt's No. 91, which had dropped back a bit during our approach, the same order was being given.

All that was necessary, upon reaching the I.P., was to fly the predetermined heading, with calculated allowance for the direction (170 degrees) and velocity (8 knots) of the wind. Since we were flying under visual conditions, the problem was simplified. The three-minute run gave Ferebee time to kill the drift and establish a perfectly stable platform for release of the bomb.

Deak Parsons came forward and looked over my shoulder and so did Van Kirk, who was exchanging conversation with Ferebee in the nose of the plane. Navigator and bombardier compared notes and agreed that our ground speed was 285 knots (330 mph) and the drift to the right required an 8-degree correction. Adjustments were made to the bomb sight, which was now engaged to the autopilot for the bomb run. Ferebee, Van Kirk, and I were working as a team, as we had many times before over Europe and North Africa. As we approached the city, we strained our eyes to find the designated aiming point.

From a distance of 10 miles, Ferebee suddenly said, "Okay, I've got the bridge." He pointed dead ahead, where it was just becoming visible. Van Kirk, looking over his shoulders, agreed. "No question about it," he said, scanning an airphoto and comparing it with what he was seeing.

The T-shaped bridge was easy to spot. Even though there were many other bridges in this sprawling city, there was no other bridge that even slightly resembled it.

Van Kirk's job was finished so he went back and sat down, hooking up his safety belt and getting on the interphone.

In this tense moment, Lewis found time to scratch a few more words in his log: "As we are approaching our primary, Ferebee, Van Kirk, and Stiborik are coming into their own, while the Colonel and I are standing by and giving the boys what they want."

Now it was up to Tom and me. We were only 90 seconds from bomb release when I turned the plane over to him on autopilot.

"It's all yours," I told him, removing my hands from the controls and sliding back a bit in my seat in a not very successful effort to relax. My eyes were fixed on the center of the city, which shimmered in the early morning sunlight.

In the buildings and on the streets there were people, of course, but from 6 miles up they were invisible. To the men who fly the bombers, targets are inanimate, consisting of buildings, bridges, docks, factories, railroad yards. The tragic consequences to humanity are erased from one's thoughts in wartime because war itself is a human tragedy.

Of course, one hopes that civilians will have the good sense to seek protection in bomb shelters. In the case of Hiroshima, I was to learn later that Eatherly's weather plane, over the city three-quarters of an hour before our arrival, had set off air raid sirens but, when nothing happened, ours were ignored.

As we approached the Aiming Point, I watched for the first signs of anti-aircraft fire or for the approach of fighter planes that might have been sent up to intercept us. I was familiar with such opposition in my combat missions over Europe and North Africa. There was no ack-ack, presumably because the enemy's anti-aircraft artillery was ineffective against airplanes flying at our altitude. As for interceptor aircraft, they were seldom sent up these days against planes that appeared to be flying only a reconnaissance mission.

By this time, Tom Ferebee was pressing his left eye against the viewfinder of the bomb sight, using a headrest we had devised at Wendover to make sure that he was always in the same position.

"We're on target," he said, confirming that the sighting and release mechanism were synchronized, so that the drop would take place automatically at a precalculated point in our bomb run.

At 17 seconds after 9:14 A.M., just 60 seconds before the scheduled bomb release, he flicked a toggle switch that activated a high-pitched radio tone. This tone, ominous under the circumstances, sounded in the headphones of the men aboard our plane and the two airplanes that were with us; it was also heard by the men in the three weather planes, which were already more than 200 miles away on their return flight to Tinian.

A moment before, Bob Lewis had made this notation in his informal log of the flight: "There will be a short intermission while we bomb our target."

Exactly one minute after it began, the radio tone ceased and at the same instant there was the sound of the pneumatic bomb-bay doors opening automatically. Out tumbled "Little Boy," a misnamed package of explosive force infinitely more devastating than any bomb or cluster of bombs ever dropped before.

By my watch, the time was 9:15 plus 17 seconds. In Hiroshima, it was 8:15. We had crossed a time zone in our flight from Tinian.

Much has been made of the fact that we arrived over the target and released our bomb after a 2,000-mile flight just 17 seconds behind the prearranged target time of 9:15. "Uncanny," wrote one correspondent, who mentioned my reputation as "a perfectionist." Actually, we pretended to be upset over the 17-second error, for operational perfection had indeed been the goal of the entire 509th.

With the release of the bomb, the plane was instantly 9,000 pounds lighter. As a result, its nose leaped up sharply and I had to act quickly to execute the most important task of the flight: to put as much distance as possible between our plane and the point at which the bomb would explode.

The 155 degree diving turn to the right, with its 60 degree bank, put a great strain on the airplane and its occupants. Bob Caron, in his tail-gunner's station, had a wild ride that he described as something like being the last man in a game of crack-the-whip.

When we completed the turn, we had lost 1,700 feet and were heading away from our target with engines at full power. Midway through the turn, with its steep bank, it was necessary to back off on the ailerons (other pilots will understand this) to avoid the danger of a roll. I was flying this biggest of all bombers as if it were a fighter plane.

Bob Lewis and I had slipped our dark glasses over our eyes, as I had directed the other crewmen to do, but we promptly discovered that they made it impossible to fly the plane through this difficult getaway maneuver because the instrument panel was blacked out. We pushed the glasses back on our foreheads in a what-the-hell manner, realizing that we would be flying away from the actual flash when it occurred. Ferebee, in the bombardier's position in the nose of the plane, became so fascinated with watching the bomb's free-fall that he forgot all about the glasses.

At the moment we released the bomb, the bomb-bay doors of Chuck Sweeney's plane also opened and out fell three instrument packages, whose purpose was to measure the effects of the detonation in terms of shock waves, radioactivity, and the like. These instruments, which sent back the results by radio, were suspended from parachutes that opened soon after their fall began. Their appearance accounted for an early erroneous report, from Japanese witnesses, that the bomb had been dropped by parachute.

For me, struggling with the controls, the 43 seconds from bomb release to explosion passed quickly. To some in the plane, it seemed an eternity. Jeppson was quoted as saying that he had counted down the seconds in his mind, apparently too fast, and had the sickening feeling that the bomb was a dud.

Whatever our individual thoughts, it was a period of suspense. I was concentrating so intently on flying the airplane that the flash did not have the impact on my consciousness that one might think, even though it did light up the interior of the plane for a long instant.

There was a startling sensation other than visual, however, that I remember quite vividly to this day. My teeth told me, more emphatically than my eyes, of the Hiroshima explosion.

At the moment of the blast, there was a tingling sensation in my mouth and the very definite taste of lead upon my tongue. This, I was told later by scientists, was the result of electrolysis—an interaction between the fillings in my teeth and the radioactive forces that were loosed by the bomb.

"Little Boy" exploded at the preset altitude of 1,890 feet above the ground, but Bob Caron in the tail was the only one aboard our plane to see the incredible fireball that, in its atom-splitting fury, was a boiling furnace with an inner temperature calculated to be one hundred million degrees Fahrenheit.

Caron, looking directly at the flash through glasses so dense that the sun penetrated but faintly, thought for a moment that he must have been blinded. Ferebee, without glasses but facing in the opposite direction from a relatively exposed position, felt as if a giant flashbulb had gone off a few feet from his face.

I continued my course from the target, awaiting the shock wave, which required almost a minute to reach us. We were racing eastward away from Hiroshima, as was Chuck Sweeney in *The Great Artiste*. Sweeney had made a similar 155 degree turn, but to the left, as soon as he had dropped the instrument packages. Because his plane was charged with the photographic assignment, Marquardt had lagged behind, with movie and still cameras poised to make a record on film of the historic scene.

We must have been 9 miles from the point of the explosion when the shock wave reached us. This was the moment for which we had been bracing ourselves. Would the plane withstand the blow? The scientists were confident that it would, yet they admitted there were some aspects of the nuclear weapon's behavior about which they were not quite certain.

Caron, the only man aboard the plane with an immediate view of the awesome havoc we had created, tried to describe it to us. Suddenly he saw the shock wave approaching at the speed of sound—almost 1,100 feet a second. Condensing moisture from the heated air at the leading edge of the shock wave made it quite visible, just as one sees shimmering air rising from the ground on a hot, humid day.

Before Caron could warn us to brace ourselves, the wave struck the plane with violent force. Our B-29 trembled under the impact and I gripped the controls tightly to keep us in level flight. From my experience of flying through enemy flak over targets in Europe and Africa, I found the effect to be much like that produced by an anti-aircraft shell exploding near the plane.

In fact, that's what Deak Parsons first thought had happened. "It's flak," he shouted, then realized like the rest of us that it was the result we had been told to expect. At a news conference next day, Bob Lewis told reporters that it felt as if some giant had struck the plane with a telephone pole. Soon after the first shock, a second struck us. It was of lesser impact, caused by what the scientists described as "an echo effect."

Now that I knew we were safe from the effects of the blast, I began circling so that we could view the results. For the record, I announced over the intercom, "Fellows, you have just dropped the first atomic bomb in history."

Caron had been trying to describe what he saw, meanwhile using a hand-held K-20 aerial camera to photograph the scene. He was not a professional photographer and only a few of his pictures proved useful. But many excellent shots were obtained from the photo plane that accompanied us.

Although Caron had told of a mushroom-shaped cloud, and said that it seemed to be "coming toward us," we were not prepared for the awesome sight that met our eyes as we turned for a heading that would take us alongside the burning, devastated city.

The giant purple mushroom, which the tail-gunner had described, had already risen to a height of 45,000 feet. 3 miles above our own altitude, and was still boiling upward like something terribly alive. It was a frightening sight, and even though we were several miles away, it gave the appearance of something that was about to engulf us.

Even more fearsome was the sight on the ground below. At the base of the cloud, fires were springing up everywhere amid a turbulent mass of smoke that had the appearance of bubbling hot tar. If Dante had been with us in the plane, he would have been terrified! The city we had seen so clearly in the sunlight a few minutes before was now an ugly smudge. It had completely disappeared under this awful blanket of smoke and fire.

A feeling of shock and horror swept over all of us.

"My God!" Lewis wrote as the final entry in his log.

He was later quoted as having said. "My God, what have we done?" These words were put in my mouth by the authors of the movie script for *Above and Beyond.*

Whatever exclamations may have passed our lips at this historic moment, I cannot accurately remember. We were all appalled and what we said was certain to have reflected our emotions and our disbelief.

It is unfortunate that there is no way to reconstruct, with

complete accuracy, the excitement that seized all of us aboard the *Enola Gay*. At my instructions, Jake Beser had used a wire recorder to make a record of everything said aboard the plane during the bomb run, and comments from all crew members after the bomb drop. He turned the spool of recording wire over to an information officer upon our return to Tinian, and it has never been heard of since.

As we viewed the awesome spectacle below, we were sobered by the knowledge that the world would never be the same. War, the scourge of the human race since time began, now held terrors beyond belief. I reflected to myself that the kind of war in which I was engaged over Europe in 1942 was now outdated.

But as I swung southward on the return flight to our base, the feeling of tenseness gave way to one of relief. Our mission, for which we had practiced diligently for so long, had been successful. All doubts about the mystery weapon had been removed.

"I think this is the end of the war," I said to Bob Lewis as I tamped the tobacco in my pipe bowl and lighted it up once more.

I jotted down a few words on a note pad, tore off the sheet, and handed it to Dick Nelson for radio transmission back to headquarters. In previously agreed-upon phrases, it simply advised that the primary target had been bombed visually with good results and that there had been no fighter opposition or anti-aircraft fire.

Meanwhile Captain Parsons was preparing his own report, containing more detail even though quite brief. Transmitted in code, his message said: "82 V 670. Able, Line 1, Line 2, Line 6, Line 9."

General Farrell, on Tinian, translated it for members of his staff and the scientists who surrounded him: "Clear cut, successful in all respects. Visual effects greater than Trinity. Hiroshima. Conditions normal in airplane following delivery. Proceeding to regular base."

The message was all Farrell needed in order to pass the momentous word along to an anxiously awaiting General Groves and his staff in the Pentagon. A few hours later, while lunching with a group of enlisted men aboard the cruiser U.S.S. *Augusta* on the way home from the Potsdam conference, President Truman got the news and exclaimed, "This is the greatest thing in history."

31 The World Gets the News

The frightful mushroom cloud that we left behind was still visible for an hour and a half as we flew southward from Hiroshima. Actually, we were almost 400 miles away when Bob Caron, who had the best view from his tail-gunner's roost, reported that the cloud could no longer be seen.

We were still groping for words to describe what we had witnessed. In our experience, we had watched many conventional bombs explode, creating what appeared to be tiny puffs of smoke thousands of feet below. But this spectacular consequence of a single bomb explosion was beyond our understanding.

Bob Lewis echoed the thoughts of all of us when he wrote, "I had a strong conviction that it was possible, by the time we landed, that the Japs would have thrown in the sponge. Because of the total destruction, I didn't feel there was room for anything but complete surrender."

Whatever tension had existed on the way to Hiroshima was now over. We talked about the end of the war and how soon we would be going home.

Another inhibition was lifted. "Atom" was no longer a word to be avoided. In answer to many questions, I told of the Manhattan Project that had produced this incredible weapon. Knowing something about radiation and recalling that he had heard that it could cause sterility, Tom Ferebee wondered aloud if we all might have become sterile from having been so close to the explosion. Deak Parsons assured him that such danger was remote.

Tom need not have worried. He and a majority of the other crewmen fathered children in numbers well above the national average in the years to come.

After more than an hour of lively conversation, in which there was speculation about the damage and the casualties our bomb had caused, fatigue began to set in. The rest of the ride back to base was a bit like a slumber party as most of us took advantage of the opportunity to stretch out, alternately, and catch some sleep.

It had been an easy mission, one of the most routine I had ever flown, except for the strain and anxiety occasioned by my knowledge of its overwhelming importance and the consequent need for precision in the bomb drop and the unusual escape maneuver. There had also been in my mind the haunting thought that we were playing with a new kind of fire—one that was generated by the elemental forces of the universe.

We had only the word of scientists about the effect of the explosion and our own safety. Only one atomic bomb had ever been set off, in New Mexico just three weeks ago. But it was different from the one we carried. Its explosive material was plutonium. Ours was uranium. The New Mexico test was near ground level. Our was set off at an altitude of 1,890 feet. Even the triggering device was entirely different. My misgivings were largely offset by a blind faith that is the last resort of the ignorant.

Now, on the return flight, I reflected on the wonders of science and rejoiced that the new weapon had surely made future war unthinkable. Just as the spear had been more deadly than the club, the bow and arrow a more formidable weapon than the spear, gunpowder had made the bow and arrow obsolete. Each technological advance in weaponry had made war more hideous but so far had not persuaded mankind to abandon this means of settling quarrels between peoples. Now certainly we had developed the ultimate argument for keeping the peace.

As we approached Tinian, Sweeney and Marquardt reduced speed so that the *Enola Gay* would land well ahead of them. They acted out of consideration for the fact that our plane would be met by a large reception committee. It was 2:58 P.M. when we touched

The World Gets the News 231

down on the long runway from which we had taken off with such apparent effort 12 hours before.

If I had given it any thought, I would have known that our arrival would be the occasion for some sort of ceremony. But I was unprepared for the welcome that awaited us when, after landing, I taxied to the hard stand from which we had departed in the early morning hours. Our welcoming committee consisted of more than 200 officers and enlisted men, including practically all the ranking military brass that could be mustered in the Marianas at the time.

In front were General Carl Spaatz, commander of the Strategic Air Force; General Nathan Twining, chief of the Marianas Air Force; General Thomas F. Farrell, deputy director of the atomic development project; Rear Admiral W. R. E. Purnell, also of the atomic staff, and General John Davies, 313th Wing Commander.

For ceremonial purposes, I was required to descend first from the plane and was caught completely by surprise when General Spaatz stepped forward to shake hands and pin the Distinguished Service Cross on my rumpled flight coveralls.

Although I managed quickly to palm the pipe I was smoking, I was hardly ready for the formality the occasion demanded, but no one seemed to mind. One after another shook my hands or slapped my back, jubilant over the success of our mission and wanting to hear more about the bomb and the destruction it had caused. Silver stars were later presented to other members of my crew and to the crewmen from the other planes that took part in the mission.

With the welcoming formalities completed, we piled into jeeps and headed for the Quonset hut that housed the officers club of the 509th for a formal debriefing conducted by Hazen Payette who, in civilian life, was a Detroit lawyer. There were food and drink, the latter including bourbon and lemonade, on the tables.

Before taking our seats, each of us submitted to a hasty medical checkup by Colonel James F. Nolan, the physician and radiologist, whose main concern was to learn if we had absorbed any radiation. He gave special attention to Ferebee's eyes after learning that the bombardier, in an exposed position, had neglected to don his goggles before the blast.

It was soon apparent that the interviewers were skeptical of our descriptions. Surely, they thought, we must be exaggerating the size of the mushroom cloud and the fact that the whole city was almost instantly obliterated from sight by the boiling mass of smoke and fire. We knew how Marco Polo must have felt when he returned from Cathay and found people of his native Venice unwilling to believe his descriptions of the Far East and its riches.

There was laughter at an exchange between Payette and Dutch Van Kirk, the navigator.

"Dutch, what time was the drop made?" Payette asked.

After consulting his log, Dutch replied: "At 091517 K." This indicated 17 seconds after 9:15 A.M., Tinian time.

"Why were you late?" the questioner asked with a straight face, knowing that the drop was scheduled for 9:15. No one would have seriously complained if we had been 17 minutes behind schedule, let alone 17 seconds. For a flight of almost 1,500 miles, such on-time performance was considered little less than miraculous.

General Groves regarded the performance as perfect. Autographing for me a copy of his book, *Now It Can Be Told*, published in 1962, Groves wrote, "I never worried about your carrying out your part of the project. Your performance and that of the 509th was perfect."

Tom Ferebee drew another laugh when he explained that he released the bomb 13½ feet northeast of the T-bridge that had been the designated aiming point!

The questioning went on for two hours as we sat around the tables of the officers' club, and the opinion was frequently expressed that we had ended the war, at least for all practical purposes. No Japanese leader in his right mind would now hesitate to accept the terms of the newly announced Potsdam ultimatum, calling for unconditional surrender. But those of us who rationalized this way did not take into account the fanaticism of the enemy militarists who tried for the next 24 hours to keep the truth of the Hiroshima disaster from the Japanese people.

A news bulletin on the Tokyo radio that evening said, "A few B-29s hit Hiroshima city at 8:20 A.M. August 6 and fled after dropping incendiaries and bombs. The extent of the damage is now under survey." Even the next morning, reference was being made to incendiaries that caused "some damage," but by midafternoon there were more accurate details. "It seems that the enemy used a new-type bomb," the radio said.

That the Japanese should try to minimize the loss of an entire city seemed incredible and no doubt influenced Washington's decision to authorize the use of a second atomic bomb without delay. Such a one-two punch, we were quite sure, would bring even the most stubborn war lord to the peace table.

Our own reports of the devastating effect of the bomb were confirmed the same night when two of our photo planes, which had flown over Hiroshima four hours after the bomb blast, returned to report that it was impossible to obtain clear pictures of the damage because the city still lay under a dense blanket of smoke, with fires burning everywhere.

The next morning, the best-kept secret of the war was no longer a secret. Over the radio came word that President Truman, then on his way home from Potsdam, had announced the dropping of an atomic bomb.

It was electrifying news in all corners of the world. The rest of the airmen on our island of Tinian were flabbergasted. Their sarcastic verse that "the 509th is winning the war" had come true. We were no longer pampered people with undeserved special privileges, but actual heroes, even to those who had ridiculed our special status on the island.

The truth, concealed from the people of Japan for the past 24 hours, was beamed to that country by the Armed Forces Radio. Even as we started preparing the second bomb for delivery on August 9, a date that had now been agreed upon, an all-out effort was made to persuade the enemy that it was useless to continue the war.

The army's psychological branch in the Pacific pulled out all the stops. Radio Saipan broadcast surrender appeals while airplanes with loudspeakers flew low over enemy cities to carry the message of the atomic destruction they faced by refusal to give up.

The Office of War Information printed several million leaflets and a Japanese-language newspaper containing one of Sergeant Caron's pictures of the atomic cloud rising over Hiroshima. These were dropped on cities all over Japan. The leaflet carried this message:

To the Japanese people: America asks that you take immediate heed of what we say on this leaflet.

We are in possession of the most destructive explosive ever devised by man. A single one of our newly-developed atomic bombs is actually the equivalent in explosive power to what 2,000 of our giant B-29s can carry on a single mission. This awful fact is one for you to ponder and we solemnly assure you that it is grimly accurate.

We have just begun to use this weapon against your homeland. If you still have any doubt, make inquiry as to what happened to Hiroshima when just one atomic bomb fell on that city.

Before using this bomb to destroy every resource of the military by which they are prolonging this useless war, we ask that you now petition the Emperor to end the war. Our President has outlined for you the thirteen consequences of an honorable surrender. We urge that you accept these consequences and begin work of building a new, better and peace-loving Japan.

You should take these steps now to cease military resistance. Otherwise, we shall resolutely employ this bomb and all our other superior weapons to promptly and forcefully end the war.

Evacuate your cities now!

Meanwhile, there was jubilation back home as American newspapers carried page after page of information about the bomb, as well as pictures of the devastation at Hiroshima. Everyone sensed that four years of war were coming to an end.

Dad heard the news by radio at his home in Miami and immediately suspected that this must have been the secret mission for which I had been preparing for almost a year. He called mother, who was at a neighbor's, and almost immediately the phone began to ring.

Soon newspaper reporters were at the door. Next came radio people. Then more newsmen.

"Did you know anything about it in advance?" they were asked.

"Not a thing," dad answered truthfully.

Having learned that the *Enola Gay* had been named for my mother, the reporters centered their questioning on her.

The *Miami Herald* carried my picture on the first page and a story about me with a headline that read, "Atom Bomb Pilot's Kin Surprised."

"Probably the most surprised people in the world at the news that Colonel Paul W. Tibbets Jr. of Miami, Fla., piloted the Superfortress which dropped the first atomic bomb on Japan were his parents," the paper said. " 'It sure was a complete surprise to us!' declared Capt. Paul W. Tibbets Sr. Tuesday night in his home at 1629 S.W. Sixth St."

A weekly feature paper, *The Floridian,* devoted most of its front cover to my picture, with a headline story that identified me as "Florida's Buck Rogers." It was mentioned that I had visited my parents in Miami the previous month, just before leaving for the Pacific.

Mother was quoted as saying that she and dad knew I was engaged in a secret mission but didn't know its nature. "If that bomb brings the Japs to time it will save the lives of our boys," she said. "When he was leaving, I told him, 'You be back for Christmas dinner.' Maybe he will be now."

In Cincinnati, it was discovered that I had attended the university's medical school there, and the newspapers interviewed my old friends Dr. and Mrs. Harry Crum.

"Paul didn't like studying medicine at all," Mrs. Crum was quoted as saying. "He ate, slept and lived aviation."

Reporters also interviewed my wife, Lucy, and son, Paul III, at their home in Columbus, Georgia. "I think my daddy is a grand guy," four-year-old Paul was quoted as saying in news dispatches. It seems just about everyone who ever knew me was interviewed except my 16-month-old son, Gene, who was pictured in the newspapers with his mother and brother.

From Quincy, Illinois, came a news dispatch quoting my 78-year-old grandmother, Mrs. Fifer, as saying, "It's all so sudden that I'm pretty excited."

One Florida newspaper carried an item to the effect that "a Miami Beach group is readying a petition which will urge Col. Paul W. Tibbets to become a candidate for governor in 1948."

That was one brainstorm that, I'm happy to say, never got beyond the talking stage. My preference for flying airplanes was as strong as ever and I planned to remain in the air force. I had no more ambition to enter politics than I did, eight years before, to become a doctor.

Back on Tinian, the second atomic bomb was being assembled even as the world was learning about the first.

It was altogether different in looks as well as explosive content.

This was the shape with which we were most familiar—a "pumpkin" like those we had been dropping in practice. Its fissionable material was plutonium, an artificially manufactured substance derived from uranium. The method of firing was also different.

"Fat Man," as this one was called to distinguish it from "Little Boy," consisted of two hemispheres of the new element that, when joined, formed a ball of plutonium that fell short of creating a critical mass. Inside the ball was an activator and around the plutonium sphere were 64 cloverleaf lens molds, wired so that all would be fired at the same instant, putting pressure from all sides on the sphere and compressing it into a critical explosive mass.

Unless the Japanese capitulated in the meantime, as some optimistically thought they would, we had scheduled the second bomb drop for Thursday, August 9. The Hiroshima flight had occurred on Monday. We made this decision Tuesday morning at a conference on Guam. Accompanying me to the meeting with Generals Spaatz and LeMay were Admiral Purnell, Captain Parsons, and Major John F. Moynahan, the 509th's public information officer.

The use of a second bomb the same week was calculated to indicate that we had an endless supply of this superweapon for use against one Japanese city after another. Actually, a third atomic bomb would not be ready until September, but we were confident two would be enough. If indeed a third had been necessary, there was serious discussion of making Tokyo the next target. Although much of that city had been burned out by incendiaries, it was still the seat of government and the center of the empire's military planning.

An important item of business that day on Guam was a press conference at which I was the principal figure. Assembled were all the correspondents assigned to this important base of military operations.

A majority were understandably unhappy that the biggest story of the war—of any war, for that matter—had broken under their noses the day before without their knowledge. The news release had been made in Washington, and their editors were already wondering why they had received nothing from the writers they had assigned to cover the war in the Pacific.

Their ruffled sensibilities were soon soothed by a patient

explanation of the absolute need for secrecy and of decisions made at the presidential level, dating back five years.

I was asked the usual questions, some stupid, some perceptive. How did I feel about introducing the most fearsome weapon in history? ("There was a sense of shock to all of us on the plane.") Was the sight more awesome than you expected? ("Yes.") How long after the bomb was released did the explosion occur? ("Forty-three seconds.") Do you think this will end the war? ("Yes, unless the Japanese have taken leave of their senses.") How was Hiroshima chosen as the target? ("It was an important center of military operations which we had spared from conventional bombing.") I also described the selection process for other potential targets, but without naming them.

Captain Parsons participated in the interview and answered technical questions about the bomb. Pictures taken at the press conference, and widely published in newspapers all over the world, showed me standing behind a table with General LeMay seated at my left and General Spaatz at my right.

While I was on Guam that day, Bob Lewis took the *Enola Gay* on a routine mission to drop one of our "pumpkins" containing conventional explosives.

Significantly, in view of the controversy that developed later, none of the newsmen at the press conference questioned the use of the atomic bomb. These reporters had seen the war at first hand and, like every soldier I met, welcomed anything that would shorten the conflict.

A dispatch from Washington that day pointed out that the bomb had been developed at a cost of $2 billion and that it would pay for itself if it shortened the war by only nine days, based on a calculation that the war was costing seven billion dollars a month.

By Tuesday night, Japan acknowledged the extensive damage caused by the Hiroshima bomb, and the Tokyo radio charged that the United States had violated international law, citing the Hague convention without mentioning that Japan was not a signatory.

Aerial photos by now had given us a fairly accurate view of the Hiroshima damage. From them, it was possible to announce that 60 percent of the city, or approximately 4.1 square miles, had been laid waste, and that only a few of the sturdier buildings in this area remained standing. It was even possible to estimate that the loss of life was in the neighborhood of 80,000, an appalling total. The actual toll has never been accurately established; the count is further complicated by the fact that there were some who died later from the effects of burns and radiation.

Oppenheimer had estimated that fatalities might number 20,000, but his figure was based on the expectation that Hiroshimans, like those in European cities subjected to bombardment, would seek refuge in bomb shelters. He calculated correctly that the bomb's explosion at an altitude of one-third of a mile would create a comparatively small amount of radiation at ground level.

Nevertheless, a great deal of nonsense was written on this subject. International News Service carried an article by a physicist who wrote that the Hiroshima area would be a lifeless valley for the next 70 years and that "any Japanese who try to ascertain the extent of damage caused by the atomic bomb are committing suicide."

Because the radiation was dissipated in all directions when the explosion took place high above the ground, rescue and fact-finding teams went into the heart of the city almost at once without suffering harm. Hiroshima was rebuilt after the war and today has a population of 900,000, three times the number who were living there on the morning of August 6, 1945.

On Tinian the next day, I went ahead with plans for the second atomic mission. LeMay assumed that I would be flying this one also, but I had decided otherwise. I told him that Chuck Sweeney would drop the second bomb. Since his own plane, *The Great Artiste*, had been outfitted with special instruments for the Hiroshima flight and would play the same role on this mission, Sweeney was assigned to fly *Bock's Car*.

That mission came close to being a fiasco, through no fault of Sweeney. Everything went wrong, starting with a fuel pump malfunction that made it impossible to use 600 gallons of fuel in the bomb-bay tanks. At the rendezvous point south of Kyushu, one of the accompanying planes failed to show up and 45 minutes were lost. Kokura was the primary target, but visibility was poor. Sweeney circled for almost an hour before giving up. The result was another loss of precious time, particularly serious when his fuel supply was limited. Finally, the bomb was dropped on Nagasaki, the secondary target, under conditions that were less than ideal. It missed the Aiming Point by a wide margin, but the damage was extensive nevertheless. Returning with a marginal supply of gasoline, Sweeney managed to make an emergency landing on Okinawa with nearly empty tanks.

The difficulties even extended to the press reports of the raid, and *Bock's Car* was robbed of its proper credit. A place was found in *The Great Artiste* for Bill Laurence, the *New York Times* reporter who was disappointed because he was unable to accompany us on the Hiroshima mission.

But Bill never knew what plane he was in. Apparently knowing the name of Sweeney's plane, he did not get the word of the switch to *Bock's Car*. Thus in his first-person account of the raid, he incorrectly indentified the plane that dropped the bomb. He repeated the error in his fine book, *Dawn Over Zero*, written the next year, in which he told of watching the bomb fall. "Out of the belly of *The Great Artiste* what looked like a black object went downward," he wrote.

The Nagasaki raid was successful in the sense that it convinced the Japanese government that further resistance meant atomic disaster and that our warning leaflets were worth heeding. Five days after Nagasaki, the Japanese gave up. For those who have contended that the enemy was already on the verge of surrender, it should be noted that a number of military leaders tried their best to keep the war going even after the two atomic bombs had been dropped.

32 End of the War

Things happened fast after the Nagasaki bombing. The Soviet Union entered the war, which, to all practical purposes, was over. Then came news of the Japanese surrender.

Visitors to Tinian included Francis Cardinal Spellman of New York, who conducted Mass in the base chapel. General Spaatz came over from Guam to visit the bomb hut and greet all the crews of the 509th.

After the signing of the peace treaty aboard the battleship *Missouri* in Tokyo harbor on September 2, scientists from the Manhattan Project were anxious to get into Japan to check on the result of our bomb drops on Hiroshima and Nagasaki. They wanted to find out the levels of radiation and determine how long it would linger. What was the most dangerous result of the new weapon: the explosive force, the intense heat, the radiation?

We secured the approval of General MacArthur to accompany the occupying forces to Tokyo immediately, and from there to visit the bombed cities.

In my security detachment were six Nisei who were born in Hawaii of Japanese parents. Because they spoke the Japanese language fluently, we took them along as interpreters.

I took two C-54s and went to Okinawa to join the big parade of planes that were flying occupation forces into Japan. We were in the second wave of aircraft that arrived in the Japanese capital. The confusion and traffic there were beyond belief. We finally got from the airport into the heart of the city, using two jeeps that I had loaded into our planes before departure. We were billeted in the Dai Ichi building, where General MacArthur would soon establish his military and civil government headquarters.

Our first job was to look for Professor Masao Tsuzuki, professor of radiology at the University of Tokyo's medical school. No one really knew where he was or even if he had survived the Tokyo bombings. Dr. Tsuzuki had studied in the United States and a thesis he had written in 1926 while conducting research at the University of Pennsylvania was well known to scientists.

Almost miraculously, the scientists who had accompanied us to Tokyo were able to locate the Japanese professor. He was well aware that his country had been rendered helpless by atomic weapons and he had a very good understanding of how they worked. He agreed to fly with me to the cities where the bombs had been dropped.

We learned that we could fly to a field near Nagasaki, but that the runways at the Hiroshima air base were in no condition to handle a C-54. Flying to Nagasaki, we landed at a naval base about 16 miles from the heart of the city. During the flight from Tokyo, I left the cockpit and went back to see our Japanese guest. He turned out to be very formal and reserved, and his attitude led me to believe that someone had told him I was the pilot of the plane that had bombed Hiroshima.

Although he bowed politely to me, he did not talk, pretending not to understand English. In his pocket he carried a set of chopsticks that he used when eating the food we served on the plane. He stopped eating when I came back to the passenger compartment and did not resume until I had left.

I took the hint and proceeded to ignore the professor for the rest of the trip. One of the interpreters told me later that the professor would do whatever was asked of him during our stay at Nagasaki, but that he appeared to do it grudgingly. His distrust of us was reciprocated. "We'll keep an eye on him all the time," the interpreter said.

At Nagasaki we went our way and the scientists went theirs. We were located near the waterfront, in an area that was meant to be the target but that actually escaped serious damage when the bomb missed its mark.

Nagasaki had been a popular resort city before the war and had been visited by English-speaking tourists from Great Britain and the United States. Furthermore, it was the home of many Japanese of the Christian faith, a fact that led to some criticism of our people who selected it as a target. In any case, we encountered a number of Japanese who spoke excellent English.

The place where we stayed was almost like a summer camp. There were bamboo buildings with thatched roofs and wooden bunks that were built about 3 feet above the ground. The place was managed by a couple who spoke our language fluently and showed us every courtesy. We had brought some food with us from the airplane and the woman prepared it in tasty fashion. I remember that our meals there included such things as fish and fresh eggs.

Uncle Sam had printed invasion currency for use in Japan, and it was accepted everywhere we went. Ferebee, Van Kirk, and I walked around the city during the three days we spent there and were amazed at the extent of the destruction. Block after block had been flattened, as if by a tornado. Strangely, however, I saw no signs of death. There were no bodies anywhere. There were not many people on the streets in the heart of the city, and we saw none who had been wounded. The reason was never explained, but I assume that the survivors, with an efficiency characteristic of the Japanese, had done a swift clean-up job and that the injured were being cared for.

Outside the areas where damage was heaviest, life was proceeding in an almost normal manner. The people were polite and didn't even seem to think it unusual that American airmen were there so soon after the long war. Their attitude was an amazing reversal of the one that had prevailed so recently, when frenzied mobs had been known to attack and kill downed American fliers. Those I met were not told, of course, that I had anything to do with the atom bomb project.

Crew members visited souvenir shops near the waterfront. I purchased a number of rice bowls and saucers that were hand-carved and lacquered to a high polish. They remain prized possessions today.

The brief visit left me with considerable respect for the people who had been our enemies such a short time before. They were carrying on and trying to live as normally as possible. They were not unlike those I had seen in England during the German bombing attacks. But if I felt no animosity, neither did I have a personal feeling of guilt about the terror that we had visited upon their land. It was unfortunate, of course, that these people had been obliged to pay such a price for a war into which their country had been led by a handful of ambitious and ruthless politicians and militarists.

We were only temporary visitors, returning to Tokyo and leaving behind a number of scientists who would probe the rubble and make measurements and study the health of the survivors. Their work goes on even to this day as studies are made of the effect of atomic warfare on the survivors, and even on their children and grandchildren.

All of us were deeply impressed by what we saw at Nagasaki and what we knew had occurred at Hiroshima. Chuck Sweeney went on a lecture tour after returning home, describing the bombings. He sent the profits to an orphanage in Hiroshima. Bob Lewis helped raise money to provide medical treatment for the so-called "Hiroshima maidens," girls who were disfigured by the blistering heat from the bomb.

Back from this trip to Japan, I found General LeMay eager for me to return to the United States and report to the Pentagon. From Washington, I flew to Roswell, New Mexico, to meet with the air crews and tell many of them goodbye because a majority wanted to get out of service and return home, now that the war was over.

I didn't have many professional soldiers in my outfit, and only a small group would be staying with me in the peacetime air force. The next move would be to start bringing in replacements and rebuild the group with permanent personnel. In Washington, I was told that the 309th would remain in existence, with headquarters at Roswell.

First, however, I was given a leave, the first in a long time. I had already moved Lucy and the boys to Roswell, and we decided to take a vacation trip into Mexico. We relaxed, saw the sights, and acted in general like the family of tourists that we were.

Now that the war was over, I foresaw the resumption of a normal family life. I was blissfully unaware of the home front tugs and tussles that lay ahead. During the preparation for Hiroshima, I had worked day and night at an exhausting pace, with a single objective that I could understand. I was soon to be caught up and tossed around in a whirlwind of military mendacity for which my wartime experience had not prepared me.

In war, the military operates with a single purpose: to defeat an enemy who is clearly defined. When peace comes, an army doesn't stop fighting. Its officers compete furiously for personal advantage and sometimes employ the same questionable tactics against their colleagues that are considered quite fair against a foreign enemy.

By this time, the dawn of the atomic age had replaced the war as the most discussed subject in newspapers, periodicals, and on the radio. I was interviewed and quoted by correspondents and commentators. Few serious questions were raised about our use of the weapon, although we heard scattered rumblings of the criticism that lay ahead. For the most part, speculation centered on the subject of how the atom could be tamed for peaceful use, and how it could become the servant rather than the destroyer of mankind.

Without soliciting personal publicity, I found it coming my way in unexpected doses. The military's public information offices encouraged me to accept invitations to tell the story of my involvement in the atomic project.

It had not occurred to me that I would be regarded as something of a hero; neither had it entered my mind that the situation was creating jealousies among certain fellow officers—particularly some who outranked me and were clearly miffed that they had not been consulted in advance on nuclear strategy.

I would be hearing from them soon.

33 Fiasco at Bikini

One day in January 1946, I received a phone call from General LeMay, who was now in Washington. He told me to report at once to General Sinclair Street at Headquarters Command at Washington's Bolling Air Force base.

A project called "Operation Crossroads" was in the works and my advice was being solicited. The operation, which involved the test-firing of two atomic bombs, was described at the time as "the greatest laboratory experiment in all history." It was indeed that. For me, it also turned out to be an example of military politics at work.

Bikini, where the tests would take place, is an atoll in the western chain of the Marshall islands in the South Pacific. Prior to 1946, it was home for 162 natives of Malayo-Polynesian origin. They lived mostly on coconuts, pandanus, arrowroot, and the fish they caught in the atoll's oval lagoon, a body of water about 25 miles long and 15 miles wide. For the duration of the test and for as many years thereafter as their home island was deemed unsafe by reason of radioactivity, these people were resettled on Rongerik atoll, 128 miles to the east.

"Crossroads" was conceived as a joint Army-Navy operation. General Street was authorized to select the air force personnel who would participate. Vice Admiral W. H. P. Blandy was commander of Joint Task Force One, which ran the show.

In response to LeMay's call, I went at once to Washington in company with Tom Ferebee. We were asked how accurately the bomb could be dropped from an altitude that would give the airplane an opportunity to escape the effects of the explosion. Based on our experience in preparation for the Hiroshima attack, we replied that we could put the bomb within 300 feet of any spot that was designated.

Then came a discussion of the target. It had already been decided that the lagoon would be filled with obsolete naval vessels in order to test the effect of atomic explosions on warships. One bomb would be dropped from an airplane, and a second would be exploded under water.

I suggested that the ships be arranged in circles, like a bulls-eye, with the target ship in the center. Each ring of vessels would be deployed at a known distance from the center.

The navy men who took part in our discussion didn't buy that idea at first. They even implied that it couldn't be done. I don't think they liked the symbolism of the navy serving merely as a target. But they finally gave in under persuasion that this would be the best way to obtain an exact measurement of the bomb's destructive power at various distances.

The target pattern would also make it possible to determine whether the bomb's effect was related to any factor other than distance. It would be possible to tell, for instance, if the radiation was more damaging to ships downwind from the blast.

Returning to Roswell, I discovered that the wheels of military intrigue had been turning in my absence. Latrine rumors were infamous during the war, but it was something I overheard while seated in a latrine that forewarned me of trouble ahead.

My old nemesis, Colonel "Butch" Blanchard, who had tried unsuccessfully to relieve the 509th of its original A-bomb assignments, came into the latrine with another colonel. Not knowing that I occupied one of the stalls, they got into a conversation that made it clear they were hatching a plan to prevent me and my crew from dropping the bomb at "Operation Crossroads."

Until that time, it had been generally assumed that, because of our experience, I would fly the plane at Bikini and Ferebee would release the bomb.

"He's already had enough publicity," I heard Blanchard say, and it wasn't long until I realized he was talking about me. In the dialogue that followed, it was clear that they were trying to figure out a way to keep me out of the spotlight. It was apparent that they feared another personal success would put me in line for advancements they would rather have for themselves.

At Roswell, we soon had an influx of senior regular officers, and it wasn't long before I was relieved of command of the 509th, which I had organized almost 18 months earlier. I was not surprised, because by this time I was fully aware that a Blanchard-and-company scheme was developing, with the help of a high-placed crony, General Roger Ramey.

The new commander and staff may have had the seniority and the West Point credentials, but they didn't have any experience with the bomb. I was retained as technical adviser to the commanding general, but it didn't take long for me to discover that my technical advice was seldom solicited, and not heeded when I volunteered.

General LeMay came to the base one day and learned, at a briefing, that I wasn't being consulted about the Bikini bomb drop. I am told that this led LeMay, who had two stars at that time, to confront Ramey, who had one star.

"Look here," LeMay was quoted as saying. "Don't be a stupid idiot. You've got to get Tibbets involved in this thing. If you don't and something goes wrong, there'll be hell to pay because you don't know anything about this business. He does."

Ramey had no choice but to keep me around. He used the familiar device of naming me technical adviser, this time to Task Force 1.5, which would have the responsibility for all "Crossroads" air operations.

LeMay had assumed, as had most others, that I would pilot the plane for the bomb drop at Bikini. Although he was on my side, he had a problem with Ramey, who, prodded by Blanchard, was determined to keep me on the sidelines. Finally, they persuaded LeMay to give them permission to use another crew, but only "if you can find a better one." That put the responsibility on Ramey but, as it turned out, he had a foolproof plan to squeeze me and my crew out of the picture.

It was announced that the crew for the test drop would be chosen on the basis of bomb-drop competition. I naïvely considered that a fair way to make the selection—and it should have been. To my surprise, it turned out otherwise.

The competition took place near Albuquerque, where the Atomic Energy Commission had a storage site with a quantity of practice bombs on hand. After the preliminary drops, my crew with Ferebee as the bombardier was one of the three finalists. Tom and I dropped 14 bombs for record. We averaged a 237-foot error from the aiming points for all the bombs dropped. From 30,000 feet, that's a better hit capability than was claimed for the Norden bomb sight.

I credit our accuracy to experience and the long time we had worked together. We knew the airplane and Tom knew the bomb sight. He knew exactly what he had to do on the bomb run to put the bomb on target. Some of his expertise was not covered in the manual, but it worked.

The crew that ranked second had an average miss of just over 380 feet. The third crew was far out, in the neighborhood of 700 to 800 feet from the target.

Those bomb shapes falling on the desert said we had won, but some sharp pencils reversed the outcome of the competition. A couple of operations analysts were called in and they figured—making allowance for an intangible and completely irrelevant factor called "ballistic winds"—that if the bombs had been dropped over the Pacific, the third crew would have come closest. In fact, they figured Tom and me right into last place.

Ironically, many of the things we had worked out in painstaking practice for the Hiroshima bombing were not heeded by the less-experienced crews competing for "Crossroads." One airplane and its crew were lost because the pilot did not understand how to perform, with precision, the diving turn that we had developed to escape the bomb's shock wave. The tail was torn off this B-29.

Much of what happened in the selection of the crew was not made public. In fact, *Time* magazine in an issue just before the Bikini test said the bomb would be dropped from the *Enola Gay*.

The pilot chosen for the Bikini mission, on the basis of the phony "ballistic winds" computation, was Major Woodrow P. Swancutt. The bombardier was Major Harold H. Wood, a former grocery clerk from Bordentown, New Jersey, who had the nickname of "Lemon Bar" because of his good fortune with the slot machines in the officers' club. Other key members of the crew were Captain William C. Harrison, the copilot, and Major William B. Adams, navigator. Their airplane was named *Dave's Dream* in memory of Captain David Semple of Riverside, California, the bombardier who was killed in the B-29 crash during the competition in New Mexico.

The bomb drop of "Operation Crossroads" took place on the morning of July 1, 1946. The navy had placed 70 obsolete vessels in the lagoon, arrayed in the bulls-eye fashion I had suggested. While my bulls-eye layout was the most effective and certainly the most obvious way to determine the effect of the bomb at various distances, it had one special requirement. The bomb would have to land on or very near the target.

The target ship at the center was the U.S.S. *Nevada*, painted a bright international orange to make it easily visible from 30,000 feet. The rest of the target fleet consisted of nine battleships or cruisers, two aircraft carriers, 12 destroyers, eight submarines, 17 landing craft, 19 merchant-type ships, and three floating drydocks or barges. Also included were one German and two old Japanese warships.

The sky was full of airplanes, many of them unmanned and radio-controlled. Their function was to fly over the lagoon for observation purposes and, in the case of the drones, to penetrate the mushroom nuclear cloud. The airplanes were based on Eniwetok, Kwajalein, and the carrier *Shangri-La*. On the decks of the target ships were sensitive instruments to measure such things as blast effect, radiation, and heat. Also on these vessels were many animals that would be sacrificed in the interests of science.

When word of this plan got into the newspapers in advance of the test, protests poured in from animal lovers. The planners persevered, however, on the grounds that it was necessary to determine the effect of atomic shock and radiation, at various distances, on living things. Angry dog-lovers won a victory when they succeeded in having their favorite animals spared from participation.

Noah would have felt at home that day at the sight of a harbor full of vessels containing 204 goats, 200 pigs, 60 guinea pigs, 5,000 rats, and 200 mice. The goats and pigs were tethered to the decks, and the smaller animals were caged.

This bombing was as well publicized as ours at Hiroshima was secret. On hand were 42,000 witnesses, including 124 writers and radio commentators, who watched from afar aboard the U.S.S. *Appalachian*. Even the Russians had an official observer in the person of Professor Simon Alexandrov.

The crew of the *Enola Gay* was probably the most interested group among the many spectators. We had arrived on Kwajalein almost a month before the test date. Naturally, we were disappointed at having been euchred out of what we considered our rightful role, but we were there nevertheless in support of this historic test operation, on which the government was spending millions of dollars.

On the morning of the test, we were up early. Long before daylight, the crew of *Dave's Dream* was briefed on the latest weather—it was drizzling but the sky was expected to clear—and went into a huddle with the so-called "ballistic winds" experts, whose computations had so drastically altered the results of the competition.

Tom Ferebee, Kermit Beahan, and I went down to the weather shack and obtained information on the expected winds aloft, then made our own computations. When we saw the figures that the other crew had arrived at, we were shocked. Trying to be helpful, Ferebee and Beahan took the other bombardier, Major Wood, aside and pointed out the obvious miscalculation. Their advice went unheeded.

Then I spoke to Swancutt. "Woody, you guys have computed the ballistic data wrong," I said. "You'd better recheck your figures." I showed him our computations and said, "Here's what we think."

Swancutt listened a bit impatiently, thanked me for the advice, and then told me politely that they were satisfied with their own results. No wonder they were so far off the mark in the New Mexico competition, I thought to myself.

Rebuffed in our attempt to be helpful, we waited impatiently for the result. Meanwhile, Ferebee and Beahan took the figures that Major Wood was going to crank into his sight and made some computations of their own.

Tom came to me and pointed to a spot on a map showing the

·location of the target fleet. "This is where the bomb is going to land," he said, indicating a point on the map 1,600 feet short and to the left of the target ship.

We were angry and frustrated at our inability to prevent the bomb drop from becoming the fiasco we feared. But we had tried our best to straighten them out, and we could do no more but wait and see.

Sunrise brought clearing skies and *Dave's Dream* took off at 5:55 for Bikini lagoon, 240 miles to the north. The bomb, known this time as "The Thing," was carefully kept from view of all those who were not involved in loading it into the plane. It was a copy of the Nagasaki plutonium bomb. On its side was pasted a foot-long pin-up of Rita Hayworth. The bomb was then given the name of "Gilda," for her most recent movie.

Dave's Dream climbed to 30,000 feet and made two practice runs over the lagoon. A flashing light aboard the brightly painted *Nevada* made the target ship clearly visible. The bomb was set to explode in the air above the target.

As the plane made its bombing run, the 42,000 observers lay prone on the decks of their ships at a safe distance, the nearest being 10 miles away. Their eyes were protected from the anticipated flash by dark glasses.

The bomb fell from the plane and 50 seconds later the earth experienced its fourth atomic explosion. To millions all over the world who listened by radio, the omnious ticking of a metronome on the battleship *Pennsylvania* served as a countdown. At the instant of the blast, the metronome became silent. Some seconds later the sound of the explosion was heard.

Back on Kwajalein, we went to the operations room next door to the communications headquarters to learn what had happened. It was almost immediately apparent that the bomb had fallen 1,800 feet short and to the left of the target—only 200 feet from the point where Ferebee and Beahan had predicted it would explode.

The only vessel within 1,000 feet of the point over which the bomb exploded was the merchant ship *Gilliam*, which sank almost immediately. Four others went down later. The bulls-eye battleship, *Nevada*, escaped with moderate damage to deck installations, while its hull and interior were not perceptibly affected. A goat tethered to the deck seemed none the worse for its experience when the ship was boarded the next day, but it died later from radiation. On one of the target ships, a movie camera that had been set up to operate automatically showed a goat contentedly munching hay at the moment of the blast, ignoring the debris that could be seen flying about when the shock wave struck.

No one expected the bomb to explode near the *Gilliam;* hence the instruments that were placed aboard that ship were not of the type to measure blast effects of such severity. When recovered by divers, they were of little use.

When results of the bomb drop reached General LeMay at his quarters, he charged out the door so fast you would have thought his coattails were on fire. He came directly to me.

"What in the hell happened?" he demanded.

"They put the wrong ballistic information into the bomb sight," I replied.

"Why did they do that?"

"I don't know," I told him. Then I showed him the way Ferebee and Beahan had calculated it and said, "This is what we computed and this is the way we said it ought to be done."

"Jesus Christ," LeMay said, and set out in search of Roger Ramey, who was actually responsible for the fiasco. Then he ordered me to get in our airplane and fly to Washington as soon as possible to report to General Spaatz.

"I don't want you on this island when all those newspaper people get back from the lagoon and start asking questions," LeMay said.

We were traveling light in those days, usually wearing just our khaki uniforms cut off at the knees. We were packed and in the air in less than an hour.

When we reported to General Spaatz, he couldn't do much more than shake his head. "We'll hear about this for the rest of our lives," he said.

The aftermath wasn't that bad, probably because there wasn't much investigative news reporting in those days. Although they knew that the bomb had missed its mark by a wide margin, the reporters didn't ask embarrassing questions, and the air force managed to leave them with the impression that the whole thing was a success.

Fiasco at Bikini 253

The facts were never brought out. They would have made interesting reading, and Ramey would have been on the spot, but LeMay and Spaatz—angry as they were about the episode—could not be expected to open a can of worms that would have reflected unfavorably on the air force. I'm convinced, however, that the navy obtained some advantage in the political arena as a result of the Bikini foul-up.

Amazingly, all this did not have an unfavorable effect on the careers of Blanchard, who attained four-star rank, and Swancutt, who became a major general before his retirement. Ramey was honored, after his death, by having an important U.S. air base in Puerto Rico named in his memory.

"Operation Crossroads" was saved by the second bomb, which was exploded 25 days later at a depth of 90 feet under water, sinking nine ships of the target fleet. It produced a million-ton hollow column of water 2,000 feet in diameter that rose to a height of more than a mile, falling back in a storm of water, steam, and radioactive debris.

It should not be inferred that all the millions spent on Operation Crossroads was wasted. A great deal was learned about the behavior and destructive force of nuclear weapons from the underwater explosion. There was even something to be gained from the air drop, which I have described as a fiasco because the bombardier inexcusably missed the target by a third of a mile under the best of visual aiming conditions. By means of some readjustment in calculations and a little guesswork, it was possible to arrive at some useful conclusions about the effect of an atom bomb dropped from an airplane on vessels at sea. Nevertheless, there was embarrassment for most of us in the air force's performance at Bikini.

34 Testing the B-47

The year was 1948. The air force was moving rapidly into the jet age, and I wanted to be a part of it. Having just graduated from the Air Command and Staff School, I was assigned to Washington, D.C., as director of operations in the office of the chief of the Air Force Requirements Division.

The director was General Thomas Power, who would later become commander of SAC. Shortly after I joined the staff, Power was transferred to London as air attaché, and his place was taken by General Carl Brandt, a tough taskmaster but a grand old guy for whom I had great respect. Because of my experience, I was placed in charge of the bombardment branch at a time when a controversy was building up over the need for an all-jet bomber force.

I couldn't see that we had a choice. Propeller-driven airplanes were limited to a top speed of around 400 miles an hour, and there was no way to protect them from the new 600 mph fighters. Already, experimental rocket planes were pushing their way through the sonic barrier, approaching speeds of 1,000 miles an hour.

Most of the argument at the time concerned the Consolidated B-36, built in Fort Worth, and the all-jet B-47 that Boeing had designed.

The B-36 was a flying monster. Early versions had six pusher-type reciprocating engines in the wing. The airplane had a high ceiling, great range, and could stay aloft for hours. Unfortunately, it lacked speed.

The B-47 didn't have the range we desired because its six jet engines burned fuel at a tremendous rate. But this shortcoming could be solved through air-to-air refueling. It was apparent, of course, that a larger longer-range jet bomber would be developed as soon as technology permitted. In the meantime, the B-47 would serve a useful purpose.

It seemed clear to me that all our planning should be directed to jets. General George Kenny was a leader in the battle for the B-36. I agree that we did need that airplane temporarily because of its long range, but it was certainly not the plane for the future. Its designers later added four jet engines, slung under the wings, giving it a total of 10 engines to increase its speed. The jets were used for the most part on takeoff and to provide bursts of speed when pursued by enemy fighters. But even with this help, the B-36 was no match for the faster jets.

As it turned out, the B-36 was retired from service without having taken part in any military action. The fact that we had it was enough, I think, to deter any would-be aggressor.

I did everything in my power to promote the development of the B-47. It was my baby, and I knew the air force needed it. I testified on its behalf before many aircraft and armament committees composed of top generals, a majority with three of four stars.

It was customary for staff officers to go before the committees to try to sell them on this or that need. It was no easy task. Those generals could tear you apart with questions. You could get shot down very easily at one of these sessions. Sometimes you would wait two or three months, gather some more ammunition, then try again.

Boeing was also active, having built a prototype for demonstration and research purposes. The generals who would be making the decisions on aircraft acquisition were given an opportunity to fly in this plane.

In recent years, many people have contended that every purchase of a military weapon—airplane, aircraft carrier, or tank—is the result of some collusion involving what is described as "the military-industrial complex." Although I acknowledge that we must guard against such collusion, which can indeed result in the purchase of unneeded military hardware, in my opinion there has been a national tendency to exaggerate the extent of this evil.

In America, there is a healthy competition among the suppliers to develop the best products, and then they must try their best to sell them. Salesmanship involves demonstrations. From the standpoint of the purchaser, in this case the military, the choice among several competing weapons is made after lengthy testing and assessment.

A majority of the military people who make the decisions are motivated by a desire to buy the best. As to the matter of quantity, there is always a tendency to ask for more than Congress is likely to authorize. This inclination is not limited to the armed services; it is apparent in almost every branch of government.

That the system has not given the United States an excess of military equipment in the past may be seen from our underpreparedness on past occasions when war came. If the United States, along with Great Britain, had not neglected its military strength in the 1930s, Hitler's ambitions would have been considerably dampened. World War II might not have occurred. Billions of dollars and millions of lives might have been saved.

I was finally able to sell the air force on the idea of buying a limited number of B-47s. The Boeing plant at Wichita, which had been shut down after the war, was reopened to produce the planes.

By this time, Boeing had worked out a successful method of aerial refueling that would give the B-47 unlimited range, providing it could make enough hookups with refueling aircraft. First tried was a system, called "probe and drogue," that had been developed by the British. This was not successful because it could not transfer the fuel fast enough. Finally, there came the "flying boom," which extended from a tanker plane to make a quick connection with a slotted fuel receptacle in the nose of the B-47. B-29 bombers were converted into tankers at first, followed by the KC-97 piston engine plane, and finally the all-jet KC-135, a modification of the military version of the Boeing 707.

By the summer of 1950, Boeing was ready to turn out the first production models of the B-47. Carl Brandt had seen my interest in the plane and knew I wanted to get it into the air force inventory, and into the hands of the pilots and crews who would use it, as soon as possible. My idea was that, if there were any bugs in the airplane, the people who were going to use it could work them out.

The previous procedure had been to let the manufacturer test the plane, then turn it over to the Air Matériel Command at Wright field in Dayton, where it would undergo tests for at least a year. I wanted to short-cut this procedure for two reasons: (1) I feared that the manufacturer's tests would show only the best side of the plane, and (2) the Air Matériel Command had already been involved in approving the plans of the Boeing people and could not be expected to find serious fault with its own specifications.

Brandt agreed with my reasoning and said, "I suppose you're the guy who wants to test it."

"You couldn't be more right," I replied.

With that, he arranged my release from the Pentagon, and in July 1950 I reported to Boeing at Wichita.

First I had to learn about jets. All my flying had been in propeller-driven airplanes. My first jet ride was in a T-33 trainer flown by Pat Fleming, an air force test pilot who had been at Muroc Air Force base (now called Edwards) in the California desert.

Pat could hardly wait to get me up in the jet. I was an old bomber pilot and he was a hotshot jet jockey. He was going to show me what that jet—we called them "stovepipes" and "blowtorches" in those days—could do.

He briefed me and put me in the front seat. When we got on the runway, he ran the engine up to 100 percent power and released the brakes. We seemed to be accelerating slowly at first, but soon the 1,000-foot markers on the runway were zipping past. He got the plane into the air, retracting the gear and flaps before we were more than a few feet above the ground.

By the time we reached the airport boundary we were doing 300 miles an hour. Then he pulled the plane into a vertical climb and started rolling it. His maneuvers made my old B-29 seem like a semi-truck. Pat finally rolled out on his back in an Immelmann. I hadn't been upside down in an airplane for years. He was giving me a workout and a look at what was new in aviation.

Then he let me fly the airplane. We made some approaches, landings, and takeoffs. The toughest lesson to learn with jets is to keep ahead of the airplane and to anticipate the landings. When a jet gets moving, it isn't easy to slow down. When you cut the power, the airplane doesn't want to stop flying. Today's jets have overcome this problem with spoilers and engine reverse thrust not available in 1950.

Upon landing, it was necessary to plan ahead. With a missed approach, it would take several seconds to get up enough power to climb out and go around for another try. In the early jets, if you jammed the throttle forward, the engine would flame out. Power had to be applied gradually.

I started thinking of a jet airplane as a boat that continues to coast through the water when you cut the motor upon approaching the dock. Jets have to be handled much the same way during landing.

After trying my wings in the T-bird, I was ready to move up to the B-47. This big six-jet airplane was nearly the size of a B-29. Its wings drooped almost to the ground and raised up to generate lift as the plane gathered speed. It was startling, until you got used to it, to see those wings flopping around in rough air.

The B-47 is a three-place airplane. The commander or pilot sits up front and handles the controls, with the copilot behind him, tandem fashion. The third crewman sits ahead of and below them, in the plane's nose. He's the busiest guy on the airplane because he is the bombardier, the navigator, the radar man, the electronics countermeasures operator, and generally the one who keeps the other two on the ball.

The ground school at Wichita was run by Boeing technical representatives, called "tech reps." They gave me a comprehensive training and really the first formal introduction I had ever had to a new airplane. Up until this time, someone always said, "This is the airplane. Get in and fly it."

The schooling went on for 30 days, a little longer than necessary because we didn't have a B-47 available at the time. When it came time for me to check out in the B-47, I was lucky to have one of the best pilots in the business: A.M. "Tex" Johnson, a big man who always wore cowboy boots and, when not flying, a big Stetson hat.

I knew what the B-47 was supposed to do. Tex Johnson showed me what it *could* do. He flew far enough away from Wichita that we would be out of sight of the Boeing people, who might not have approved of the demonstration that was in store for me. We did slow rolls, loops, Immelmanns—just about everything you would say was impossible in a big airplane with six engines.

Tex was a natural pilot and handled the bomber as if it were a fighter. In fact, he often referred to it as a fighter with five extra engines. When the fun was over, he started to teach me some of the things I needed to know about this remarkable airplane with the flapping swept-back wings. There was the wing warp, for instance. At low altitudes and high speed, that big wing would twist so that it sometimes created a reverse aileron effect. It was important to recognize this and make the proper correction at once.

Flying at high altitudes—higher than I had ever flown before—I had to learn to cope with a phenomenon called "the coffin corner." It was a sometimes frightening situation that would develop occasionally at high altitudes where too much speed would create a dangerous supersonic buffet and too little speed would cause the plane to stall. There was often only a few knots' difference in the speed that would trigger one or other of the hazards, and the pilot would have to exercise great skill in extricating himself from the "coffin corner" by descending very gradually to an altitude where the air was more dense.

In the landing pattern, there was also the need for careful computation of the approach speed, depending on the weight of the plane—which varied, of course, with the fuel load. The copilot would compute the fuel remaining and the gross weight of the plane, passing the figure to the pilot, who would maintain his approach and landing speed accordingly. If he remained in the traffic pattern for the purpose of making a number of practice landings, he had to recompute the weight every time around. Coming over the fence just three knots above the recommended speed could add 900 feet to the landing distance. Most runways in those days were no more than 6,500 feet long.

There were safety factors built in, however. Jato (jet assist-takeoff) bottles on the fuselage could provide extra thrust for a heavy takeoff from a short runway. Then there was a drag chute that could be deployed to shorten the landing roll.

This was a new world of flying for me, and I enjoyed it.

We started our test program by wringing out the airplane, finding out the problems, and what to do about them.

I insisted on taking one airplane and flying it for 1,000 hours, using enough crews to keep it in the air all the time it wasn't being worked on by the ground crews. This accelerated program soon showed us all the bugs and kinks that might develop in two or three years of operational service, and it is now standard procedure for at least one plane of each new model that is developed for the air force. Prior to the introduction of my plan, it took about seven years for tactical units of the air force to get an airplane after it was ordered. We cut that time to three years with the B-47, and the engineers at the Wichita plant told me it was one of the best things that had happened in aircraft testing and procurement.

I lived with the B-47 for three years. Colonel Mike McCoy picked up the first of these airplanes for the Strategic Air Command and I checked him out. He flew it to his group at Pinecastle Air Force base in Florida. Mike, who was a great pilot, later pulled one of the airplanes apart when he inadvertently exceeded its stress limits, losing his life in the crash near Orlando. Pinecastle is was named McCoy Air Force base in his memory.

In 1951, Boeing field at Wichita was renamed McConnell Air Force base in memory of two brothers, both bomber pilots: Captain Fred J. McConnell and Lieutenant Thomas L. McConnell. Fred was killed in a private plane crash in 1945, and his brother died in 1943 in a bombing raid on Bougainville in the Pacific.

McConnell became the training base for B-47 crews. They were sent from SAC bases all over the country for transition training in the six-jet bomber. We developed a cadre of real specialists at McConnell, and they turned out SAC crews that were doing some of the most precise flying ever required of regular air force outfits.

This too was an innovation. Normally when a new airplane was introduced into the line units, a few crews from the unit would qualify and then go back to their base to train the rest of the outfit. Under our system, every crew got the same training and all members had to meet the same high standards. We turned out top flight crews and General LeMay's program kept them sharp. They had to meet and maintain the standards or they didn't fly.

In 1953, the air force was at the peak of its buildup for the Korean war. There had been 2,372,292 airmen in service in 1944 when our flying forces reached their wartime peak. That figure dropped to a low of just over 300,000 in 1947. Now we were back to nearly a million.

It was known from experience that a rapidly expanding force

Testing the B-47

means a higher accident rate. But General LeMay, the SAC commander, was determined that there would be no letdown in the quality of flying even when the air force was growing.

Training programs like the one at Wichita, and the continuous checking and rechecking of flight crews, gave us a large force that was well trained and capable and helped convert our bomber forces to jets with a maximum of safety and effectiveness.

The switch to jet bombers paid off handsomely. Aerial refueling was developed to the point where planes were making hookups around the clock in all kinds of weather.

When the B-52 was first planned, it was to be a turbo-prop bomber, by which the power would be supplied by putting a standard propeller on a jet engine. This would have given the airplane more range, but less speed. As we showed the air force and Boeing what we could do with the B-47, it was decided that the B-52 would also be a pure jet airplane, but with eight engines instead of six.

The Russians meanwhile developed a number of turbo-prop bombers. I like to think that our experience with the B-47 enabled us to skip this expensive and unnecessary step in the modernization of our bomber fleet, giving the United States a decisive lead over the Soviets at that time.

This advantage has now disappeared and, in this day of long-range ballistic missiles with multiple nuclear warheads, the importance of a new and higher-performance manned bomber is hotly debated. Whether the cancellation of the B-1 supersonic bomber program was a wise decision remains to be seen. Reliance on missiles—ballistic or cruise—is an option we did not have in the early fifties.

A great deal of this earth had slipped beneath my wings while I was at the controls of Boeing airplanes (the B-17 and the B-29), and the B-47 measured up to the rest of the breed. I still had a lot of air time ahead of me in that airplane, but in 1953 my active flying was again interrupted for awhile. I was ordered back to the War College.

35 "Above and Beyond"

One of the engines of the B-29 was on fire, the hydraulic system was out, the wheels wouldn't come down. The pilot's wife was talking to the air policeman at the main gate when she heard the crash sirens, saw the plane come in on its belly and skid to a stop. Then she saw the crew members piling out of the various escape hatches and running for safety.

The man who came out of the pilot's seat was called Paul Tibbets, but his real name was Arlington Spangler Baugh. If you were old enough to go to the movies in 1952, or if you are a fan of the late television films, you probably know him as Robert Taylor.

Ever since the bombing of Hiroshima, Hollywood had wanted to make a movie based on the atomic mission. It would have been impossible, however, without the cooperation of the air force. The security problem was one of the reasons most often given for withholding that cooperation.

The break came when the Strategic Air Command decided something had to be done about the high divorce rate among flight crews. Curtis LeMay had taken over SAC, and under his command the duty became tough and demanding. Crews spent long hours on alert, away from their families. They were rotated regularly to advance bases overseas, where they stayed for weeks at a time. Theirs wasn't the kind of life that led to stability in marriages, but

SAC was convinced that, during this Cold War period, the training and discipline were vital to national defense.

Beirne Lay, Jr., a World War II air force veteran and a skilled writer who had done such a great job on *Twelve O'Clock High*, knew of the problem because he was close to LeMay. He was also aware that we had similar discipline and training requirements in the 509th. He suggested that it might help SAC's problem and the morale of its men to do a film story about the atomic bomb project that would focus on the strain it put on family life. I was in favor of this and gave the project my support. I knew if Beirne worked on the script, it would be an accurate portrayal.

As it turned out, the movie *Above and Beyond* was about my wartime experiences. Metro-Goldwyn-Mayer made the picture with Robert Taylor playing my role and Eleanor Parker cast as my wife, Lucy.

Although sensitive at first when I found the moviemakers taking certain liberties with the facts, I soon came to learn that this approach is routine. When history is transformed into entertainment, it's not unusual to jazz things up a bit to heighten suspense and excitement—but usually within the framework of probability. Shakespeare took considerable liberty with English history, and Longfellow embellished the Paul Revere story.

Robert Taylor wanted to meet me as a means of preparing himself for his part, so I made two trips to Hollywood while the picture was being filmed. The movie star and I hit it off from the start. We actually had a great deal in common. He was four years older than I, but he also had his beginnings in the same part of the Midwest that I came from: Missouri and Nebraska. He was the son of a doctor and had considered going into medicine when he was young. In fact, one of his early nicknames was "Doc." He was also a gun lover and an avid skeet-shooter.

He had earned a flying license before the war and went into naval aviation as an instructor at New Orleans. He tried several times to get into combat flying during the war, but his value as an actor prevented this. He used to make naval cadet documentaries when he would have preferred to spend his time training students in the fundamentals of flying.

After the war, MGM furnished him with a new twin Beech which became his special toy. He would drop in at airports all over the country. He used the plane for hunting and fishing trips, or sometimes just to find a good place to eat lunch. Barbara Stanwyck, his wife at the time, complained that he spent all his spare time polishing his guns and his airplane.

The $75,000 plane was part of a deal he made with MGM when he got out of the navy. The studio even hired one of his old navy buddies, Ralph Couser, as his full-time copilot. The airplane was named "Missy" for Barbara Stanwyck, but she never gave evidence that she appreciated the honor. She once complained that Bob would stay up in the air forever if that was possible, and added, "He can do anything a bird does except sit on a barbed-wire fence."

I don't know if it is true that aviation broke up their marriage, but Robert Taylor and Barbara Stanwyck had been divorced only a few months before the filming of *Above and Beyond* started. This domestic rupture may have given him some special feeling for the part he was to play.

Beirne Lay didn't actually write the script for the movie, but he outlined a series of events that was to be included. His ideas were turned over to the producer and director, Melvin Frank and Norman Panama, two very talented and understanding young men. They explained to me that some of the incidents had to be rearranged to make the story flow better; and I agreed that the changes didn't detract from the basic honesty of the story.

They asked me to be technical adviser in the making of the picture, but I felt that would be about the worst thing I could do. The fact that I was still in the air force might influence my decisions. I also didn't believe I could take an objective view of a story that was primarily about my life.

For the job I recommended Charley Begg, who had been commander of the ordnance squadron that assembled the bomb. He had been with us all the time and had a good opportunity to observe the stresses and strains at work on the flight crews and their families. He was an intelligent and perceptive officer who had occupied a front-row seat to the entire development. His only shortcoming might be in the technical aspects of the plane's operation. Chuck Sweeney, who flew the Nagasaki plane, gave advice on the flying aspects of the movie.

The incident in the film where I blew my top because someone let Lucy use the telephone in my office was true but slightly exaggerated. Some of the other officers' wives on the base at Wendover had pressured Lucy to find out things from me, and my reaction was always that "it's none of their damned business." Another episode, previously mentioned, concerned the atomic scientist who was asked by Lucy to unplug a stopped-up drain because I had told her that the scientists on the base, in their white laboratory coats, were "sanitary engineers." The Norstad incident in North Africa was accurately portrayed, although Norstad's name was not used.

There was a number of accomplished actors in the film. James Whitmore played Major Bud Uanna and wanted to meet the man whose part he portrayed, but this proved to be impossible since Uanna had become a CIA agent in the meantime and, for all practical purposes, had disappeared. Most people who see the movie rerun on television these days are surprised to see that LeMay is played by Jim Backus, who was convincing in that role. This was long before he became known as the voice of the cartoon character, Mr. Magoo.

During the early part of the Hiroshima flight, where Captain Parsons was arming the bomb, Hollywood introduced considerable turbulence to add to the suspense. This wasn't exactly accurate, but it was an effective way to portray the feelings of the crew when the mightiest explosive in the world was coming to life in the bomb bay of their airplane. Most of the crew members were not identified by name in the movie because of some problems encountered with Bob Lewis over payment for the use of his name.

Eleanor Parker had been nominated for an Academy Award for her part in *Detective Story* a year before she appeared in *Above and Beyond*. She was in the process of separating from her second husband, and there was speculation in the movie magazines that she and Taylor were more than just friends. I don't know whether they were or not, but they worked well together in the film. One of Taylor's biographers said his portrayal of me was the closest he ever came to an Academy Award performance.

Taylor disliked making personal appearances, but he volunteered to go on the road and promote *Above and Beyond*. I'm convinced that he did this out of a sense of patriotism, knowing that the picture might help in the recruitment of air force personnel, as well as boost morale in the Strategic Air Command.

When the movie opened in New York, I attended the premiere. Taylor and I appeared together on Ed Sullivan's "Toast of the Town" television show and clips from the film were shown. It was unprecedented for a studio to permit a major star to appear on live television, which was then viewed as a threat to the future of the motion picture industry.

I think Taylor convinced the movie people that the appearance would be beneficial. An MGM press release said, "The engagement of Taylor for the Sullivan show, according to a vice president of MGM, is regarded as an experiment to see the value of television in the promotion of pictures."

In general, *Above and Beyond* received favorable reviews. The Film Estimate Board of National Organizations said in a news release:

"The strain, the tension, the dire need for top secrecy and the grueling discipline demanded by preparation to drop the first Atomic Bomb are shown here in compelling human terms. Although the training scenes, and the redesigning and testing of the B-29 are authentic and absorbing, the film focuses on the toll of human beings and their personal relationships. As the lieutenant colonel in charge of the project, Robert Taylor plays his finest role as he watches his unexplained insistence on superhuman discipline gradually alienate his wife, family and friends. Only by implication does the film touch upon the enormity of the A-Bomb problem itself, but the picture is impressive in its emphasis on quiet realism rather than showy heroics. Superior photography enhances the taut drama, with the explosion over Hiroshima as an awesome climax."

Another review noted that "Taylor plays his role with 'set jaw' and determination—a man with singleness of purpose."

Of course, all the reviews weren't that favorable. The National Congress of Parents and Teachers said the movie "lacks the technical brilliance and emotional depth and intensity essential for star rating."

Well, that's "show biz," or so I'm told.

I personally found my part in making the picture mostly a rewarding experience. It brought me a little notoriety that I didn't feel I needed at that point in my career—mainly because I found it somewhat embarrassing. I was uncomfortable with the idea that I was being portrayed on movie screens all over the country as a legendary figure at the center of a tremendously important moment in human history. The very idea of a famous actor, Robert Taylor, starring in the role of Paul Tibbets, gave me a bit of a chill. People so portrayed are usually well settled in the graveyard, and I was very much alive with an important part of my life still ahead of me.

When Robert Taylor died of lung cancer in 1969, I felt that the nation had lost a patriot, the film industry an excellent actor, and aviation a useful friend.

And now I have something in common with Alexandre Dumas's Armand, Killer McCoy, Billy the Kid, Johnny Eager, Marcus Viniquius, Ivanhoe, and Sir Lancelot. We have all been played by Robert Taylor!

36 Trouble-shooting Years

I had flown the Atlantic many times, but now I was crossing by ocean liner. It was a leisurely trip and one I enjoyed, for ever since I had outgrown my boyhood tendency to seasickness aboard dad's yacht, I had been fascinated by boats and ships of every description.

My destination was France and an assignment to which I looked forward with a sense of excitement. I was to be a member of the North Atlantic Treaty Organization (NATO) staff in Paris.

The year was 1954, and I had just completed an academic year at the War College in Montgomery, Alabama. Departure from my homeland came at an opportune time. For the last few years, Lucy and I had known that we would never make it together in the long run. Consequently, when military orders arrived designating NATO in France as my new assignment, I told her I wanted to go alone and that she and the boys should remain in Montgomery.

It was not a happy situation but one I had to accept. Our marriage had lasted 17 years, and now both Paul and Gene were reaching ages I felt would let them have an understanding of what was taking place. Once Lucy and I had been separated for a period of time—other than the war years—a divorce suit could be initiated quietly and unnoticeably. This was, in fact, done without fanfare in 1955.

Now I was headed for France and a new life: one that was different from anything I had ever experienced. I made up my mind that I was going to get acquainted with the French people and find out how they lived. I was happy with the opportunity to become familiar with another culture. Until then, I had seen France only from the pilot's seat of a B-17.

In the easy camaraderie that develops on shipboard, I made the acquaintance of a number of Americans then living in France, who invited me to visit them. I thanked them for their offers of hospitality and promised to look them up, but made a mental note to avoid a social life that would keep me tied too closely to the American community. Now that I had a chance to meet Europeans and learn about their customs, I intended to make the most of it.

There was one American acquaintance, however, whom I was depending on to steer me in the right direction once I reached Paris. He was my old friend Bill Rice, with whom I had roomed and shared adventures in Algiers during the early days of the North African invasion. Bill was a Bostonian who had spent a great deal of time in France, where his father owned a house. Educated at Harvard and the Sorbonne, he spoke French like a native.

When I left North Africa, he told me, "There's money to be made in Algiers. I'm coming back after the war and going into business." I thought he was kidding at the time but, sure enough, that's what he did soon after the end of the war. We had kept in touch, and when the NATO assignment came up I sent him a note telling him I would soon be in France. He replied promptly with a letter ending with a breezy promise, "I'll see you in Paris."

Upon arriving in France, I learned that I would be assigned to Allied Air Forces Central Europe (AFCENT) in Fontainebleau, about 30 miles south of Paris. As soon as I became settled, I dropped Bill another note, giving him my address. Back came a letter saying he and his wife would arrive in a few days. "We'll put our car on a boat to Gibraltar and drive on up," he wrote. When they arrived, he made it clear that they intended to stay until I got acquainted with enough people to feel at home in this country where I didn't even understand the language.

I mentioned that I had brought my shotgun and would like to resume my old hobby of skeet and trap shooting. Bill didn't know anything about this sport, but he soon found a friend who steered us to one of the city's best shooting clubs—the Bal Trap Club de Paris.

It was difficult to get acquainted because only two or three of the members seemed able to speak even a few words of English. Nevertheless, they made me welcome in a polite but not warmly cordial way and as soon as I demonstrated that I knew how to handle a shotgun, they permitted me to participate in their shooting program. The French are safety-conscious and require all shooters to buy a government liability insurance policy after proving their knowledge of safety procedures.

The club had practice shoots on Wednesday and Saturday afternoons and a competitive match on Sundays. I participated in most of them and, although I proved to be one of the better shooters, I soon had the feeling that I would never really get acquainted with my fellow competitors.

Then unexpectedly one Saturday morning, while we were practicing, one of the men with whom I had a speaking acquaintance asked me if I had plans for lunch that day. His name was André Thiriet, and he understood English better than most of the other club members.

By this time, Bill and his wife had returned to Algiers and I was on my own. I had no special plans, intending to go to a restaurant where I usually ate, so I readily accepted André's invitation to join him and his wife at their home.

This luncheon broke the ice. With André identified as my friend, others also became sociable. To my surprise, I discovered that many of the club members spoke English very well. When I mentioned this change in attitude, André explained. "We French are naturally a suspicious people," he said. "We don't accept strangers at first. We stand off and take a look before deciding whether we really want to be friends."

Now that I felt myself a part of the group, I was at ease and my ability to relax was reflected in my shooting. Actually, I was the best shooter in the club, having been a military instructor in this sport. Soon I was being asked for advice, and I was able to respond with tips that improved the other members' scores.

Even with my experience, it took a couple of months to get into the swing of European-style competition. For one thing, the ranges were more difficult. Instead of having the sky for a background, I found that the ranges in Europe are usually located in a forested area where the clay birds are difficult to follow. In skeet, as soon as I learned the European rules, I seldom missed a target. The competition usually consisted of a combination of trap and skeet and, even with two or three misses in a string of shots at trap, my skill at skeet usually enabled me to win the match.

The next year, I won the French national championship at Vichy, then entered the international match for the European title, which I also won. After returning to the States, I learned that the French championship was won the following year by a member of the club whom I had trained. I remember only that his last name was Wasson. He was a cheese-maker from Normandy.

Once I had joined the crowd on a social basis, new friends decided I should have feminine companionship. I was invited to parties, to which the hosts usually invited a woman to be my partner. In this way I met my present wife, Andrea Quattrehomme. At first we needed an interpreter because she spoke English sparingly and I was still struggling with the French language.

She was a charming young divorcee, very intelligent, who had a secretarial position in Paris. Her father was with the French national railroad system, in charge of control operations at a rail center about 90 miles northeast of Paris. We got along well and were soon seeing each other on a regular basis. She picked up the English language rapidly and I made a bold effort to become proficient in French. Things went so smoothly between us that I proposed and she accepted. Before a wedding date was set, however, it became apparent that I would soon be returning to the States.

My NATO assignment involved many meetings and the writing of numerous papers to support the American position that airpower was the key to Western Europe's defense. No more Maginot Line philosophy. World War II had proved the futility of such defenses but, surprisingly, there were those among our allies who still insisted on the need for a chain of land fortifications.

I was sent to Paris for a specific purpose. Our government wanted to use my name and reputation as an expert in strategic bombing to convince our friends, particularly the French, that their defense was best achieved through air power and deterrent nuclear weapons rather than with huge land armies.

I finally succeeded, but only after two years and many a tiresome multilingual conference. The papers I had to write in support of the American position were among the most ridiculous duties of my military career. I consider them ridiculous because the papers were repetitious, presenting the same arguments time after time, but in different words.

General Lyman Lemnitzer, whom I had known from my North African days, was NATO commander at the time. General Norstad, of less pleasant memory from North Africa, was his deputy but later took Lemnitzer's job. I had a number of contacts with Norstad in Paris, always pleasant enough but strictly formal.

Norstad even went along with a proposal by my immediate superior, Major General Carl Truesdale, to keep me in Europe and place me in a key assignment within Allied Air Forces, Central Europe. To do so would have meant an immediate promotion from colonel to brigadier general—but a tug-of-war developed between Paris and Washington, with the folks in the Pentagon insisting that I return home. After several weeks of transatlantic bickering on the subject of my future, I went to General Truesdale one day and said, "Damn it, Carl, cut the orders and send me back to the States." I had grown tired of the hassle.

Once in Washington, I found out why I was so urgently wanted there. Frank Armstrong, my old commanding officer from the Polebrook days in England, had a problem, and he thought I was the best one to solve it.

In 1956, General Armstrong, the prototype for the fictional hero of *Twelve O'Clock High*, was in charge of the Second Air Force. He had become embarrassed by the fact that one of the B-47 wings under his command was at the very bottom of the chart in the Strategic Air Command rating system. SAC had a way of rating its outfits at regular intervals from the standpoint of efficiency, discipline, morale, and overall performance. It was General LeMay's way of keeping all of his outfits on their toes—through competition.

I was placed in charge of the 308th Bomb Wing at Savannah, Georgia, with the understanding that I was to shake it up and shape it up. The situation I faced on assuming command at Savannah was somewhat like the one Armstrong had encountered when he took over Polebrook in 1942. Working as a team, he and I had put that B-17 outfit back on its feet, and now that he was running the Second Air Force, he needed someone to work similar magic at Savannah.

Soon after my arrival in Georgia, Andrea flew to the United States. On May 4, 1956, we were married in the chapel at Hunter Air Force base in Savannah by the base chaplain. A longtime friend of mine, Major Ray Abernathy, stood up with us during the ceremony. Mother and father came up from Orlando to attend.

I was pleased that Andrea was well able to make the adjustment from Paris to Savannah. Her intelligence, poise, and pleasant personality were well suited to her new role as wife of the commander of an American air base. Her linguistic adaptability was much better than mine had been in France, and it wasn't long until she was speaking English as fluently as I, although with a delightful French accent.

Within a year the Savannah wing moved from the bottom to the top of the SAC totem pole. That I succeeded in imposing strict discipline and a sense of pride on a unit that had gone to pot was a feather in my cap. It didn't win me the promotion that many of my fellow colonels thought I deserved. It did, however, earn me a reputation as a trouble-shooter.

The assignment at Savannah involved an occasional flight overseas to inspect units of my outfit that participated in reflex missions, as they were called, to overseas bases. In December 1958, about two and a half years after I took on the job, I was in England on such an inspection trip when I was roused from my sleep in the middle of the night at the Columbia Club in London by a telephone call from General John P. McConnell, commanding general of the Second Air Force.

"What are you doing?" he asked in the hillbilly drawl of a typical Arkansas native, which he was. In addition, he was a former Rhodes scholar and sharp as a tack.

"I'm sleeping," I told him in a foggy voice.

"My God, I forgot what time it is over there," he apologized, then asked, "When are you coming back?"

I told him I expected to return in a couple of days.

"When you get back, come and see me at Barksdale," he said, referring to an important SAC base in Louisiana.

Before I went back to sleep, I began wondering why the Second Air Force commander wanted so much to see me that he would put in a phone call to London. I decided to return to the States at once and find out.

I got my copilot and navigator up early the next morning, and

I'm sure they weren't happy to have their London stay cut short. We went to the air base, fueled our B-47, and headed west across the Atlantic.

At Savannah, I stopped long enough to shave and change clothes, then went on to Barksdale. When I walked into General McConnell's office, he couldn't believe it.

"I told you not to hurry back," he said. Then he explained why he had called me.

"I want you to take over the air division at MacDill," he said. MacDill is at Tampa, Florida, and things weren't going well there. It was Polebrook and Savannah all over again. My reputation as a trouble-shooter would be put to another test.

There was a further challenge this time. The promotion that had been so long denied me was now certain. An air division command called for an officer of general rank, and McConnell had the promotion in mind when he called me. I soon had the star of a brigadier general on my uniform.

Tampa, with its pleasant climate and sandy beaches on the Gulf coast, is a pleasant place to live—so pleasant, in fact, that many air force officers settle down there upon retirement. Unfortunately, some of them have a tendency to sample the joys of retirement while still on active duty at MacDill.

That's what I discovered when I arrived to take command of the air division on January 1, 1959. The tactical organization was a shambles and discipline was nonexistent.

I started by tightening the screws. The incompetent were warned. Then came courts-martial. Prisoners were put to work cleaning up the base, whose appearance had been neglected. I cracked down on personnel who had been passing bad checks and getting away with it.

The slot machines in the officers' and NCO clubs were well patronized, but the clubs never seemed to make a profit from them. I found that some of the club officers had keys, and the cash was going into their pockets. They were driving Cadillacs. Whiskey distributors were giving kickbacks to those who were in charge of ordering supplies.

The bars opened at 8:00 A.M. and stayed open most of the night. I reduced the hours drastically and forbade the sale of hard liquor until 4:00 P.M.

People who had been getting away with murder screamed and raised hell. The local newspapers called me to see what was happening. A congressman threatened an investigation of my dictatorlike tactics.

But General McConnell was pleased. After hearing reports of what I was doing, he called one day and said, "Hey, you're a mean son of a bitch, aren't you?"

When I agreed, he said, "Keep it up!"

In fact, I kept him informed of every step in my campaign to put this sad installation back on its feet. I made many enemies on the base because so many were involved in the inefficiency and downright corruption that had been allowed to flourish. In fact, I became the most unpopular officer on the base. I fired the loafers and malcontents and kept many from being promoted. Some technical and master sergeants who were loafing out their last two or three years before retirement in sunny Tampa found themselves shipped to Alaska or some less-than-desirable overseas base.

Some of these people would storm into my office and say, "You can't do this to me because I'm going to retire here."

One such case comes to mind. I asked if he remembered another master sergeant who had left a couple of weeks before.

"Of course," he said.

"Well," I replied, "he came in here and told me exactly the same thing. He's in Thule now." Thule is in northern Greenland, only 900 miles from the North Pole.

I remained at MacDill for two years. By that time our division was the largest in SAC and ranked with those in the top bracket of the command's management control system. Then in 1961 I was summoned to Washigton to head up the office of management analysis in—believe it or not—the air force comptroller's office.

General LeMay had just been appointed chief of staff of the air force, and he wanted the same sort of management control in Washington that he had maintained in the Strategic Air Command. He knew that I understood this type of operation.

We called our new operation the Office of Strategic Analysis. I had a team of more than 60 people working for me, and every quarter we would evaluate one of the major commands by making personal visits, after which I would report in person to LeMay.

It was a job that I enjoyed because it involved flying opportunities. My last task in this assignment was to check the National Guard outfits that had been sent to Germany during the period of tension after the building of the Berlin Wall.

In 1962, I was called upon to develop what came to be called the National Military Command Center in Washington. The center was responsive, on a 24-hour-a-day basis, seven days a week, to any situation that threatened to develop into a crisis anywhere in the world. Funneled into the center was sensitive information from our command overseas and from secret sources behind the Iron Curtain.

I was at my Pentagon desk on November 22, 1963, when a telephone call from Dallas gave me word of President Kennedy's assassination. I knew of his death at a time when the news services were still speculating on the seriousness of his injury.

It was with a sense of relief that this desk assignment came to an end in August 1964. My next job would take me halfway around the world to a country I had never visited: India.

37 Mission to India

I arrived in New Delhi in August 1964, at a time when relations between the United States and India were at a low ebb. The Vietnam War was heating up, and Communist influence was a factor in India's seething political situation. Jawaharlal Nehru was the prime minister and Krishna Menon was an influential figure in politics. Menon was also the proprietor of a left-wing newspaper.

It didn't take long for Indian reporters to find out that I had been the pilot of the airplane that dropped the atom bomb on Hiroshima. Communists all over the world had found the atom bomb a convenient subject with which to revile the United States. With anti-American sentiment being fanned in Menon's paper, and in a number of others that were actually Communist-controlled, I became a convenient symbol of the fiendish brutality of the hated capitalists.

With the rank of brigadier general, I was the number two man in the U.S. supply mission to India. This outfit, operating under the name of the Military Assistance Group (MAG), consisted of 114 people, as I remember it, with an army major general, Charles Johnson, in charge, and army personnel predominating.

I made many friends in India, including some newspaper people who were out of sympathy with the radical left, which had gained such influence. Noting that I was taking the brunt of stepped-up left-wing propaganda, one of these friendly newsmen sought to assure me that America in general, not Tibbets, was the real target.

One day he offered congratulations and told me I had just set a new record.

"Krishna Menon attacks a great many people in his newspaper," the man told me, "but the attacks seldom last through more than four or five issues. You have broken the record." He had kept count and found that I had been mentioned unfavorably for 11 weeks in a row. Among other things, the paper had suggested editorially that I should not be allowed to breathe the air of India.

It has been written that I was called back to the United States as a result of these attacks. That is not true. I remained in New Delhi for almost two years, returning home in June of 1966 at a time when the mission was about to close.

During my 22 months in New Delhi, the relationship between our country and India went from bad to worse. Indira Gandhi was a rising politician whom I met several times at social functions in the capital.

The work of our mission was made difficult by the political climate. General Chandri, India's army chief of staff, was a graduate of Sandhurst, Britain's famous military academy. The air marshal, Argan Singh, was a bearded and turbaned Sikh. He was polite but aloof and avoided me as much as possible, with the result that I had to deal mainly with his subordinates. The U.S. Air Force was not doing him any great favors, and the neighboring Pakistanis, with whom India was in conflict, were using U.S. military equipment. The Indian airmen, on the other hand, were flying Russian-made MIG 15 jets, which we weren't allowed to approach. They also had some old British aircraft, and we had given them some obsolescent C-119 cargo planes.

Despite the frustrations, I managed to requisition a considerable volume of equipment and supplies for India's air force; but I failed to secure all that was wanted. I did arrange to have many Indian airmen sent to the United States for training at our technical service schools.

One of our tasks was to furnish help with the building of a radar line in the Himalayas near the border of China. Altogether, I believe we did a constructive and helpful job under difficult conditions. But the tension remained to the point that the duty was often unpleasant.

For the headaches that went with this assignment, there were a few pleasant compensations. Andrea and I were afforded comfortable living quarters in a house owned by the U.S. embassy. Although the summers were very hot, the weather was delightful in the fall and winter, when I found opportunities to shoot and hunt and play an occasional game of golf.

I was the guest on several occasions of Karni Singh, the maharajah of Bikaner, who lived in a rambling palace with 82 bedrooms about 250 miles west of New Delhi, with a hunting lodge nearby. He had been a member of India's shooting team in the 1962 Olympics and his lands included trap, skeet, archery, and pistol ranges. It was good grouse-hunting territory, and there was a lake that was a duck-shooter's paradise. Singh's family had been influential and prominent in India for many years; his grandfather was a confidant of Britain's King George V.

Despite these pleasant interludes, my stay in New Delhi was not among the happiest assignments of my military career. Consequently, I was not disappointed one morning in June 1966, when General Johnson called and told me to clean out my desk; that the mission with its personnel, which had been reduced by this time to a mere sixty, was going to be closed.

I was not prepared, however, for the telex that arrived a few days later from Washington, assigning me to head up the Department of Defense Transportation office in the Pentagon. I was to have the distinct honor of being in charge of all ports of embarkation, both aerial and surface, in the military establishment.

If India had been bad, from the standpoint of a military career officer, I considered the new appointment to be absolutely degrading. The job was actually outside the air force. When these orders arrived, I decided that never would I take this transportation job.

Immediately, I filled out the necessary papers for retirement and mailed them to the air force director of personnel in Washington. After 29 years and seven months of service in the air force, I was making a clean break with a military career that had supplied me with many moments of excitement, exhilaration and, on the other end of the scale, disappointments.

With 90 days of accumulated leave, Andrea and I flew to Europe, where we visited her sister in Karlsruhe, Germany. There I received word of my mother's death.

The news left me with a feeling of deep sadness and loneliness, because Enola Gay Tibbets had been a special kind of inspiration to me since earliest childhood. I regarded her as a close friend and confidante throughout my life, and she reciprocated by displaying a firm confidence in everything I undertook.

After flying back to Miami for the funeral, Andrea and I returned to Europe, bought a Volkswagen station wagon, and bummed around the continent for several weeks before returning to the United States. At the age of 51, I was confident of finding another career outside the military but was in no hurry to start looking for a job.

I managed to avoid displaying any bitterness over the fact that my military service ended with the rank of brigadier general when friends, who were acquainted with my record, expected me to win two or even three stars. I found consolation in the fact that I had participated in the most successful air force operations in history—in Europe, North Africa, and the Pacific—and had been rewarded with the opportunity to fly the best airplanes in the world and even participate in their development.

My selection to head up the atomic bombing unit had been a tribute to my record as a competent pilot and planner of military operations. The task had been carried out with precision. The inevitable publicity created jealousies on the part of certain officers who, not having been considered for the atomic assignment, were now in a position to throw roadblocks in the path of my future progress. The Bikini incident was the tip-off.

At War College, where everyone was evaluated by other members of his class, I was rated an outstanding officer, with the commander adding his endorsement to this appraisal.

Only once did I receive an effectiveness rating of less than "outstanding" from a senior officer under whom I served. The exception was a staff assignment for which I had no enthusiasm, and for this I received the next highest rating of "superior."

At least three times I was turned down by the promotion board in Washington after being recommended for higher rank. In an air force shrunk to peacetime size, West Pointers are inclined to stick together and block the advancement of "outsiders." In my case, however, there was another complication in the form of a detrimental report from General Norstad, then a colonel, after our unpleasant confrontation in North Africa in 1942.

After being turned down twice for promotion to major general, I suspected some derogatory remarks by Norstad had been inserted in my secret file in Washington, but I had no proof. When I asked a civilian friend, who was one of a very small group with access to these records, he checked my folder and confirmed my suspicions.

"I see why you didn't make the grade," he said. "There's a notation from Norstad that hasn't done you any good."

All this is water over the dam, of course. In the air force, I was associated with many a competent and dedicated officer, and my admiration for that branch of the service is in no way diminished by a few who, in peacetime, have exercised political influence considerably out of proportion to their military competence. My air force career was filled with many satisfying hours, the best of which I spent at the controls of an airplane. I never lost my love for flying.

My role as pilot of the *Enola Gay* over Hiroshima produced mixed reactions, of course, not only in India, but throughout the world for years to come. Yet, ironically, to many people the term "Hiroshima pilot" conjures up the image of a man whose life was perhaps even more influenced by the world reaction to the atomic bomb than was mine. Long after I had found a way to express my love of flying in a civilian role, he was still being used as an unwitting pawn in a worldwide propaganda game. At this point it seems appropriate to examine the sad case of Major Claude Eatherly.

38 The Sad Case of Major Eatherly

I have been asked many times about Claude Eatherly, the so-called "Hiroshima Pilot" whose personal misfortunes were shamelessly exploited by some of the world's leading left-wing propagandists. So successfully did they falsify the record that many people were led to believe that he had suffered a mental breakdown from remorse over his part in the killing of innocent civilians.

It was written by people who knew better that he was the pilot of the plane that dropped the bombs on Hiroshima and Nagasaki, and that he commanded the entire operation. These falsehoods were published in book form and in magazines all over the world, along with the fiction that he was held prisoner by the U.S. government to prevent him from speaking out.

Major Eatherly was a competent airplane pilot with a happy-go-lucky personality and a weakness for liquor, gambling, and women—not necessarily in that order. No account of the 509th would be complete without a chapter about the bizarre career of this popular officer who did, indeed, develop mental problems some years after the war and spent considerable time in Veterans Administration hospitals. He also served time in jail for crimes that were no doubt related to his mental condition. There is no evidence, however, that his difficulties were in any way touched off by his experience on the day the bomb was dropped on Hiroshima. Actually, Major Eatherly did not take part in the attack and did not

The Sad Case of Major Eatherly   283

see the bomb blast that was supposed to have haunted him through many sleepless nights.

I was aware of a certain instability in Eatherly's character during the training period at Wendover. This was most evident in off-base activities, however, and most wartime commanders come to expect occasional erratic behavior from their more high-spirited subordinates.

On my desk one morning was a report from the Officer of the Day, informing me that Buck Eatherly was in trouble with the law. I wasn't surprised, for he had been in trouble before.

The last time I had summoned Eatherly to my office for a "chewing out," it had been for speeding violations. He had his own car and liked to drive it between Wendover and Reno during off-duty hours at speeds up to 100 miles an hour. The state police had trouble catching him but, when they did, they handed him tickets that he proceeded to ignore.

I don't know how much it cost him to settle all those traffic fines, but he probably figured that it was a good investment. He was known to be lucky at the gaming tables and the sooner he got to the casinos, the more money he made.

This time, however, it was liquor permits. State liquor agency inspectors had discovered that he had somehow accumulated 15 permits to purchase liquor—14 more than he was entitled to. Don't ask me how he managed it. Let's just say that he was uncommonly resourceful. I ordered him in for an explanation.

He knew in advance why he was being called in. As he came through the door, he had the look of a contrite schoolboy who has been caught throwing paper wads across the classroom. It was a half-sheepish look, but there was no sign of fright. He knew that despite my reputation as a strict disciplinarian, I wasn't going to have him shot at sunrise.

"Look here, Buck," I said, using the nickname by which he was best known. "You're not only getting yourself in trouble, you're putting me on the spot. We have a special kind of operation here at Wendover, and we can't afford to get in a jam with the local authorities."

Eatherly was apologetic. "Sorry it happened, colonel," he said, "but the enlisted men in my outfit don't seem able to qualify for these permits and I was just trying to help some of them out."

I had heard the same story from other sources. Fellow members of his squadron loved Eatherly for good reason. They knew he would go through hell and high water for them.

Before my "chewing out" session was over, he had expressed just the right amount of regret, promised never to do it again, and left my office with a smile on his face.

I had not attempted to put on an act for Buck's benefit. I had reason to treat him with restraint. I recognized that his transgressions were largely the result of a high-spirited tendency to thumb his nose at rules, which he perceived to be intended for lesser men.

I didn't want to kill his spirit because I liked much of what I saw. That spirit might well come in handy sometime in the future. Some of the more unruly aspects of his character, which led him occasionally to run afoul of the law, might prove useful when he ran afoul of the enemy.

He was an excellent pilot with the capability of carrying out any mission to which he was assigned. Meanwhile, I knew I would have to put up with his off-duty misbehavior, which would include an occasional fistfight at the officers' club.

One incident, of a more serious nature, did not come to my attention at the time. In his well-documented book, *The Hiroshima Pilot*, author William Bradford Huie quotes Eatherly's radar operator, Albert Barsumian, as saying Eatherly once ordered him to cause a malfunction in the radar system in order to give them additional liberty time in Havana.

I have been asked what I would have done if I had known about the incident at the time. I'm not sure. If the plane's equipment had acutally been damaged as the result of his order, it would have been a serious matter. I probably would have fired him as a command pilot and assigned him to a remote base in Canada that had been set up to take care of problem personnel.

On the other hand, if the equipment had merely been disconnected, and not actually damaged, I might well have let him off with minor punishment. Many a military pilot has been known to report phony mechanical troubles in order to lay over a couple of days at an interesting port of call. And Havana was a considerably more exotic place to relax than Wendover, Utah.

Major Eatherly's plane, *Straight Flush*, was one of three to take off from Tinian shortly before two o'clock on the morning of August

The Sad Case of Major Eatherly 285

6, 1945. Their assignment was to report on weather conditions over three proposed target cities in Japan.

Arriving over Hiroshima a few minutes after 7:00 A.M., Eatherly found a big break in the cloud cover and sent back a radio message to that effect. He did not select the target city, as some have implied. Hiroshima had already been chosen as the primary target, weather permitting. The alternatives were Nagasaki and Kokura.

The *Straight Flush* headed back for Tinian immediately and was 225 miles away when I arrived over Hiroshima. Eatherly and his crew were disappointed at being too far distant to see the flash of the bomb or the mushroom cloud that rose over the city. He had no part whatever in the bombing of Nagasaki. Yet the legend has developed, and has been repeated many times, that Major Eatherly dropped both atomic bombs.

In all fairness, it must be explained that he did not initiate the fiction. Frustrated and mentally disturbed after being discharged from the air force in 1947 under unpleasant circumstances, he turned to crime. When he was arrested for breaking into two post offices in Texas, the story of his role as a member of my atomic bomb strike force was given wide publicity.

I read with interest and a sense of deep personal regret the newspaper reports of my former subordinate's difficulties after his discharge from the Air Corps. For much of the documentation of what happened to him after we parted company, however, I am indebted to the carefully researched book, *The Hiroshima Pilot*, previously mentioned.

Author Huie picks up the story from the time that Eatherly came home from the Pacific, apparently disappointed that he and his crew did not share in the tremendous Hiroshima publicity. His radio operator, Patrick L. Bowen, wrote, "I think that much of Claude's personal tragedy stems from this. Claude Eatherly was the sort who needed some recognition. He deserved it, and he was deeply hurt when he didn't get it."

Bowen said that "Claude expected to spend his life in the air force, and repeatedly he sat with me and begged me to stay in the air force with him."

So much for the theory that his mental difficulties stemmed from remorse over Hiroshima. Actually, it appears that he wanted more credit for his secondary role in that mission. But his troubles really began after his application for a regular air force commission was turned down in August 1946. Remaining in service with his reserve commission, he began to sense that he might soon be released from active duty, as had been many of his fellow officers.

In the hope of remaining in service, Eatherly managed to secure a transfer to Meteorology School at Keesler field, Biloxi, Mississippi. Then on December 3, 1946, he was relieved of duty as a student "for cheating on written class examinations." He was required to resign his commission, but because of his war record, he was spared the disgrace of a dishonorable discharge.

Civilian life was a disaster for Claude Eatherly. In 1947 he became involved in a gun-running enterprise that involved a conspiracy to drop bombs on Havana in support of a coup to overthrow the government of Cuba. Jailed briefly in New Orleans for firearms act violation, he returned to his native Texas and took a job as a salesman of petroleum products.

This and other jobs did not last long because of his erratic and sometimes criminal behavior. From 1949 through 1961, he was in and out of the Veterans Administration hospital at Waco, Texas, an essentially psychiatric institution, eight times. He was frequently arrested on charges that ranged from forgery to robbery.

Left-wing writers in Europe made the most of these episodes, claiming that he was being imprisoned in a mental hospital by the military to keep him from speaking out against atomic warfare, and ignoring the fact that he was repeatedly released and that he was saying what he pleased. Unfortunately, the more respectable newspapers and magazines in this country repeated the sensationalized propaganda, which soon came to be accepted as fact.

The first published report contained a number of errors and exaggerations and, from these, the story grew until Eatherly came to be pictured as an American Dreyfus who had turned to crime in order to call attention to his greater crime against Japan. It was even said, quite falsely, that he was being hounded and persecuted by the American military in an effort to silence him. His misfortunes were magnified into a cause célèbre.

The initial news story, containing just enough fiction to set off a worldwide chain reaction, appeared on the first page of the Fort Worth *Star-Telegram* of March 20,1957. It said, in part:

The Sad Case of Major Eatherly 287

The Air Force pilot who led the world's first atomic bombing mission into Hiroshima was in Tarrant County Jail Wednesday—charged with a crime against his country.

He is Claude R. Eatherly, 38-year-old resident of Van Alstyne.

Eatherly, a decorated hero of World War II, is accused of breaking into post offices at View and Avoca in West Texas.

He was transferred here from the Veterans Hospital in Waco to await trial in Abilene next month.

Nervously puffing on his pipe in a jail cell, the former Air Force major and B-29 pilot reluctantly described to a reporter his part in the Hiroshima bombing.

His crew was one of four assigned to fly reconnaissance ahead of the bombing plane over several potential target cities.

Eatherly's mission was to go to Hiroshima.

Finding bombing conditions there suitable, he flew back to a rendezvous point with the other scout planes and the bomb-carrying plane, Col. Paul Tibbet's *Enola Gay*.

Together, the five bombers made the historic raid on Hiroshima.

Another paragraph in the same news story said: "For his wartime services Eatherly was awarded the Distinguished Flying Cross and other honors."

This was incorrect, as was the mention of his flying back to a rendezvous point and participation in the raid on Hiroshima. But these were minor errors compared with the flagrant and deliberate distortions that were to come.

From the day of that newspaper account, which was picked up by the wire services and published all over the world, the story mushroomed incredibly. Based on half-facts, and with newspaper headlines describing Eatherly as the "Hiroshima hero," the theory was soon advanced that he had suffered mental torture because of his terrifying experience. Pressed by newspaper reporters, a Veterans Adminstration psychiatrist speculated that this was indeed a possibility.

An Associated Press dispatch on December 13, 1957, described Eatherly as "a man hand-picked to usher in the atomic age."

The next step in his elevation to superhero status occurred when the reporter who covered the Texas case won NBC televison's "Big Story" award. For some reason, Eatherly's real name was not used in the dramatization and the show was described as "a silly lie" by Eatherly's brother, Joe. Nevertheless, it helped to fix in the public mind the belief that the man who bombed Hiroshima had been driven to insanity, haunted by the memory of his dreadful deed.

Not surprisingly, the sad and distorted story wound up as the script for a Hollywood movie entitled *Medal in the Dust*. Even though the picture was never filmed, the script was widely circulated and some of its most farfetched episodes became part of the growing Eatherly legend. Fact and fiction became hopelessly intertwined.

In 1962, *Parade* magazine published what it called "the first complete, authentic report on the saga of Claude Eatherly." Claiming that its reporters had spent nearly a year gathering the facts, the magazine published a story that, incredibly, was based in large part on the fictional movie script.

Meanwhile, the Eatherly story received wide circulation in news magazines in this country and abroad. *Newsweek* headed its report "Hero in Handcuffs," and repeated misstatements that the *Straight Flush* had participated in the attacks on Hiroshima and Nagasaki; also that Eatherly had received the DFC.

The following year, Eatherly became the hero of a book, *Formula for Death*, published in France and England. The author was Fernard Gigon, a French journalist, who told a false story concerning the pilot's $237-a-month pension. "He regards this pension as a premium for murder, as a blood payment for what he did to the Japenese cities," Gigon wrote. "He has never touched this money."

At about the same time, a Viennese philosopher, Gunther Anders, was inspired to write a book, *Off Limits to Conscience*, published in Germany, with an introduction that described Eatherly as the commander of the Hiroshima raid. A British version, published under the title *Burning Conscience*, was reviewed by the Oxford *Mail*, which wrote: "Eatherly. Major Claude Eatherly. Remember the name? We should remember, for he was the man chosen by the Allies to drop the bomb on Hiroshima."

The *London Times Literary Supplement* said Eatherly "sent money to Hiroshima, visited it in person." The Communist *London Daily Worker* said that "Major Eatherly has been framed by the U.S. military because of his insistence on making public his remorse at having taken part in the Hiroshima raid."

The Sad Case of Major Eatherly 289

Both statements were nonsense. Left-wing writers all over the world had a heyday with the Eatherly story, and many well-respected publications accepted the distortions and falsehoods as fact. Honest liberals, tortured in their own minds by America's use of the atom bomb, were quick to accept the inventions of the propagandists.

Strangely, false versions of Eatherly's war record found their way into the *Congressional Record* through insertions by Rep. Frances Bolton (R-Ohio) and Sen. William Proxmire (D-Wis.)

The British philosopher Bertrand Russell, who wrote many antiwar treatises in the latter years of his life, was recruited at age 90 to express dismay at the unhappy fate of Major Eatherly.

It was probably inevitable that the anti-American propagandists, in their zeal to spread falsehoods to the far corners of the earth, should have drawn me and others of my outfit into their web of fabrications.

In 1959, a Vienna newspaper, *Wiener Illustrierte*, reported that I was in a lunatic asylum, having become insane from remorse. Another report, at about the same time, said Tom Ferebee had found solace in a monastery. Another unnamed member of the *Enola Gay* crew was said to have entered Walter Reed hospital for an operation to remove cataracts that had developed as the result of radiation from the Hiroshima bomb.

Our embassy in Vienna cabled Washington for guidance "concerning the defamatory article about Colonel Tibbets." Word went back that I had been on continuous active duty with the air force since the war and was presently commanding SAC's Sixth Air Division at MacDill. Lt. Col. Ferebee, far from doing penance in a monastery, was also at MacDill as commander of the 306th Armament and Electronics squadron.

I had lost track of Claude Eatherly for the 11-year period between the publication of Huie's book and the 30th anniversary of the A-bomb drop in 1975, when *People* magazine carried a picture of him and said that he "seems to have found serenity" at his home near Houston, where he lives with his second wife and two daughters. A throat malignancy in 1974 robbed him of his voice, said the magazine, which reported that "he may be facing death from cancer."

Despite all the problems created by his erratic life-style, I was saddened to learn of his death in July, 1978. Mentioning his radio message about the weather over Hiroshima, *People* said: "Minutes later the bomb-bay doors of the *Enola Gay* opened, and a metallic mass about 10 feet long tumbled out. When it exploded Major Eatherly and his crew were 9 miles away. Before the war ended, the dapper young pilot had flown 160 combat missions."

In one paragraph, the magazine committed three needless errors of fact, one in each sentence. Instead of being "minutes later," the bomb was dropped more than an hour after Eatherly's *Straight Flush* had arrived over the city of Hiroshima and 52 minutes after he had advised me by radio that the weather was favorable. When the bomb exploded, Eatherly's plane was 225 miles, not 9, from Hiroshima. As for his combat missions, the correct number was six—not 160. All six were to Japan to drop a single conventional explosive bomb, nicknamed "pumpkin."

If Eatherly's mental troubles were indeed the result of disappointment over failure to receive needed recognition, as his radio operator said, it is ironic that he wound up with more publicity, albeit of a dubious nature, than any other member of the 509th.

Fortunately, I was better able than Claude Eatherly to make a successful transition to civilian life. Best of all, my present job outside the air force allows me to indulge the love of flying that has been so strong since my boyhood.

39 Executive Jet

On April 21, 1976, I became president of Executive Jet Aviation Inc., an all-jet air-taxi company located at Columbus, Ohio. This new position was the summit of a second career for me and, like the military service from which I had retired, it still involved airplanes.

The story of EJA, if told in its entirety, would require another book. In fact, the equivalent of a book has already been written about it in newspapers, magazines, and trade journals. A few pages seem appropriate here because it is an interesting company and a place where I am most happy, working with people and airplanes to provide a much-needed service to a large segment of U.S. business and industry.

Executive Jet's history started with a dream that soon developed into reality. Early promise was followed by scandal with touches of sex and high living, tragedy and near-defeat. Finally, there was a rebirth of the company under new leadership. To the business world, the EJA saga was exciting and then unbelievable as new management gave the company a new image.

To understand the story of EJA, you have to know something about its colorful founder.

Olbert Fearing Lassiter was born in Elizabeth City, North Carolina. His first name was that of a Viking hero, and Fearing was the name of a family friend. He preferred being called Dick, a name he adopted at a tender age when he learned that Olbert was getting him into fistfights he could get along better without.

I first knew Dick as a high school classmate of my sister in Miami, where he was living and being reared by his grandmother. In those days of 1933–36, Dick was hooked on airplanes, motorcycles, and flashy cars. His flying began at age 15 when, in 1933, he soloed in a pontoon-equipped Aeronca. His military career started with the Florida National Guard, from which he transferred to the Army Air Corps, where he became a pilot in 1940.

When the war broke out, he started his combat career as a fighter pilot, flying Lockheed P-38 Lightnings. He became an ace with seven confirmed kills.

His next combat assignment was in bombers, where he continued to display skill and daring. On one occasion, while flying a daylight raid on Nagoya in 1945, his B-29 received 236 flak holes; two engines failed, and several crewmen were killed or wounded. Nevertheless, he flew the plane through a typhoon, crash-landed it at Iwo Jima, and walked away to fly again two days later.

After the war, in quest of recognition and excitement, Dick set speed records in both closed-course and transcontinental distance flying. In 1952, he broke into the movie crowd as technical director of the successful film *Strategic Air Command*. Because of Dick's lust for excitement and fast living, Jimmy Stewart, the picture's star, dubbed him "Rapid Richard," a nickname that stuck from then on. Popular and flamboyant, he scored a big hit with many movie personalities, and throughout the ensuing years he maintained close contacts with Hollywood and the stars.

Upon completion of *Strategic Air Command*, Dick was assigned to SAC headquarters at Offutt Air Force base in Omaha, and once again our paths were to cross.

I was in Wichita, in charge of a detachment conducting accelerated service tests on the Boeing B-47. One morning in 1952 my phone rang and the caller asked, "Do you know Dick Lassiter?"

I recognized the voice as Curt LeMay's and replied, "Yes sir."

Not being known as a great conversationalist, LeMay came to the point. "Will you take him in your outfit, because if you don't, I'll have to court-martial the bastard."

By the tone of his voice and the manner of approach, I knew LeMay was seeking help, so I agreed and was told to come to

Omaha at once. Two hours later, in his office, LeMay gave me the whole story with a twinkle in his eye and the trace of a smile on his face.

The night before, a brigadier general had gone to the officers' club for a drink. Dick was already there, and his German shepherd dog, Bo, was waiting outside. Bo, a well-mannered and obedient dog, was Dick's shadow, having been given to him by the director of *Strategic Air Command* as a token of appreciation for Dick's help with the picture.

The b.g.—his name was Curly Edwinson—was known to have a low boiling point, and he became irritated on seeing the dog just outside the club entrance. Curly came into the bar and in a loud and demanding voice wanted to know who owned that "damned dog" out front, knowing very well it was Dick's.

As politely as a colonel should, when talking to a general, Dick acknowledged ownership. Thereupon Curly warned Dick that if the dog was still there when he left, he would "kick the hell out of him." Dick angrily replied that anyone threatening harm to Bo would have to take him on first.

The challenge had been issued and was promptly accepted. Curly was slightly taller than Dick and outweighed him by 30 pounds. He thought he was tough and, even though he knew Dick worked out in the gym with weights and played handball every day, he wanted to prove that he was the better man. What Curly did not know was that Lassiter was a former Golden Gloves welterweight champion.

On the other hand, Dick Lassiter was not known as a barroom brawler. Although normally mild-mannered, he was incensed by Curly's obscenities and suggested they "step outside" to settle the matter. Curly accepted and preceded Dick to the lawn as other officers left the bar to witness the anticipated action.

Once outside, Edwinson stopped and turned to face Lassiter, then swung a wild haymaker. Dick easily ducked and counter-punched with a dynamite left that knocked Curly to the ground. Enraged, Curly scrambled to his feet and rushed at Dick, shouting and cursing. Dick sidestepped and hit him again. Curly was out cold, and the fight was over.

As LeMay recounted the incident to me, omitting none of the details as they had been relayed to him by witnesses, he admitted that Curly got what he deserved. Nevertheless, he could not let both men remain at Offutt without taking disciplinary action against them. In that case, both would no doubt be demoted.

It was LeMay's opinion that justice had been served and that the incident could be overlooked only through Lassiter's departure. I understand that, at a later date and an appropriate time, LeMay admonished Curly for his failure "to adequately assess an enemy's capabilities" before attacking.

Dick and I got a C-54 transport, with LeMay's help, packed it with his furnishings, and took off for Wichita and what turned out to be a mutually beneficial working relationship, as well as a lasting friendship. The B-47 Project WIBAC—code for Wichita Boeing Airplane Company—continued into 1954 and was absorbed into the Air Training Command as McConnell Air Force base was built there. Dick stayed for awhile after I left and then went back to SAC. He had a tour at Thule in northern Greenland, after which he was assigned to Westover Air Force base in Massachusetts. In 1960, he was assigned to command the 801st Air Division at Lockbourne (now Rickenbacker) Air Force base at Columbus, Ohio—a city with a long-standing reputation for friendship to the military.

Dick Lassiter hit it off right away with the Columbus civic leaders. As a brigadier general and the ranking officer at Lockbourne, he headed what was considered one of the community's major industries.

One member of the Columbus Airport Commission remembers touring the base with him in his command car. While driving along the flight line, the alert phone in the car buzzed. The passenger, thinking that he might become the first local citizen to learn of the start of World War III, was relieved to learn that the call was from the commander of a SAC installation in Alaska, reporting to Lassiter on his efforts to get a pair of white wolves for the Columbus zoo.

As early as 1958, Lassiter started thinking about what he would do when he left the air force. One of his plans was to establish a civilian jet service that would make use of the know-how he developed on jet operations as a test pilot and member of the Strategic Air Command.

After his tour at Lockbourne, he was assigned to the Pentagon.

The defense center's atmosphere was confining for a man who liked to wheel and deal and be his own boss. "I started right then thinking damned hard of something else to do," he told a friend.

Executive Jet Airways was incorporated in Delaware shortly before Lassiter's retirement from the air force in 1964. He decided to locate in Columbus because of the friendships he had made there. Moreover, the city was centrally located in relation to potential customers, there was an available pool of jet pilots and mechanics separating from the air force at Lockbourne, and there was a hangar available at Port Columbus International airport.

His first airplane would be a Lear jet, since he was a friend of Bill Lear and had worked closely with him on the development of the new business jet. The military and the airlines were well into the jet age by this time, but jets in the business fleet were a new concept. Many people believed that the cost of training crews and the expense of buying and operating jet equipment would keep them out of general aviation.

Executive Jet Airways came into being with Lassiter as president and chairman of the board. The general manager was Philip F. Lovett, a retired colonel who had been operations officer at Westover and for the VIP fleet maintained by the air force at Andrews Air Force base near Washington. J. Sheldon Lewis was general sales manager. The maintenance manager was Dwaine E. Gould, a retired lieutenant colonel.

Lassiter's idea was to sell jet transportation on a contract basis. Companies would buy his services, and he would have a jet where they wanted it when they needed it, and take their people wherever they wanted to go. He adopted the SAC idea of having airplanes alert around the clock, ready to respond to an emergency anywhere in the world. The operation received publicity in many magazines.

Lassiter sold the idea to friends he had made during his military career. The board of directors included such men as Jimmy Stewart, Arthur Godfrey, General LeMay, and James Hopkins Smith, former assistant secretary of the navy, and Monroe J. Rathbone, former chairman of Standard Oil of New Jersey. LeMay even came to Columbus to ask the Airport Commission for concessions on behalf of the new company. It was one of the few arguments LeMay ever lost.

Plans were made to open offices and to base jets in five cities around the country. An alert facility with sleeping quarters was established at Port Columbus. It was much like a SAC facility, except that it wasn't bombproof and there was no barbed wire.

The alert quarters were soon abandoned. Executive Jet learned that most trips made by American businessmen are planned in advance, and it was rare when the need for jet transportation arose in the middle of the night. When there was a need to get an airplane off in a hurry, it was adequate to have a crew on alert at home.

One thing that remains from the early days, reminiscent of the air force, is our status board showing the location of all our airplanes and the time remaining for the crews to stay on duty before they must be given a rest period. It works in the military and it works for us.

Lassiter also started an operation in Switzerland with the idea that it would cover all of Europe. He wanted to develop business there, and he planned to fly American businessmen while they were in Europe. The Lear jets did not have nonstop ocean-flying capability, but Lassiter hoped EJA would pick up businessmen near their homes and take them to airports to board international flights. When they arrived at their European destination, an executive jet would be waiting to speed them to their final destinations abroad.

I received a phone call from Lassiter late in 1966, just about the time I was getting a bit restless in my retirement. EJA's operation in Switzerland was not working out, and Dick wanted to talk to me about it. The call came as a surprise. He asked me to attend a meeting of the EJA board in New York. There I met a number of the board members, including Perry Hoisington, a retired major general, and Bruce Sundlun, a former B-17 pilot who was then a Washington attorney and secretary and corporate counsel of Executive Jet.

Dick wanted me to size up one of the men from Switzerland who was advising on the operations there. He came across to me as a real phony. Dick had the same idea and asked it I would take over the Swiss operation in the hopes of straightening it out. I agreed to try, but first visited Columbus to learn more about EJA's operation.

Arriving in Switzerland, I found the situation to be worse than described. Swiss regulations were being disregarded and government officials were upset. I started changing things and soon our operation was acceptable. However, there were other problems.

Flying in Europe is hindered by a maze of custom and clearance regulations. In addition to clearance at points of departure and arrival, it is necessary to obtain advance clearance from every country flown over. Imagine a flight from New York to Los Angeles for which you had to run paperwork for every state in between.

But even without such problems, the European operation was doomed. The business just wasn't there. The Europeans didn't want to do business with an American firm, and the anticipated American business didn't develop. We finally sold out to a Swiss corporation, maintaining a small interest in the company, which continued to use our name.

Aside from the business headaches, I spent an enjoyable two years in the beautiful city of Geneva. Andrea had opportunities to visit relatives and friends in her native France, and we managed a few sight-seeing excursions into neighboring countries.

There was, however, one unforgettable experience that came close to causing me embarrassment. Upon departure from the United States, we had engaged a moving company to take care of the shipment of personal effects. Some were packed in crates and boxes. There were also a couple of trunks containing an accumulation of odds and ends.

When we began unpacking in our newly rented house in Geneva, I was surprised and chagrined to discover my long-forgotten submachine gun, tucked away in the bottom of a trunk. It was the weapon that had been issued to me 24 years before at Bangor, Maine, just before I started my wartime flight overseas. I had fired it only once in anger—at low-flying Nazi planes that were strafing our barracks in North Africa—and on one other occasion on a rifle range as a means of getting acquainted with its operation. After the war, I had kept it as a souvenir, stowing it away out of sight and out of memory.

Now I was in a foreign country with a weapon of a type that was certainly illegal for a civilian to possess. Since it had passed through customs with my other belongings without challenge, the disposition of the gun was of no immediate concern, but when it came time to leave the country, I knew I would have to face up to the problem. A week before the customs inspectors were scheduled to come to the house and look over the goods that were being packed for shipment to the States, I took the precaution of taking the machine gun out of the house and placing it in the trunk of the car. I would find a way of disposing of it before we left.

The next day being Sunday, Andrea and I decided to drive across the border for lunch at a French countryside restaurant that was well known for its fine food.

At the border checkpoint, I had to wait while the French customs agent questioned the driver of the car ahead of me. When he lifted the trunk lid of that car, I suddenly remembered the contents of my own trunk.

I must have turned white, for Andrea, observing my agitation, asked, "What's the matter?"

"I've got a machine gun with two 20-shot clips of ammunition in the trunk," I told her. "How am I going to explain that to the customs man?"

The good Lord must have been riding with us that day because, when it came our turn to be inspected, the man in uniform simply smiled and waved us through with a cheerful "Bonjour!"

I wasn't about to test my luck a second time by returning that afternoon with the gun still in the car. The road to the restaurant led past a water-filled rock quarry. I pulled off the road, opened the trunk, and stripped the machine gun into its smallest component parts, then tossed them, one at a time, into the deep water. What a relief!

When EJA was formed, it was a closely held secret that the financing came from the American Contract Company of Wilmington, Delaware, a wholly owned subsidiary of the Pennsylvania Railroad. It was soon apparent that the railroad was getting no return on its investment. I saw what was happening and I didn't approve, but I was in no position to do anything about it. LeMay resigned from the board in the summer of 1967 in what some people interpreted as a prelude to his entry into national politics the following year. An exodus of other big names on the board soon followed.

I told Dick I wanted out because I felt some of the things that were happening were flagrantly illegal. He understood my feelings, and we parted on a friendly basis in 1968.

Lassiter proceeded with grandiose plans, buying Boeing 707 and 727 airliners and even talking about the purchase of a giant Lockheed C-5. To operate big planes, he needed a supplemental air carrier certificate, but in this he was blocked by the Civil Aeronautics Board when EJA's Penn Central connection was discovered. The railroad, which had invested $22 million in Executive Jet, was ordered to dispose of its interest, which it eventually did at a considerable loss.

Stuck with big jets that he was barred from using for domestic operations, Lassiter leased them to International Air Bahama, a Lichtenstein corporation that he had persuaded a number of foreign investors to organize. Cut-rate service was offered between Nassau and Luxembourg. The service was excellent, the stewardesses were pretty, but the lease money wasn't getting back to Executive Jet. Lassiter was living high.

With EJA going deeper in the hole financially, it was apparent that something would have to be done. Harry Pratt of the Detroit Bank and Trust Co., which held the Penn Central interest in an irrevocable liquidating trust, discussed the problem with Bruce Sundlun, a Washington attorney and a member of the Executive Jet board of directors.

The bank, representing the majority of shares in the company, authorized Lassiter's removal as president. Pratt and Sundlun went to Columbus, and in a surprise midnight raid on June 30, 1970, seized the Executive Jet headquarters at Port Columbus and started examining the company's records. Another agent of the bank took over the New York office.

Sundlun was the only person with a knowledge of the operation available to the bank, and he was promptly named president of the company. It was expected that he would liquidate the assets; instead, he decided to find out if the business could be saved.

The situation was worse than he expected. No financial statements had been published in 1968 and 1969, but an audit indicated that the company had lost about $4 million each year on revenues of $13.5 million. Sundlun set out to bring order out of the confusion.

One of EJA's senior pilots, who had been with me in Switzerland and then returned to Columbus shortly after I left Europe, called one day to inform me of what had taken place. Surprised and interested, I phoned Bruce. After an enlightening conversation, Bruce asked if I had the interest and "gambling instinct" to come to

Columbus. My job would be to help him "make EJA swim." The offer was a challenge that I was quite willing to accept. Since I had left the company and returned from Switzerland, Andrea and I had been living in Florida.

Engaging as Dick Lassiter was, and the possessor of many qualities that I admired during our long friendship, candor compels me reluctantly to mention the flaws that contributed to his downfall. Starting with his ego-expanding experience in Hollywood, where he tasted deeply of the exotic life of the movie capital, he developed grand illusions that were often out of phase with reality. It would have taken more willpower than many men possess to have overcome the temptations a quixotic fate served up to him.

The money he raised for his jet-taxi enterprise permitted him to live like a millionaire, and he sometimes found it difficult to distinguish between his own resources and those of EJA. A weakness for beautiful women contributed to his problems, according to more than one magazine article that appeared at the time the EJA difficulties were making headlines. One of his so-called mistresses was identified only as "Bahama Mama," a stewardess for the transatlantic airline he had started. There were others. Additional expenses resulting from his free-swinging life-style were incurred to pay for furnished apartments in New York and elsewhere, and for hotel suites in foreign cities, his favorite being Rome, where he died in 1973 as the result of a brain tumor.

The way EJA was turned around under Bruce Sundlun's guidance is one of America's business success stories of the decade. He managed to get the big jets off the books and finally brought the company into the black sufficiently to make it a salable asset. Nevertheless, Detroit Bank and Trust was not successful in attracting buyers.

Finally, the bank turned to Sundlun himself. He and two partners, Robert L. Scott, Jr., of Philadelphia, and Joseph S. Sinclair of Providence, borrowed $1.25 million to buy out Penn Central's interest. The sale was approved by the court handling the railroad's bankruptcy.

Today, EJA is a dynamic company doing business with approximately 250 contract flying customers. We regularly fly throughout the United States, parts of Canada, the Caribbean area, Central and parts of South America, at the rate of more than 3 million miles a year.

In the summer of 1977, EJA flew its 55-millionth mile. In addition to our flying customers, we have many aircraft owners and operators who bring their aircraft to us for routine maintenance. These number as many as 300 a year. Annual recurrent air and ground training for many of these pilots is conducted during one of their visits. EJA has matured now and is a respected company in the eyes of the business world. We have earned a good reputation in the industry and I intend for it to remain that way.

At Columbus, Andrea and I live comfortably in a pleasant suburban area less than 10 minutes from my office at the airport. I still have a number of fine shotguns and often, on weekends, engage in my longtime favorite sport as a member of a skeet club at nearby Groveport.

Although my present duties keep me chained to an office desk most of the time, I manage to find opportunities to get behind the controls of a Lear jet often enough to keep my pilot's license current.

It may be difficult for friends who knew me in my cigarette-, cigar-, and pipe-smoking days to believe that I have kicked the nicotine habit. My decision to quit smoking came about in 1959, when I went for my annual physical examination at MacDill Air Force base. After taking my cardiograph, the doctor showed me the results in the form of crooked lines on graph paper and said ominously, "Do you see those little blips? If you get three of them in succession, you're through flying."

When I asked why, he said, "These blips tell me that you smoke too much and drink too much coffee."

Surprised that he could make such accurate deductions from the tracings on that piece of paper, I confessed that I was indeed a heavy smoker and coffee drinker.

Then he said, "If you will slow down, in six months this will disappear and you will have no more problems. You're all right at the moment but you had better not keep it up."

On the spot I decided, "This is it. I'd rather fly than smoke or drink coffee."

I went home, emptied my pipe, tossed my cigarettes into a waste basket and my lighter into a dresser drawer. I haven't smoked since. For a time I switched from coffee to tea but, after subsequent physicals in which the warning blips had disappeared from my cardiograms, I resumed my old coffee-drinking habit, but in moderation.

As for drinking, I like a glass of beer on a hot day; also, when living in France, I developed a taste for wine. My favorite is Beaujolais. But I have not touched hard liquor since college days when I was blinded, along with several fraternity brothers, after we had consumed a jug of bootleg moonshine. We wound up in a hospital, where it was four days before I regained my eyesight.

My weight today is 163 pounds, about the same as it has been throughout much of my adult life. My hair, once dark, is salt and pepper. Bifocals are required, and my hearing, dulled by airplane engines and shotguns, is augmented by an aid in each ear. My fascination for airplanes has not changed, by my perspective of them has as I become less active and involved in flying. It appeared prudent to leave the flying to the younger men. I made this decision in late 1986. By this time Executive Jet was a solidly established business and an attractive acquisition target for the right purchaser. We were approached by several potential purchasers and the company was sold to a New York based leasing and financing company. I remained on a consulting basis for another 12 months. As I look back, I do not know what I would change. Today I see a strong and vibrant organization, and satisfaction from something well done is sweet.

40 Reflections

There are voices which assert that the bomb should never have been used at all. I cannot associate myself with such ideas. Six years of total war have convinced most people that, had the Germans or Japanese discovered this new weapon, they would have used it upon us to our complete destruction with utmost alacrity. I am surprised that very worthy people, but people who in most cases had no intention of proceeding to the Japanese front themselves, should adopt the position that, rather than throw this bomb, we should have sacrificed a million American and a quarter million British lives in the desperate battles and massacres of an invasion of Japan. Future generations will judge these dire decisions, and I believe if they find themselves dwelling in a happier world from which war has been banished, and where freedom reigns, they will not condemn those who struggled for their benefit amid the horrors and the miseries of this gruesome and ferocious epoch.
—Winston S. Churchill, in an address to the House of Commons, August 16, 1945.

One day in the summer of 1975, a friend invited me to join the Confederate Air Force, a Texas-based organization of serious-minded but fun-loving fliers who have restored a fleet of obsolete World War II aircraft. Knowing it to be dedicated to the preservation of these historic airplanes, and its membership to include such wartime air force leaders as Jimmy Doolittle and

Nathan Twining, I accepted the invitation and was commissioned a colonel, the honorary rank assigned to all members.

That fall, I attended the CAF's annual air show at Rebel Field, Harlingen, Texas, and witnessed an exciting reenactment of many episodes from the war, including the attack on Pearl Harbor and the bombing of Hiroshima. For the former, six replica aircraft with the red meatball insignia of the enemy comprised the attacking fleet. These were the same planes that had been used in filming the motion picture, *Tora! Tora! Tora!* A restored B-29, the only one of the old Superforts still flying, made the simulated atomic attack. A smoke bomb was set off in the center of the field to represent the mushroom cloud.

The performance was so interesting that I returned for the 1976 event, at which time I was offered the opportunity to be checked out in the B-29. I agreed enthusiastically, for I had not flown one of these famous old bombers for 30 years. Going over the checklist, which seemed strange after years of flying jets, I was surprised at the ease with which I was able to recall the old routine. This plane, named "Fifi," had been salvaged from an airplane graveyard at China Lake in the California desert and restored to flying condition at considerable expense.

After three successful takeoffs and landings, I was invited to fly the plane in the simulated Hiroshima attack that same afternoon. When I agreed, the information was passed along to the air show's public address announcer, who concluded his narration with a tribute to the wartime fliers who had lost their lives, then added:

"As the B-29 approaches, the explosion of the atomic bomb goes off, ending some of the darkest days of America's history. At the controls of the Boeing B-29 Superfortress is General Paul Tibbets, who was the pilot of *Enola Gay* that dropped the atomic bomb on Hiroshima."

The Associated Press coverage featured the fact that I had piloted the airplane in a reenactment of the Hiroshima bombing. This set off an immediate reaction from an organization in Japan that calls itself the Japanese Congress Against Atomic and Hydrogen Bombs.

Ichiro Mortake, president of that organization, sent a cablegram to the Confederate Air Force, demanding that there be no repetition of the air show. He described the bombing of Hiroshima and Nagasaki as a "historical crime to mankind" and suggested that the United States "should think of compensation for this crime." His protest was publicized worldwide, and the American embassy in Tokyo expressed its regrets while pointing out that the Texas air show was privately sponsored.

The Confederate Air Force issued a statement, regretting that some Japanese people were offended, but adding: "We feel that this demonstration was altogether proper and presented in an appropriate manner. We do not owe an apology to anyone." It noted that the war, started by the Axis powers, cost 30 million lives, both civilian and military, between 1939 and 1945.

A great many Japanese do not share Mortake's view that the atomic bombings were unwarranted and criminal. A free-lance Japanese photographer, Y. "Jake" Yamada, attended all four days of the Texas show and flew one B-29 mission. He found nothing offensive about the simulated A-bomb drop and expressed surprise at the reaction in Tokyo. His picture-stories of the event have appeared in a number of Japanese publications.

Japanese tourists visiting the National Atomic Museum at Albuquerque have been known to applaud filmed scenes of American nuclear accomplishments. My own experience, on being interviewed by Japanese writers and television commentators, has convinced me that there is very little bitterness on the part of our former enemy. A majority of Japanese welcomed the end of the war.

One must sympathize with any movement designed to reduce or eliminate human slaughter. Nuclear warfare is indeed inhuman and ought to be banned. By the same token, other forms of warfare, such as the dropping of fire bombs and the shooting of soldiers with cannon and rifles, are likewise uncivilized and should be outlawed. Those who try to distinguish between civilized and uncivilized forms of combat soon find themselves defending the indefensible. To suggest that one specific act of war is barbaric and thereby illegal is to imply that other forms of slaughter are acceptable and consequently legal.

One also runs into trouble in arguing that it is unthinkable to take the lives of innocent civilians but all right to kill soldiers and sailors whose glorious mission it is to kill or be killed. This sad logic ignores the fact that the soldiers and sailors are really civilians who were conscripted and put in uniform, many against their will.

Interestingly, those who protest most vigorously our use of the atomic bomb against Japan deplore the killing of so many people in just two raids. One is given the impression that a thousand planes, rather than two, should have been used to accomplish the same result. Their complaint that so many were killed is answered by those who contend that the use of this terrible weapon actually saved a million or more lives by shortening the war.

It is even possible to suggest that Mr. Mortake might not be alive today, to lead his protest group, had it not been for the atom bombs. Many Japanese lives would have been lost if it had been necessary to invade the Japanese home islands. The people of Hiroshima and Nagasaki would not have been spared because, had these cities not been reserved for A-bombings, they certainly would have been destroyed by conventional explosives or incendiaries. Of course, one cannot overlook the plight of those who were seared and disfigured by nuclear exposure, nor is it possible to deal lightly with the suffering of those who live on with lasting scars from the flames ignited by nighttime terror raids on Tokyo and other Japanese cities.

One frequently voiced argument against use of the bombs at Hiroshima and Nagasaki is based on the contention that the Japanese were already on the verge of surrender. However, the Potsdam declaration, calling for unconditional surrender and spelling out the consequences of prolonging the war, was firmly rejected by the Japanese. Although it did not hint at our possession of a new superweapon, the ultimatum threatened "prompt and utter destruction."

It is true that Japan had approached the Soviet Union to be an intermediary, naïvely unaware that the Russians were on the verge of entering the war in the Far East. There is evidence, however, that Tokyo was interested only in a peace that would permit its military leaders to go unpunished.

"Unconditional surrender is the only obstacle to peace," said an intercepted message from Foreign Minister Togo to Ambassador Sato in Moscow. This statement has been curiously interpreted by some to mean that Japan was ready to surrender if only assurances were given that the emperor would not be dethroned or treated as a war criminal. In truth, the leaders of the Japanese government were interested in a number of other conditions, including a promise of no war trials and no occupation of the home islands by American troops.

The question of whether the enemy was ready to surrender, except on the most favorable terms, was answered by the cabinet's attitude even after the atomic bombs were dropped. General Korechika Anami, the minister of war, suggested that the real test lay ahead and that better terms could be achieved after U.S. invasion forces had suffered heavy casualties. The cabinet was evenly divided, and finally the emperor himself broke the deadlock and voted for surrender.

In the more than 40 years since Hiroshima, I have received many letters from people all over the world. Some have condemned me as a war criminal, but the vast majority have expressed thanks that my crew dropped the bomb that ended the war. Many expressed their gratitude in personal terms, acknowledging that they might not be alive today had it been necessary to carry out plans for an invasion of the Japanese homeland.

It has been estimated that the conquest of Japan by conventional means would have cost over a million casualties, both Allied and Japanese. Those Marines who witnessed the fanatical resistance of Japanese soldiers on Guadalcanal, Iwo Jima, and elsewhere will testify that the enemy was capable of fighting to the last man and that the struggle for the home islands would have been unthinkably bloody.

The decision to use the atomic bomb was not made without giving careful thought to the consequences. President Truman and his advisers were well aware of the possible adverse reaction to the introduction of a frightful new weapon into the world's already awesome arsenal of destruction.

They knew that the scientists who had developed the bomb were divided on the question of whether it actually should be used. They also considered the suggestion for a demonstration blast to persuade the Japanese that further resistance was futile.

This proposal was rejected by a scientific panel of the Interim Committee that had been formed, under the chairmanship of Secretary of War Henry Stimson, to consider all the disturbing questions related to the use of the bomb. The panel's report, signed by Robert Oppenheimer, said that "we can propose no technical demonstration likely to bring an end to the war; we can see no acceptable alternative to direct military use."

Oppenheimer later hedged under pressure, saying that the report was based on an assessment of the military situation supplied by Stimson, an active proponent of the bomb's use. He also said the committee did not have before it a statement by a committee of scientists, headed by James Franck, which argued that a surprise atomic attack on Japan was "inadvisable." However, a summary of the Franck report had been presented to the committee by one of its members, Arthur Compton. Furthermore, Oppenheimer was well aware of all the arguments it contained, having discussed the question frequently with such opponents as Leo Szilard, Neils Bohr, and Franck himself.

Curiously, it was Szilard who drafted the letter that Einstein wrote to President Roosevelt in 1939, describing recent nuclear experiments and suggesting that "extremely powerful bombs of a new type" could be constructed. It is ironic that the scientists who uncorked the bottle should disown their mad genie. With their slide rules and equations, they were perfectly aware in advance of its true nature.

As for the question of morality that has haunted the United States ever since 1945, volumes have been written to support each side of the controversy. There has been a notable lack of objectivity, writers preferring to sift through old records to find fragments of evidence to back up their preconceptions.

It was President Truman who made the decision to drop the bombs, with the concurrence of Britain's Prime Minister Churchill, who later wrote: "The historic fact remains, and must be judged in the after-time, that the decision whether or not to use the atomic bomb to compel the surrender of Japan was never an issue. There was unanimous, automatic, unquestioned agreement around our table; nor did I ever hear the slightest suggestion that we should do otherwise."

The punishment aspect of our war-winning strategy had been mentioned by Churchill in a speech to the U.S. Congress in 1943 when he said: "It is the duty of those who are charged with the direction of the war to overcome at the earliest moment the military, geographical and political difficulties, and begin the process, so necessary and desirable, of laying the cities and other munitions centers of Japan in ashes, *for in ashes they must surely lie before peace comes back to the world.*"

Expectations of heavy casualties, if invasion had been necessary, were based on the Japanese use of suicide tactics in the final months

Reflections   309

of the war. Kamikaze planes and manned torpedoes had destroyed a substantial number of American warships. On the day before the announcement of the Hiroshima attack, *The New York Times* carried a dispatch from Manila that said: "Indications are growing that the Japanese military still has sufficient control of the domestic situation to prevent Japan's surrender [from] the weight of our bombing attacks alone. There is increasing evidence that the Far Eastern enemy is as little likely to submit to air attacks alone as was Germany." Later the same dispatch said that "hard and probably extremly bloody land fighting against a skilled and determined foe is now being taken for granted here."

But all this happened more than 40 years ago. I am writing about ancient history as time is measured in this fast-moving age of technology, in which the nuclear hazard has been compounded by the development of intercontinental ballistic missiles.

The bombs we dropped on Hiroshima and Nagasaki were primitive by today's standards, as was our method of delivery. Powerful missiles will now propel thermonuclear warheads for a distance of 5,000 miles in 20 minutes. No point on earth is beyond reach. The oceans no longer protect us.

A typical ballistic missile may carry a warhead yielding 20 megatons or more of explosive power. This is equivalent to 20 million tons of TNT, or more than a thousand times as powerful as the Hiroshima A-bomb, which had a yield of less than 20 kilotons (20,000 tons). Each of the 20 cruise missiles that can be carried by one B-52 jet bomber is in the 100 kiloton range.

There seems to be no limit to the size or power of a thermonuclear (hydrogen) bomb. The largest on record, set off in 1962 by the Soviet Union, developed an explosive force of 58 megatons, more than 3,000 times that of the Hiroshima bomb.

During the past few years, the United States and the Soviet Union have engaged in a series of talks on the limitation of strategic weapons. An interim agreement limits each side to 2,400 offensive strategic delivery vehicles (intercontinental ballistic missiles, submarine-launched missiles, and bombers). Of these, 1,320 may have multiple warheads, each independently targeted, called MIRV's.

Such arsenals are believed sufficient to destroy our civilization and possibly wipe out all life on the planet. It is more than a coincidence, and of special interest to the inhabitants of such cities as New York, Detroit, Leningrad, and Minsk, that Washington and Moscow are the only cities that, by treaty, may be protected by antiballistic missiles.

With such a clause written into the ABM agreement, logic indicates that both nations plan to avoid targeting their rival capitals in event of nuclear war. While some cynics may hastily conclude that the political leaders of the U.S. and the USSR are thus taking pains to save their own skins, the rationale is more likely based on the obvious need to have someone still alive to get on the hot line and cry, "Hold, enough!"

If there were no such islands of life in a world gone mad, the missiles would keep on flying in both directions until all stockpiles were exhausted, leaving the world in radioactive ashes beneath an immense mushroom cloud.

It is a sobering thought that our two bombs, feeble by today's standards, were the curtain-raiser on what many view as the supreme human tragedy. Mankind's best hope is that the prologue was so frightening that the main show will be canceled.

President **Reagan** expressed the hope that all nuclear weapons may someday be abolished. His is a praiseworthy goal, but one that must be accompanied by a drastic reduction or, better yet, elimination of conventional armaments. Two world wars have occurred in this century without nuclear impetus, and the suffering has extended far beyond the battlefields.

Today, it is clear that the existence of atomic weapons has been a war deterrent. Certainly they are an equalizer in Europe against the superior manpower of the Soviet Union. Nuclear disarmament by both sides would leave the NATO allies vulnerable if not helpless.

It is widely hoped that future war on a worldwide scale can be prevented by maintaining a balance of terror between the potential adversaries. Yet the very existence of enormous stockpiles of these weapons is enough to make the world uneasy. However unthinkable the prospect, one can never be sure that someone may not, in a suicidal moment, someday push the button.

This is why a way must be found to eliminate war as a means of settling quarrels between nations.

Index

Abbeville, raid on, 90
Abernathy, Ray, 273
Above and Beyond, 227, 262-67
Adams, William B., 249
Air and Space Museum, 9, 23
Air Cadet Training, 41-48
Alamogordo, New Mexico, 149-50, 152, 168, 185
Albury, Don, 163
Alexandrov, Simon, 250
Algiers, 101, 103, 105, 112, 114, 118, 120, 123-26, 129-30, 132, 134, 137
Allen, Eddie, 140
Amiens, raid on, 90
Anami, Korechika, 307
Anders, Gunther, 288
Armstrong, Frank, 79, 82, 87, 89, 148, 159, 169, 272
Arnold, H. H. "Hap," 84, 133, 159, 169, 184, 187
Ashworth, Frederick L., 198
Ateliers d'Hellemmes locomotive works, raid on, 97
Areliers et Chantiers shipyard, raid on, 92
Atkinson, Hampton H., 120, 128
A-20, 54, 62-64, 66
Atomic bomb
  proposed, 160
  first chain reaction, 160
  manufacturing sites, 155
  secret laboratory, 160
  "Trinity" test, 185, 189
  first use in war, 225

Baby Ruth bars, 19-23
Backus, Jim, 265
Bartlett, Sy 79
Batista Field, Havana, 172
Beahan, Kermit, 163, 194, 250, 251
Beasley, Bill, 52
Begg, Charley, 264
B-18, 54, 66-67, 70
Beser, Jacob, 163, 206, 212, 228
Bikini, 245, 286
Birch, Francis, 199, 201
Biskra Air Base, 119-20, 128, 133
Bizerte, raids on, 115-17, 127-28, 130-32
Blanchard, William "Butch," 186-88, 246
Blandy, W. H. P., 245
Bluie West Eight, 75-76
Bluie West One, 75-77
Bock, Frederick, 196
Bock's Car, 10, 196, 238, 239
Boeing-Wichita, 145-48, 151, 158, 256-57
Bohr, Neils, 308
Bolton, Frances, 289

312 Index

Boomerang, 103, 107, 112
Bowen, Patrick L., 285
Brandt, Carl, 256
Brode, Robert, 198
B-10, 51, 53-54, 62
B-17 Flying Fortress, 66-68, 70-72, 74, 77-78, 80, 82-84, 87, 90-93, 97, 103-05, 107-08, 110-11, 116, 118-19, 122, 128, 130, 146-47, 159, 188, 261
B-18, 68
B-24 Liberator, 78, 97
B-26, Marauder, 121-23
B-29 Superfortress, 9, 122, 130, 134-40, 152, 155, 157-58, 162, 165, 168, 170, 182, 184, 186, 188-89, 197, 201, 206, 209, 212, 217, 226, 257-58, 292
B-47 jet bomber, 254-56, 258, 261, 272, 274
BT-2, 51
BT-9, 44-45
Burning Conscience, 288
Butcher Shop, 80, 82

"Cannon," 199
Caron, George, 163, 206-07, 213, 224, 226-27. 229

Cate, J. L., 113
Cayeux, raid on, 97
"Centerboard," 196
Chandri, General, 278
Chiang Kai-Shek, 148
Churchill, Winston, 7, 102, 105, 185, 303, 308
Cincinnati, University of, 35-36
Clark, Mark, 102-04, 106-07, 112, 114, 134
Classen, Tom, 162, 184
Code Names, 156, 183, 196, 199, 202
Compagnie de Fives-Little, raid on, 97
Compton, Arthur, 308
Confederate Air Force, 303-05
Connors, Wayne, 103-04, 107-08
"Coronet," 18
Couser, Ralph, 284
Cowan, Maynard, 142-44
Craven, W. F., 113
"Crossroads," 245, 248-53
Crum, Charley, 35
Crum, Harry, 35-37, 185, 235

Crum, Mrs. Harry, 185, 235
Crum, Louis, 35
Curtis, Ted, 129, 132
Cyanide capsules, 205

Darlan, Jean Francois, 111, 114
Dave's Dream, 249-251
Davenport, Iowa, 12
Davies, John, 183, 231
Davis, Doug, 19-23
Del Genio, Nick, 207
Des Moines, Iowa, 12, 14
"Dimples," 202
Doolittle, James H., 101, 108, 110, 111, 121-23, 128-29, 132-34, 141, 303
Dougherty, Dora, 176-77
Downey, William B., 203
Drucat airfield, raid on, 90
Duncan, Asa, 110, 122
Duncan, Claude, 122
Duzenbury, Wyatt, 163, 207

Eaker, Ira, 82, 84, 87-88, 90
Easterly, Elliott, 203
Eatherly, Claude, 164, 192-93, 196, 218, 281-90
Eatherly, Joe, 288
Edwinson, "Curly," 293-94
Egtvedt, Clair, 68
Einstein, Albert, 160, 308
Eisenhower, Dwight D., 58, 60, 101, 105-10, 112, 142
Enola Gay, 6, 8-10, 197-98, 200, 204-05, 208, 210, 217, 220, 230, 234, 237, 248, 250, 281
crew of, 206
Ent, Uzal G., 152, 154-57, 159-62
Ervine, Bill, 183
Ewbank, Eugene, 140
Executive Jet Aviation Inc., 291-302

Farrell, Thomas F., 198-99, 206, 208, 210-12, 228, 231
"Fat Man," 9, 201, 222, 236
Ferebee, Tom, 82, 135, 163, 185-86, 188, 194, 197, 202, 206, 221-23, 232, 242, 246, 248, 250-51, 289
Fifer, C. Arthur, 13, 28
Fifer, Mrs. C. Arthur, 13, 27-28

Index 313

Fisch, Frank, 44-47
509th Composite Group, 169, 182, 186-87, 190, 193, 203, 213, 216
   authorized, 156
   to Wendover, 162
   activated, 163
   security, 163-67
   to Tinian, 181
   is Winning the War, 191
   insignia, 200
Fleming, Pat, 257
Florida, University of, 32, 35
Folke-Wolfe 91, 97, 190
Formula for Death, 288
Fort Benning, 49-62, 65
Franck, James, 308
Franck Report, 308
Frank, Melvin, 264
Full House, 204, 218
Furman, Robert R., 195

Gandhi, Indira, 278
George VI, 106
Gibraltar, 122, 142
   Mark Clark's mission, 101-106
   with Eisenhower, 107-112
Gigon, Fernard, 288
Gilliam, 251, 252
Giraud, Henri, 111
Godfrey, Arthur, 295
Golden, Bill, 56-57
Gosnell, Helen, 176-77
Gould, Dwaine E., 295
Great Artiste, The, 196, 203, 208, 212, 222, 226, 238-39
Green Hornet Line, 176
Groves, Leslie R., 159, 163-64, 169, 171, 179, 184, 189, 195, 196, 199, 228, 232
Guderian, Heinz, 61

Halifax bomber, 85
Hamblen, A. L., 102
Harris, Arthur, 84
Harrison, William C., 249
Hayworth, Rita, 251
Heard, Rusty, 34, 42
Heater, Gabriel, 151
Henderson, Frank, 26-31
Hirohito, Emperor, 192, 201

Hiroshima, 6, 8, 19, 133, 184, 192, 195, 208, 217-221, 228, 233-34, 238, 243, 266, 288, 300, 309
   Aioi "T" Bridge, 196, 222-23, 232
   bomb drop, 224
   bombing re-enactment, 304
Hiroshima Pilot, The, 284-85
Hoisington, Perry, 296
Holmes, Julius C., 102
Hope, Bob, 162
Huie, William Bradford, 284-85
Hydrogen bombs, 309

Indianapolis, 194-95, 201
Iwo Jima, 212, 215-18, 307

Jabbitt III, 204, 218
Jackson, Ralph L., 30
Jeppson, Maurice, 206, 214-15, 220, 225
Jiminez, Federico, 26
Johnson, A. M. "Tex," 258
Johnson, Charles, 277, 279
"Judge," 199
JU-88, 112, 124

Kaltenborn, H. V., 151
Karis, Christopher, 137
Kelly Field, 47-49
Kennedy, John F., 276
Kenny, George, 255
Knox, John, 73, 79, 108, 110

Lancaster bomber, 85
Lansdale, Jack, 152, 154
Lassiter, Olbert F. "Dick," 291-96, 288-300
Laurence, William, 201, 208, 214-15, 239,
Lawrence, Ernest O., 171
Lay, Beirne, 79, 96, 263-64
Leahy, W. D., 200
Lear, Bill, 295
LeMay, Curtis, 182, 184, 186-89, 192, 196, 199, 236-37, 243, 246-47, 252-53, 260, 262-63, 275, 292, 294-95, 298
LeTrait, raid on, 92-93, 98-99
Lemnitzer, Lyman, 102-03, 110, 272
Lewis, J. Sheldon, 295

314 Index

Lewis, Robert, 163, 174, 187, 197, 206-07, 210, 214-15, 219, 223-25, 227-29, 237, 243
Lille, raid on, 96-99
Lipsky, John, 92
"Little Boy," 9, 200, 209, 222, 226
Lockhart, Gene, 93-96
Lohr, Thomas F., 110-11
Longfellow, Newton, 77, 94-96
Longueau railroad yards, raid on, 90
LoPrinzi, Vince, 9
Los Alamos, 155-56, 160, 167, 175-79
Lovett, Philip F., 295

MacArthur, Douglas, 241
MacDill Air Force Base, 66, 69, 71, 274, 275
Mackenzie, DeWitt, 98
MacFarland, F. N. Mason, 110
Maison Blanche Air Base, 112, 114-15, 118
Manhattan Project, 154-55, 159, 169, 176, 229
Marquardt, George, 203, 212-213, 217, 220, 222, 230
Marshall, George C., 60, 198
Mast, Charles Emmanuel, 102, 104
McConnell, Fred J., 260
McConnell, John P., 273-75
McConnell, Thomas L., 260
McCoy, Mike, 260
McKnight, Chuck, 212-13, 217
McNair, Lesley J., 60
Medal in the Dust, 288
Menon, Krishna, 277-78
Messerschmitt (Me 109) fighter, 83, 86, 91, 93, 97
Metcalf, G.B., 87
Miami, Fla., 11, 14-16, 18, 20-22, 34, 50-51, 53, 68, 98-99, 173-74
Molder, Lieutenant, 111
Montgomery, Bernard, 101, 109
Mortake, Ichiro, 304-06
Moynahan, John F., 236
Munn, Allen, 12
Murphy, Robert D., 102

Nagasaki, 8, 10, 184, 192, 195, 217-18, 285, 288, 309

bombing of, 239
postwar visit to, 241-43
Narsarssuak, Greenland, 77
National Atomic Museum, 9, 305
National Military Command Center, 276
NATO assignment, 136, 268, 271
Nehru, Jawaharlal, 277
Nelson, Richard, 207, 228
Nevada, 249, 251
Nimitz, Chester, 182
19th Transport Group, 141
90th Squadron, Third Attack Group, 62
93rd Bomb Group, 97
97th Bomb Group, 70, 73-74, 78, 79, 87, 89, 98, 118
Nolan, James F., 195, 231
Norden Bomb Sight, 22, 80, 163, 171, 221
Norstad, Lauris, 126, 127, 129-31, 133, 135, 149, 187, 171, 180-81
Now It Can Be Told, 232
Nuclear Arms Limitations, 309-10
No. 91, 208, 212, 222

Off Limits to Conscience, 288
Office of Strategic Analysis, 275
0-46, 50, 51
0-47, 51, 52
Oppenheimer, J. Robert, 160, 177-78, 185, 275, 199-200, 307-08
Oppenheimer, Jean, 178
Oppenheimer, Katherine, 177-78
Osborne, Neil, 44

Panama, Norman, 264
Parker, Eleanor, 263, 265
Parsons, William, 154, 156-57, 160, 174, 198-99, 201-06, 211-12, 214, 219-20, 222, 226, 228, 230, 236-37, 265
Patton, Beatrice, 55-56
Patton, George Smith, 55-61, 101
Payette, Hazen, 231-32
Pearl Harbor, 65
Pennsylvania, 251
Pennsylvania (Penn Central) Railroad, 298-300
Petain, Henry, 101, 114
Phillips, Charles T., 122
Pinecastle (McCoy) Air Force Base, 260

Index 315

Polebrook Air Base, 78-79, 83, 94, 103, 107, 148, 159, 209, 272
Porter, John, 202
Power, Thomas S., 135-36, 254
Pratt, Harry, 299
Prestwick, Scotland, 77-78, 145
Proxmire, William, 289
P-38, 75-78, 119, 292
P-39, 74
P-47, 149, 162, 169
PT-3, 42, 44-45
Purnell, William R., 198, 231, 236

Quincy, Illinois, 5, 11-12, 15, 28, 34

Ramey, Roger, 45, 247, 252-53
Ramsey, Norman, 154-55, 198, 202-03
Randolph Field, 40-47, 62
Rathbone, Monroe J., 295
Red Gremlin, 82, 103, 106-08, 112, 117, 121, 196
Richardson, Kendall, 26
Rice, William, 123-25, 269-70
Ridenour, Carlyle H., 122
Rommel, Erwin, 61, 101, 109
Roosevelt, Franklin D., 7, 127, 133, 148, 151, 185, 308
Rosenthal, Joe, 216
Rotterdam, raids on, 91-92
Rouen, raids on, 80, 82-84, 90, 209
Russell, Bertrand, 289

Sadowski, Hubert, 26
Sato, Naotake, 306
"Scale," 199
Scott, Robert L. Jr., 300
Seibert, Bill, 47
Semple, David, 249
Seraph, H.M.S., 105-06
Seville, Gordon, 140-41
Shooting (skeet and trap), 56-58, 269, 271, 301
Shumard, Robert H., 206, 213
Sigma Nu fraternity, 33
"Silverplate," 156
Sinclair, Joseph S., 300
Singh, Argan, 278
Singh, Karni, 279
16th Observation Squadron, 49
Slater, George, 41, 43

Smith, C. R., 141
Smith, James Hopkins, 295
Smith, Robert, 14
Smithsonian Institution, 9, 23
Sondre Stromfjord, 76
Sotteville, raid on, 82
Spaatz, Carl, 81-82, 84, 96, 103, 105, 118, 127, 182, 195, 231, 236-37, 240, 252-53
Special Bombing Mission No. 13, 196, 210
Speer, Albert, 87
Spellman, Francis Cardinal, 240
Spitfire V, 75, 81-82, 91, 97, 104, 112, 121
Split, Orville, 67
Stanwyck, Barbara, 264
Stiborik, Joe, 206, 213, 223
Stimson, Henry L., 184, 307
Straight Flush, 196, 204, 218, 220, 284-85, 288, 290
Strategic Air Command, 292
Street, Sinclair, 245
Sullivan, Ed., 266
Summers, John C., 110-11
Sundlun, Bruce, 293, 299-300
Suribachi, Mount, 216-17
Surrender Leaflets, 233
Swancutt, Woodrow P., 248, 250, 253
Swaybe, Ralph, 59
Sweeney, Charles, 163, 174, 196, 203, 212-13, 217, 220, 222, 225-26, 230, 238-39, 243, 264
Szilard, Leo, 178, 185, 308

Tafaraoui Air Base, 118
Task Force 1.5, 247
Taylor, B. B. "Buckshot," 59
Taylor, Ralph, 218
Taylor, Robert, 262-264
Thiriet, Andre, 270
Thomas, Lowell, 151
308th Bomb Wing, 272
393rd Bomb Wing, 272
393rd Bomb Squadron, 157, 162, 170
Tibbets, Andrea Quattrehomme, 271, 273, 297-98, 301
Tibbets, Barbara, 11, 13
Tibbets, Enola Gay, 11, 14, 38-39, 53, 172-74, 197, 235, 273, 279, 280

316 Index

Tibbets, Gene, 167, 235, 268
Tibbets, Paul W. Sr., 11, 38-39, 48, 53, 153, 235, 273
Tibbets, Lucy Wingate, 52-53, 139, 167, 235, 243, 265, 268
Tibbets, Paul III, 53, 139, 167, 235, 268
Timberlake, Ted, 48
Tinian Island, 181, 185-86, 190, 193, 212, 224, 228
   installations, 182
   takeoff from, 211
   return to, 230-31
Togo, Shigenori, 306
Tokyo firebomb raid, 6, 189, 306
Tokyo Rose, 190
"Top," 199
Top Secret, 212
"Topic," 199
"Torch," 101-02, 107, 109, 113
"Trinity" A-bomb test, 199, 228, 230
Truesdale, Carl, 272
Truman, Harry S., 7-8, 178, 185, 228, 233, 307-08
Tsuzuki, Masao, 241
Tunner, William H., 49-50
Turley, Bob, 56
Twelve O'Clock High, 79, 263, 272
29th Bomb Group, 66
Twining, Nathan, 231, 304

"Urchin Fashion," 199
Uanna, William "Bud," 163, 265
UC-78 (Bamboo Bomber), 70

Vandenberg, Arthur, 133
Vandenberg, Hoyt, 129, 133, 135
Van Kirk, Theodore "Dutch," 82, 134-35, 163, 188, 194, 197, 202, 206, 207, 211, 214, 217, 222-23, 232, 242
Van Pelt, James, 163
"Victor," 202

War College, 261, 268, 280
Warfield, John D., 12-13
Welsh, William, 155
Wendover (Utah) Air Base, 157, 161-67, 172-75, 181, 186, 193, 197, 284
Western Military Academy, 18, 24-31
Whitmore, James, 265
Wikel, Jesse, 117
Williams, Bob, 173
Wilson, John, 218
Wilson, Roscoe "Bim," 159, 169
Wilton shipyard, raid on, 91
Wolfe, K. B., 148
Wood, Harold H., 248, 250
Woodward, Jim, 56
Workman, E. J., 149
Wright, Jerauld, 102

Yamada, Y. "Jake," 305
Yankee Doodle, 82
"Yoke," 199
Young, Don, 204-05

Zipp, Marvin, 49-50, 54